OPERA
IN THE FLESH

Opera IN THE Flesh

SEXUALITY IN OPERATIC PERFORMANCE

SAM ABEL

WestviewPress

A Division of HarperCollins*Publishers*

Queer Critique

Copyright © 1996 by Westview Press, Inc., A Division of HarperCollins Publishers, Inc.

Published in 1996 in the United States of America by Westview Press, Inc., 5500 Central Avenue, Boulder, Colorado, 80301–2877, and in the United Kingdom by Westview Press, 12 Hid's Copse Road, Cumnor Hill, Oxford OX2 9JJ

A CIP catalog record for this book is available from the Library of Congress.
ISBN 0-8133-2900-0—ISBN 0-8133-2901-9 (if published as a paperback)

The paper used in this publication meets the requirements of the American National Standard for Permanence of Paper for Printed Library Materials Z39.48-1984.

10   9   8   7   6   5   4   3   2   1

In loving memory of my parents,
Robert and Evelyn Abel

Vivi ancora! Io son la vita!
Ne' miei occhi è il tuo cielo!
Tu non sei morta!
Le lagrime tue io le raccolgo!
Io sto sul tuo cammino e ti sorreggo!
Sorridi e spera! Io son l'amore!

and
for Craig

O *namenlose Freude!*
Mein Mann an meiner Brust!

CONTENTS

Part Four
Means and Ends

FIGURES

PREFACE

It is a daunting task to name, in a few paragraphs, all of the people who put their mark on a book that has been nearly a decade in the making. Were I to enumerate all of the ideas inspired by friends, all of the suggestions taken from colleagues, all of the late-night debates that shaped my thinking in these pages, this preface would expand to truly operatic proportions. Still, with the understanding that these few words of thanks are poor payment for great intellectual gifts, I will attempt to redress a fraction of the debts I owe.

My deep gratitude goes to the friends and colleagues who read earlier drafts of the book and shared their opinions and evaluations with me. Most of all, my thanks to Rebecca Schneider, who read an early version of the manuscript and then, over lunch, told me in two sentences what the book was really about. Fred Kolo read the same draft and informed me, with cheerful bluntness and unfailing accuracy, what I should keep and what I needed to toss. Talia Rodgers offered support during the early stages of writing, and Diana Taylor provided similar encouragement to get me through the later stages. Eve Kosofsky Sedgwick and the other members of the "Queer Performativity" seminar at the School of Criticism and Theory at Dartmouth in 1992 supplied theoretical fuel, jarred loose my thinking, and gave me permission to write about my feelings. I had the good fortune to live for a time near Susan McClary and Rob Walser; their work and conversations sparked many intellectual fires. Thanks also to my many friends, family members, and professional colleagues who provided valuable feedback at various stages of the writing in response to drafts and in conversations about opera, most notably Philip Brett, Bill Cook, Daniel Katz, Sarah Katz, Tom King, James Loehlin, Craig Palmer, Joan Parker, David Román, Peter Saccio and Jim Steffensen, Steve Scher, Thanalakshmi Subramaniam, Gary Thomas, and Simon Williams, along with several anonymous readers. And special thanks to Gordon Massman, who believed in this book and went to the mat for it.

I received archival support and research assistance from a number of quarters. Thanks to Dartmouth College and its generous support for junior faculty (even those of us in the humanities) through the Walter Burke Research Initiative Grant, which provided me with the resources to travel in Europe for research and operagoing. I received much friendly help from the staffs at the Theatre Museum in London and the Picture Library at the Victoria and Albert Museum. The archivists at Covent Garden were most gracious in allowing a crazy American to root through their boxes of old illustrations. I have fond memories of the administrative staff at the Museo Teatrale at La Scala and the research assistants at the Civica Raccolta delle Stampe Achille Bertarelli at the Castello Sforzesco in Milan, who were remarkably kind and understanding when confronted with my limping attempts to speak their language. The staff at the Harvard Theatre Collection provided its usual invaluable help. Bonnie Wallin of the Special Collections Department of Dartmouth's Baker Library has been a constant help in my work, and Kathy Hart at the Hood Museum of Art at Dartmouth unearthed some very useful treasures for me, most notably the amazing print that plays an important role in Chapter 4.

A few more thanks are due. To my teachers, particularly Errol Hill, Marvin Carlson, Peter Saccio, and Sam Smiley, my thanks for getting me into this business in the first place and for their continuing support and encouragement as I wend my way through the maze of academia. To my colleagues in the Department of Drama at Dartmouth and the Department of Communication Arts and Sciences at DePauw, my thanks for providing support and encouragement and an environment that made my writing possible. To my many students at Dartmouth, DePauw, and Moorhead, my thanks for providing a sounding board for new ideas and for teaching me to look at opera with new eyes. To Tom Fitzpatrick, my dear colleague in operamania at DePauw, undying thanks for many hours of conversations and, especially, for twice letting me fulfill my fantasy of singing in an opera. Most of all, to my large, crazy, and remarkable family—maybe the last great nuclear clan left in this country—my thanks for the love, unquestioning acceptance, support, and faith they have given me, and for making my life a hell of a lot of fun. Special thanks and love to my two sisters: Joan, for being my regular date at the opera and my favorite opera conversationalist; and Judy, for her unflagging support, belief, energy, and enthusiasm; and to both of them for giving me my first opera recordings.

I have two dedications for this book, the first looking to the past, the second to the future. My retrospective dedication is in memory of my parents, Robert and Evelyn Abel. No one (other than my two sisters) was ever blessed with parents more supportive and more giving or who took more joy in their children's accomplishments. Through the example of their lives, I learned what love means. I only regret that they did not live to see this book published, because it would have made them so happy.

My forward-looking dedication goes to Craig Palmer, my husband, my lover, my best friend, and my favorite opera-queen-in-training. This book and our relationship have grown hand-in-hand. I started drafting the manuscript just as we met, and my most productive writing happened when, after months apart, the two of us crammed ourselves into *La Bohème*–like accommodations in Hamburg and St. Louis. He is my muse and my guardian angel, who blesses me daily with his energy, his remarkable smile, his impassioned debate, his gentle touch, his unstinting support, and his relentless insistence that I slow down and let life happen, on occasion, without my hyperactive participation. I love him beyond measure, and I look forward to happy decades of operagoing together.

Sam Abel
Hartford, Vermont

Part One

Opera and the Body

1

EMBODYING OPERA

*A singer's voice sets up vibrations and resonances in the listener's body.
... The listener's inner body is illuminated, opened up: a singer doesn't
expose her own throat, she exposes the listener's interior. Her voice enters me, makes me a "me," an interior, by virtue of the fact that I have
been entered.*

—Wayne Koestenbaum
The Queen's Throat[1]

Opera and Bodies

This book is about the way the human body responds to opera. It is about
the way an audience that listens to and looks at opera in the theater responds physically and erotically to the bodies singing and performing opera
on the stage. It is about opera as a kind of theater and about why opera is
unlike any other kind of theater. It is my attempt to find words to express
the deep, irrational, and intensely physical passion I feel for that deeply irrational, physical, and passionate art form, opera. This book is my way of
trying to verbalize an aesthetic experience that seems to me beyond words,
an experience far more physical than discursive.

My feelings for opera do not adapt well to the strictures of discourse. I
am not even sure that words exist to express my experience of opera. Other
art forms submit much more readily to analysis. I can say in a few sentences
exactly why I love Shakespeare and Beckett, Van Eyck and Picasso, Brahms
and Stravinsky. But when it comes to explaining my adoration of opera,
simple formulas escape me. I become tongue-tied, the way I become in the
early stages of love—or, more accurately, sex. These pages map my current
struggles to pin down my passion for opera, my intense admiration for its
aesthetic forms and beauties; but much more they express my astonishment

3

at how opera makes me lose myself, how it consumes me in a way matched only by sexual desire. I want to know why opera feels to me so much more physical, so much more embodied, than any other art form. I want to know why opera feels so much like sex.

I am certainly not the first person to notice the connection between opera and physical desire. The literature surrounding opera (and, more broadly, music) resounds with sexual imagery. Critics call musical themes and cadences masculine or feminine; sonata movements and arias come to a climax; music seduces its audience. But, as Susan McClary argues forcefully in her landmark book *Feminine Endings: Music, Gender, and Sexuality,* this language of desire remains largely hidden, a set of secret codes, and few mainstream musicologists acknowledge its presence overtly.[2] According to the official line, as delivered by the loftiest exponents of high art, opera has no traffic with anything so crude as desire. Opera, they say, is not about carnal knowledge; like all great art, it deals with pure passions (whatever those are). Or rather, since opera is supposed to be nothing other than music, it is not really about anything at all; the narrative is incidental to the platonic effluence of sound. Physical feelings aroused by opera are aberrations, failures of the art to live up to its ideals. No art is perfect. In other words, let's just pretend these nasty feelings don't exist and stick to our vision of opera as an elevated, exclusively intellectual experience.

Till the last few years, most opera books have left intact the wall of silence around opera's physical nature. They offer either dry musicology, or gossipy history about great productions and houses, or tales of the peccadilloes of great (and not so great) singers. None of these approaches tells me much about opera's erotic impact. Biographies of opera stars and accounts of past productions amuse me, but they do not reflect my immediate experience of opera. And though I find the voyeuristic tone that pervades so much opera history titillating, these chronicles reveal the sex lives of opera people offstage, not the sexuality of opera itself. Most musicology, on the other hand, strikes me as fatally formal, entirely abstracted from the physicality of opera. Analyses of Wagner's chromaticism tell me what happens musically in *Tristan und Isolde* but not why my back arches during the "Liebestod."

What I miss most in opera criticism, in other words, is theater. Until recently, only a few works offered a serious analysis of opera's theatricality, most notably Joseph Kerman's groundbreaking *Opera as Drama.*[3] Kerman's book has, in many ways, fathered this one. *Opera as Drama* was published in 1956, one year before I was born. It was one of the first books about opera that I read in college; it struck me then, and does still, as both revolutionary, in its defiance of standard critical approaches, and conservative (in the best sense), in its reclaiming of opera's original theatrical impulses. Through Kerman, I learned to unite my love of opera with my vocation of theater; I am deeply in his debt. But we all must break away from our parents; Kerman's way is not my way. I can admire Kerman's analysis, but I cannot take his critical approach. Most of all, I cannot embrace his condescending attitude toward Puccini and Strauss. I love Puccini and Strauss precisely for the attributes that Kerman uses to dismiss them: their shameless theatricality and passionate emotionalism. Kerman loves opera for its form, not for its feeling. He sees opera as drama, but he never really gets to opera as theater, a performed physical exchange between singer and audience. Opera for me is not formal and analytical; it is messy, overblown, melodramatic, theatrical.

In the last few years, several writers have challenged the stultifying orthodoxy that pervades opera criticism. Susan McClary joyfully jars loose several hundred years of patriarchal assumptions about music and its relation to society in *Feminine Endings,* defying the turgid status quo of mainstream musicology. Catherine Clément unearths the deeply misogynistic nature of operatic narrative in the disturbing polemic *Opera, or the Undoing of Women.*[4] Michel Poizat, in *The Angel's Cry: Beyond the Pleasure Principle in Opera,* uses Lacanian psychoanalysis to ask why opera arouses such passionate desire in its audience, concluding that opera is a quest for *jouissance,* the rare, orgasm-like instant of eroticized pleasure induced by the climactic moment of an aria.[5] Anne Rice's novel about the intrigues of the eighteenth-century castrati, *Cry to Heaven,* stares unblinkingly at the castrato's wounded scrotum, unmasking the terrifying sexuality of opera's great hidden secret.[6] Much in these books is subjective, passionate, erotic, impressionistic, difficult. They all have evoked emotional, at times unpleasant, responses from critics, who sense the danger inherent in their discourse. I do not agree with everything they say. But in their iconoclastic embrace of opera's dangerous physicality they begin to articulate what I feel in the opera house. Mostly, what I take from these books is the revelation that opera is about the human body, that opera is *embodied.*

For me, though, the most energizing recent book about opera is Wayne Koestenbaum's *The Queen's Throat: Opera, Homosexuality, and the Mystery of Desire.* It appeared just as I finished my first draft of this volume, and it forced me to rethink much of my analysis. On the surface, Koestenbaum offers to explain the appeal of opera to gay men, but he does a great deal more. The book is a hymn to opera's eroticism. As I read it, I was almost overwhelmed by Koestenbaum's passion for opera. I rejoiced at the precision of his poetic expression, at the depth of his feeling. I felt pain, both in empathy for his anguish and out of jealousy: I wish I had Koestenbaum's command of metaphor, and I have had to suppress my desire to quote in these pages every line of his book. I also identify closely with the book and its author. Koestenbaum and I come to opera with the same demographic profile: We are both white, middle-class, East Coast, Jewish, gay, intellectual, Ivy League–educated, Ivy League professors writing about opera from fields other than music.

But if we come to opera from the same place, we differ sharply in our outlook. Koestenbaum approaches opera with a pessimism in which I cannot join. He argues that opera is dead, a relic of the past. Koestenbaum posits opera's death as the central condition of its cultural production, the cause of its erotic appeal to gay men, whose lives (he argues) are defined by rejection and spiritual death. Opera for me is not dead, not a relic of the past, not a subject of despair. Nor do I see my sexuality as a source of pain or rejection. My passion for opera grows out of joy, not anguish. To me, opera's sexuality—and my own—is a matter of life, not death.

This book, then, is also my reply to *The Queen's Throat*. Koestenbaum's book, I would argue, is not really about opera per se; it is about a particular vision of gay sexuality, about how opera functions as a cultural icon for a certain generation of closeted, self-deprecating, urban gay men. Koestenbaum uses the erotic nature of opera as a means to explore his idea of gay sexuality, a dark and troubling vision of disjuncture, loneliness, and failure. My purpose here is exactly the reverse. Rather than using opera to explore gay sexuality, I propose in this book to use sexuality, gay and otherwise, as a means to explore my experience of opera, an experience that (although it may encompass some darker elements) is fundamentally life-affirming, joyous, and celebratory. Koestenbaum eroticizes opera as a function of shame and secrecy, but I want to make opera's eroticism public. I find too much life in opera to bury it in the closet.

Like Koestenbaum, I am not a musicologist; my background is in theater. The sum of my training in music is a handful of guitar and recorder lessons in grade school, one college course in elementary music theory, and a lot of nontechnical reading. I can hear basic musical structures and harmonic configurations; I can pick out a melody on a keyboard if it is in C major (and in other keys, under duress and given sufficient time). I experience music sensually and intuitively, whereas I view dramatic narrative, under the influence of my schooling, analytically and structurally. Opera's potency as theater lies for me in music's power to dislodge my logical faculties, to return me to the dizzying emotionality that first made me love both opera and theater. When I go to the spoken theater I respond as a critic. When I go to the opera, I respond from the gut.

My aim, then, is to articulate this visceral response to operatic performance. I cannot, however, presume to speak for the emotions and feelings of other audience members. I can observe how other people behave in the opera house, and I can listen to them describe their reactions. But when it comes to physical responses, I can only speak with certainty about myself (and that task is difficult enough). And so I choose here to write mainly in the first person, about my individual response to opera. I write in the first person not because I think I am a typical opera audience member or because I think there is something unique about my reactions, but because my own feelings are what I know. And I write about my own experience in the hope that my feelings will resonate with those whose experience of opera is like mine—and perhaps with those who respond to opera in fundamentally different ways or with those who do not respond to it at all. And so, in this spirit of self-understanding, and with apologies to Wayne Koestenbaum, I, too, must begin my tale with autobiography.

Opera and My Body

I first learned about opera from my mother, though I can't remember how or when. My mother adored romantic opera, Verdi and especially Puccini; *La Bohème* was her favorite, with *La Traviata* close behind. But during my childhood she rarely went to the opera and did not own recordings—not even a record player. Opera belonged to her youth; it was not something for a mother of three children, not something for an older woman with responsibilities, not something she shared with my father. For her it was a treasured memory of past pleasures, her open secret. For my mother, opera was something rare, a passion reserved for special occasions. Most children have illicit, guilty fantasies about their parents having sex. I had dreams about my mother at the opera.

My first live experience of opera came when my mother took me to see Beverly Sills sing Violetta in *La Traviata* at the Opera Company of Boston; I was ten, I think, or thereabouts. Most details of that performance escape me now; I remember a huge, two-level set, the enormous auditorium, but few specifics. What lingers in my memory is the size of the performance. Everything seemed big to my small body, and the biggest thing of all (even bigger than Sarah Caldwell in the orchestra pit) was the overwhelming presence of Sills as Violetta, her physicality, her body on stage making amazing sounds, distant yet sharing the same space with me. The power of that singing body joined with my thrill at seeing my mother's overt ecstasy, her joy in sharing her joy. In that moment opera assumed a physical existence, something more than a public performance of a story told through music; opera became for me the embodiment of passion, family, and love.

Opera came more regularly into my life about the time I hit puberty. My bachelor uncle, my mother's youngest brother, worked in a shoe warehouse, but he also sang as a cantor for a Jewish congregation on Saturdays. He also sometimes sang tenor in the chorus for Caldwell's company in Boston and performed a few leading roles with community troupes. He sang in the chorus of Schoenberg's *Moses und Aron,* which I was told was too difficult for my young ears: an illicit opera. I went instead to see him perform Radames in a community production of *Aïda* when I was about twelve. Again, my memories of that high school auditorium performance are dim. Mostly I remember the last scene of the opera, the death scene, as my uncle was smothered in the crudely staged tomb. The performances and production values could not remotely compare to Sills and Caldwell, but it did not matter. I was enthralled all the same.

When I was thirteen, I bought a cheap stereo with my bar mitzvah money. My older sisters owned opera LP sets from the fifties, some of which, abandoned in a fit of closet-cleaning, formed the beginning of my collection: *Aïda* with Leontyne Price, *La Bohème* with Anna Moffo (the soprano idolized by Koestenbaum), *Madama Butterfly* with Victoria de los Angeles. I saved my money and bought an opera recording: the complete *Ring* with Wilhelm Furtwängler conducting. I didn't know quite what I was letting myself in for. I think I bought it, at the time, more for its massiveness than for any appreciation of Wagner. Carrying it home on the train, I felt as if I owned something important. My ownership of that set inflamed my desire to own more opera sets, a desire that I fulfilled as quickly as my finances allowed.[7] Ultimately, I gave away all my LPs when I switched to CDs, but I still like my recordings in bulk, an assertive physical presence in my life; my opera sets threaten to take over an entire wall of my living room.

Through my teens, I went to hear the Boston Symphony Orchestra at Tanglewood and to their open rehearsals at Symphony Hall, learning the sensual pleasures of live performance. I loved my records, but not even their weighty bulk could compare with the real thing, being in the same physical space with the performers. When I got my driver's license, a high school buddy and I got permission to borrow my mother's car, and we spent a long weekend at Tanglewood on our own, sharing accommodations in a cheap rooming house, lying on the lawn, staring at the stars in the cool evening air, communing with the music and each other. We repeated this exercise a few times, and we always chose weekends featuring huge vocal events: Mahler symphonies, Beethoven's Ninth. Looking back at this youthful rite of passage, it's hard to tell what gave me a greater thrill, the music or the repressed, and entirely unfulfilled, desire generated by a weekend alone with my friend. Or maybe we (or at least I) used the music to substitute for desires buried too deep to acknowledge.

About the same time as my engagement with opera, I began participating in theater regularly. Theater started as a high school hobby, or so I told myself and my concerned and protective parents, and ended as a career—if one considers the demimonde of drama in academia as a theater career. I don't remember ever wanting to be an opera star, but then I'm no singer. Theater became a way to enact my growing passion for opera without embarrassing myself in public. When I started making theater on my own, directing college productions and writing plays for children's groups, my creations looked rather operatic. The more I studied theater in college the more my taste grew toward broadly drawn farce and melodrama rather than the subtler (and more respectable) manners of high comedy and tragedy. Even without the music, I yearned for theater to create the physical impact of opera.

With an undergraduate degree in theater and no taste for business, medicine, or law, I chose the one remaining option for a dutiful Ivy League graduate and started work on a Ph.D. I went to Indiana University, the Mecca for opera students, to study the history of spoken theater. I did not study opera there and had no contact with the Music School, other than religiously attending performances. Ostensibly, I went to Indiana not because of opera but because they gave me money. But I suspect that my growing passion for opera influenced my choice. In retrospect, I also suspect that I went into theater because I saw it as a kind of opera without music (though I managed to include music theory in both my master's and doctoral theses). Opera is a secret passion for many of us in academic theater; it's the kind of theater we like best, though we dare not say so. The social norms of our field tell us that we're supposed to like Shakespeare and Sophocles more than Verdi and Strauss, but given the choice some of us would rather be at the opera house. I went to Bloomington to be near my illicit passion.

I also went there to avoid dealing with my sexuality. I was one of those clueless gay workaholics, the people who keep sexuality off their minds by burying themselves in their work. (I had no sex life, but I finished my Ph.D. when I was twenty-six.) Through high school, college, and graduate school I had plenty of opportunities to confront my desires, but I systematically avoided them. My remarkably functional heterosexual family provided such positive role models that I could not see myself in any other framework. Unlike Koestenbaum, my youth was not filled with conscious, anguished struggles about my sexuality, which opera then symbolized and sublimated. My childhood and young adulthood were filled with clumsy attempts at heterosexuality, more comic than traumatic, accompanied by a willful ignorance of my own same-sex desires. Thus opera increasingly became for me not a symbol for anguish and unfulfilled desire but the site of my most successful erotic experiences. If I could not see my desires for other men, my desire for opera was readily apparent and easy to fulfill.

Finishing graduate school and joining the "real world" gave me the financial resources to pursue my passion for opera on a higher level (which I began to do immediately) and the psychological motivation to overcome my repressions and deal openly with my sexuality (which took a bit more time). I had my first postrepression sexual encounter—not surprisingly—with an opera singer. And for the first time, I had an experience that matched the way I felt at the opera, the same irresistible draw, the same racing heartbeat, the same sense of floating on air when the performance was over. Looking back, I cannot claim the opera queen's history; I did not come to love opera specifically because I am gay. Nor did I find in opera a reflection of my experiences as a gay man; I discovered opera long before I had any such experiences. Instead, I came to opera because I found there a different kind of sexuality, a public performance that offered to me the same attractions that I would later find in person-to-person sexual relations.

I offer the following essays, then, as my attempt to travel again that journey of discovery, the road that led me to opera and to sexuality. They are my way of paying homage to opera, of giving thanks for the pleasures—intellectual and physical—opera brings to me.

2

THE PARADOX OF THE FAT LADY

The diva's body has never lost its representational magnetism for many of us as an alternative body-identity fantasy, resolutely embodying as it does the otherwise almost entirely anachronistic ideal, formed in early nineteenth-century Europe, of the social dignity of corpulence, particularly that of the serenely fat bourgeois matron.

—Michael Moon and Eve Kosofsky Sedgwick
"Divinity"[1]

The opera ain't over till the fat lady sings.

—Traditional saying

Visions of the Fat Lady

Opera is a hotbed of paradox. It stages subtle intimacy between lovers with loud music, enormous scenery, and overwrought acting. It is theater but not "legitimate" theater; it is music but not "pure" music. Opera's narratives abound in horrendous character inconsistencies, plot disjunctures, and motivational absurdities, all of which melt into insignificance in the sweep of its emotional intensity. Samuel Johnson rightly calls opera illogical and absurd, yet its greatest popularity came during the eighteenth century, the Age of Reason. Opera means elitism, the exclusive territory of the upper classes who can afford to sit in the orchestra. Yet opera is, at its very core, a popular genre, its every aspect catering to "low" tastes for grand spectacle, sensual display, exciting action, and passionate eroticism. Opera inspires absolute devotion or absolute hatred from its listeners, rarely anything in between; opera is my life, yet it produces physical illness in my friends.

These paradoxical tensions become even more intense in the realm of opera's sexuality. Why, for example, do the most masculine roles in nineteenth-century opera belong to tenors, men with voices closest to the female range; and before that, to castrated men, sometimes with voices higher than the heroines? Why do women in opera play men's roles so often, though the reverse situation happens only with great rarity? How can aging divas portray young ingenues, wooden tenors dashing heroes, and overweight sopranos women dying of consumption, with no protests from the audience? And how can opera get away with staging sexual transgressions such as adultery and incest with so little protest from the audience, even during the height of the Victorian era? How does opera manage to be entirely sexual underneath a face of complete chastity, thoroughly subversive in its eroticism behind a mask of sexual normalcy?

Most ambiguous, most maddening, most intriguing of opera's paradoxical images is the infamous "Fat Lady" of the opera. The Fat Lady has become, of late, opera's central icon, an immediately recognized symbol for the entire cultural institution of opera. The popular catchphrase in which she is embodied, "The opera ain't over till the Fat Lady sings," seems to be of fairly recent origin, though the stereotyped image of the obese diva can be traced back much further. This slogan, through which the Fat Lady has entered popular discourse, may not even have originated in opera; it seems to have made its way into American speech via professional sports.[2] But the image has stuck to opera and has come to represent everything about opera. For much of the non-operagoing public, the entire world of opera reduces to this single figure. Even for me, and I should know enough to escape such a simplistic stereotype, the Fat Lady means opera. As a symbol, the Fat Lady has become virtually transparent, as much a normative element of cultural iconography as Uncle Sam and Aunt Jemima—and just as troubled an image.

Who is the Fat Lady? She is the prima donna of prima donnas, the necessary element of opera's physical manifestation, the one who must sing in order for the opera to be complete. She is, first of all, a reductio ad absurdum of Wagner's Brünnhilde in *Der Ring des Nibelungen;* her iconography draws from the stereotyped excesses of Wagnerian Nordic mythology. Her various manifestations paint a remarkably consistent picture. She always looks the same: a grotesquely overweight Wagnerian dramatic soprano, screeching a piercing E above high C at the top of her capacious lungs, with her mouth distended to a distressing degree. She is not pretty. She may smile or scowl, but either way her appearance is terrifying. She wears a daunting metallic breastplate, a voluminous skirt, and a horned helmet; she wields an enormous spear, sometimes an equally large spiked shield. Mostly, she's just big. She is not merely fat; she is gargantuan. She dwarfs everything around her, singers and scenery. She is bigger than life, as big as opera itself. She is no phantom of the opera; she is the imposing visual representation of opera's fleshly materiality, an evocation of its immensity and that of the huge opera houses and grandiose personalities that signify opera in popular discourse. She is too big to avoid, too weighty and too heavily armored to ignore.

This portrait of the Fat Lady operates as a familiar commodity in popular iconography, employed gleefully both by opera's devotees and its detractors, in cartoons, films, and magazine and television advertisements. She bellows from the stage in the pages of the *New Yorker* and the *New York Times,* virtually every time a cartoonist wants to evoke the image of opera. She towers over terrified animals on the cover of *The Anna Russell Album.* She glowers from the covers of two popular recordings entitled *Heavy Classix,* which bill her as the original heavy metal musician and warn us to play her thunderous music only at top volume. In a metonymic shift, she transmogrifies into a huge horse bearing a cross-dressed Brünnhilde/Bugs Bunny in Chuck Jones's brilliant cartoon short "What's Opera, Doc?"[3] She sells soft drinks and basketball shoes on television. Like the devil, she appears at the mere mention of opera.

This much-trafficked image of the Fat Lady conflates a wide array of contradictory and exaggerated gender-role stereotypes. She is, first, an overblown evocation of the feminine, everything society tells us women should be, carried to a frightening extreme. Her huge breasts imply both an overwhelming sexual fecundity and a monstrous maternalism. She is the Freudian feminine out of control: a breast fetishist's wet dream, the overbearing mother whose capacious bosom threatens to smother her hapless children. Her voluminous skirt covers veritable acres of taboo territory. She has the siren's stratospheric vocal range but with excessive volume, the piercing soprano that can shatter glass. Her gaping mouth evokes terrors of unknown and unspeakable female sexuality, the *vagina dentata* retranscribed to the mouth. She is the patriarchal fantasy of femininity, the siren-mother gone foul, Barbie off her anorexic diet and on steroids. She is the seductress-turned-harpy, the mother of our nightmares.

These extreme signs of the feminine, however, become negated at the same moment they appear by conflicting signs of the masculine. The Fat Lady is as butch as she is femme. She is excessively maternal, but she has no children. Her breasts are encased in metal, steeled against any attempts at sexualizing them (and so all the more erotic for being forbidden). Her skirts provide an equally impenetrable barrier to her lower regions. She is overlaid with a profusion of phallic symbols: spear, horns, spiked shield, outstretched arms, especially her voice. Even in silent drawings, her phallic voice is palpable. It soars into the female range, but with a decidedly masculine thrust and volume. The Fat Lady's voice is her most potent weapon, and she wields it aggressively. She carries a spear but has no need for it. Her voice has enough power to beat down any potential rival with a single "Hoio-toho."

In short, the Fat Lady embodies an overdetermined gender image, a primer of obvious and contradictory sexual stereotypes. Contemporary feminist criticism provides ample tools for dismantling the Fat Lady's iconography. We can dismiss her as a compilation of every negative image that society attaches to women: the sex machine and the sex monster, the goddess and the whore, the overbearing mother and the evil seductress, the ridiculous cartoon and the serious threat to male authority.

Despite (or because of) these obviously reductive stereotypes, the power and pervasiveness of the Fat Lady profoundly disturb me. I shudder at the possibility of collapsing all of opera, four centuries of artistic creation, into a single image, the grotesque figure of a ridiculous woman.[4] No other art form is subject to this kind of reduction; no single stereotype, gender-based or otherwise, embodies the public perception of painting, sculpture, theater, dance, film, or instrumental music. The only figure who comes close to representing an entire art form is Shakespeare, who often stands as an icon for the theater. Shakespeare is not all of theater, but there is a certain logic in the identification, as he is the West's most popular playwright. But the Fat Lady is not a real person and she does not create opera; she is a derisive gender stereotype, a pander to society's basest assumptions about women. The reductive prejudice of this symbol is transparent, laughable. Like the Fat Lady of the circus sideshow, the Fat Lady of the opera cannot possibly be taken seriously.

The Fat Lady's Body

Or can she? The one element missing from this analysis of the Fat Lady's iconography is how this image connects to opera. Why does this particular grotesque and monstrous parody of Wagner signify "opera"? How has the Fat Lady come to embody opera's physicality, and why particularly at this moment in history in the popular discourse of American culture? The ubiquity of the Fat Lady is particularly significant because far more people recognize this icon than ever go to the opera. Relatively few people in the United States attend opera, but the Fat Lady has achieved wide public recognition. The average consumer of her image in popular discourse probably has no idea why she wears armor and horns, and certainly very few could describe the original Wagnerian Brünnhilde whom the Fat Lady parodies. The Fat Lady means opera not because of her connections to Wagner. She means opera specifically because she is a fat woman who sings. Her power as a symbol, then, comes initially not through the workings of opera but as a function of the way this culture constructs female obesity.

In the public trade in images, the body of the fat woman carries multiple and conflicted meanings. The popular media and the circles of high fashion ridicule and exclude images of large women. In a political economy that glorifies thinness, fat women have little power in the sexual marketplace. (In response to this systematic exclusion, a counterindustry has arisen to return self-esteem to large women, with Richard Simmons and Roseanne as high-profile gurus.) Yet if the dominant discourse attempts to remove sexual capital from the overweight female body, the popular image of the fat woman also can imply excess sexuality, especially reproductive sexuality. The iconic large woman evokes the image of a primal earth goddess, the planet in miniature, voluptuous and nurturing. In this mode, the large woman also symbolizes motherhood, especially ethnic motherhood (the Eastern European Jewish mother, the Italian mother, the Irish mother, and so on), with all the attendant sexual images wrapped up in the psychology of the mother figure. In each case, as mother, earth goddess, or fashion outcast, popular discourse denies to the large woman the sexuality of a so-called "normal" woman: She is seen as having either an excess of sexual power or none at all.[5]

Michael Moon and Eve Kosofsky Sedgwick, in their freewheeling dialogue/essay "Divinity," explore the complex dynamic that surrounds the image of the fat woman's body in contemporary culture. Female obesity, they argue, represents both plenitude and abjection. The image of the large woman embodies the excesses of consumer culture and, at the same time, is rejected by consumerist society for being too obvious a symbol of its excess. In this analysis, "Human fat, and especially fat-gendered-female, [represents] economic accumulation and waste in post-Enlightenment Western culture."[6] Consumer culture fetishizes the fat woman, then reviles her for being a blatant embodiment of the fetish:

> Visible on the one hand . . . as a disruptive *embolism* in the flow of economic circulation, the fat female body functions on the other hand more durably (and through the same etymologic route) as its very *emblem*. Like the large, dangerous bodies in Malthus, the modern fat female body represents both the efflorescence and the damaging incoherence of a social order, its function sharpened by representational recastings and by the gender specification, class complication, and racial bifurcation that accompany the shifts from nineteenth-century Europe to twentieth-century U.S. models.[7]

The iconic body of the fat woman engages the paradox endemic in rampant consumerist culture. The late-twentieth-century consumerist wants to have everything without looking as if he has everything, especially in the person of his crowning possession, his wife. (I once overheard a conversation in a five-star restaurant, where a wealthy man, referring to his spouse, used the term "Trophy Wife" rather than her given name—to her face. Tro-

phies, of course, must look impressively svelte.) Large women violate this
paradigm by looking like, if not actually being, excessive consumers.

This paradoxical construction of "fat-gendered-female" in modern consumer culture becomes an ideal vehicle to express opera's similarly conflicted physicality. Like the large woman, opera means both glorious plenitude and embarrassing excess. Contemporary society sees opera as both
imposing and overdone. The public wants massive entertainment, every
pleasure in extreme measure (it is no accident that the most successful video
rental chain in the United States is named "Blockbuster"). Opera fills this
bill, in more than full measure. Opera consumes more resources than any
other live art form and revels in its excess. Opera also consumes every other
art form, Wagner's *Gesamtkunstwerk* as an aesthetic consumerist fantasy.
For opera, too much is never enough. On the other hand, the sheer size of
opera is embarrassing. Opera has more scenery, more music, more emotion,
more everything than any self-respecting art form should have. No one
should spend that much money on a stage production, not when there are
homeless people in the streets. The stage director Constantin Stanislavsky
admonished his actors to keep things simple with the maxim "less is more";
but in opera more is emphatically more. Opera, at least as it is practiced in
houses of international note, is the conspicuous consumer of high culture,
the form that devours everything it sees, causing jealousy and rejection
from other corners of the art world. The people who can't stand opera usually cite its excesses as the leading cause for their disgust.

But if opera is embarrassingly excessive, it embraces its embarrassment
and banks on the public's secret desire for the excess that underlies the
shame. People who make opera know that it is excessive, and they flaunt its
excesses when they can and as much as they can, because that is just the
way the public wants it. The absurdly overproduced opera stagings of
Franco Zeffirelli come immediately to mind, especially the over-the-top hy-
perorientalism of his production of *Turandot* at the Metropolitan Opera.
Here the scenery is so large and profusely detailed that one can hardly see
the singers; the chinoiserie so patently fake and overdone that no one could
possibly take it seriously. And the crowds go wild, applauding the scenery
before anyone sings a note. Scenic excess makes sense for opera. It is merely
a logical extension of the embarrassing physical and emotional plenitude of
resources that pervade all aspects of the art.

It is, of course, possible to produce opera on a smaller scale; not every
opera company can afford—or even desires—to stage opera on a Zeffirelli
budget. I have seen entirely satisfying opera productions played against almost no scenery, and the intimacy I find in Europe's smaller houses often
provides a much better balance between singer and orchestra than do caves
like the Met. But even when produced on a shoestring, even if there is only
a tinny piano instead of an orchestra, opera *feels* bigger than any other

kind of stage performance. The fact that opera unites music, verbal narrative, and theatrical presentation—its necessary elements—when any one of these media alone constitutes an art form, creates a sense of excess consumption. And grandiose production is certainly the rule at the Met and the major European houses, the theaters that generate the most powerful popular conception of opera. Opera, as practiced in its iconic form, replies to its embarrassment by aggressively amplifying its causes. The Fat Lady revels in excess and sings her extravagance shamelessly.[8]

This tension between plenitude and embarrassment also informs opera's sexuality. If the Fat Lady is, in herself, a paradoxical gender image, she also presents opera's monumental sexual paradox. Like the Fat Lady, opera abounds with age-old gender stereotypes, long ago put to rest by feminist analysis. The same monsters and seductresses embodied by the Fat Lady inhabit the opera stage: the winsome, helpless victim, the self-immolating martyr, the castrating witch, and all the rest. Feminist theory knows these characters by rote, and Catherine Clément takes them apart piece-by-piece in *Opera, or the Undoing of Women*. I step away with embarrassment when I see them in spoken theater or narrative fiction. Yet I enjoy their excessive representation in opera; their very obviousness makes them acceptable. Opera's sexual discourse is open, reductive, silly, and yet in its excessiveness it becomes endlessly attractive.

Clément critiques opera's female characters as reductive stereotypes, but I would argue that the case is exactly the reverse. These stereotypes seem so right in opera not because they are reductive but because they are excessive. Opera adopts the sex-role stereotypes of the spoken theater and amplifies them beyond the point of believability. Violetta in *La Traviata* is not just one victimized, consumptive, fallen woman of the nineteenth century; she is *the* fallen woman, the archetypal representative of every fallen woman on stage and in literature. Brünnhilde (the real one, not the Fat Lady cartoon) is not just any androgyne; she is both a full-blown masculine warrior and a completely passive feminine lover, for the duration of three very long operas. Both of their death scenes are embarrassing—too long, too sickly sentimental, too loud, too simplistic—but that excess is also their theatrical power.[9]

No phenomenon in opera displays the excess-embarrassment dynamic more than the castrati, the star singers of the seventeenth and eighteenth centuries, castrated in boyhood to preserve their soprano voices. The spoken theater of the same period toyed frequently with androgyny: Shakespeare's boy actors and their complex cross-dressing games, or the fops of the Restoration comedy. But only opera took the extreme step of literally creating androgynes to put on the stage, a step so embarrassing that the church banned the practice, yet simultaneously created the greatest demand for castrated singers in church choirs. Everyone involved in the actual med-

ical practice consistently denied their involvement while turning out castrati by the hundreds.[10] The public hysteria that surrounded the castrati in
their heyday was equally embarrassing and excessive, and so, of course, im-
mensely satisfying for the screaming fans in the audience. The success of the
castrati relied on the audience's combined horror and amazement at the extreme measures taken to create extreme beauties of singing. When the hysteria died down at the end of the eighteenth century, shame took over with
a vengeance, and the opera world did everything it could to pretend that
the castrati never existed.[11] But the castrati are, in fact, only the most obvious example of opera's persistent dynamic: seizing an embarrassing excess
and delivering it to an eager audience in more than full measure.

The Fat Lady, then, is a camp icon for opera's embarrassing plenitude. To
non-operagoers, she represents everything bad and overdone about opera,
which is to say everything about opera. To opera devotees, she also embodies operatic excess, in all its paradoxical complexity, and that is her attraction. As with all camp icons, the Fat Lady engages an insider/outsider dynamic. On the one hand, those outside the camp community of opera
lovers perceive the Fat Lady as a ridiculous amplification of the negative;
they never get beyond the overblown vision to see the complexity she represents. Those within the camp community, on the other hand, see her as
both an embodiment and a subversive parody of opera's excess, a self-reflexive commentary on the complex physicality of opera.[12] She is a prime
example of, to use Judith Butler's term, "gender trouble," a simultaneous
embodiment and violation of societal gender norms, an image that becomes
subversive by presenting these norms so blatantly that their constructedness
becomes obvious.[13] The opera fan develops a double vision, an ability to
love the excessive, both in itself and as a critique of more moderate kinds of
excess. The overdetermined gender signifiers that adorn the body of the Fat
Lady are a camp performance of the sexual excess of opera itself.

Desiring the Fat Lady

If the Fat Lady represents opera's conspicuous consumption of resources,
she also represents the audience's enormous appetite as consumers of
opera. The excesses of opera induce my desires in a self-reinforcing chain:
The more sensual display opera gives me, the more I crave. If, as Bertolt
Brecht once observed, opera is "culinary theater," then those of us who
feast upon it want our meals in bulk. This desire, according to Wayne
Koestenbaum, engages the image of the overweight soprano. We desire the
body of the diva in just the way we desire food. We invest in the body of the
singer the vastness of our craving; her body becomes the physicalization of
our desire. He observes, "We consider the diva fat because *we* are the hungry ones; we want to ingest the diva through our voracious, vulnerable

ears. And so we project onto the diva's body an image of our own cannibalistic orality, an image of how grotesque we consider our desires to be."[14]

Some opera fans feel a powerful urge to reify the Fat Lady, to take this stereotypical image of conspicuous consumption and impose it on actual opera divas. This desire projects the stereotype onto the reality, and it asserts that opera singers (at least female ones) really are always fat. Some observers even offer physiological arguments that posit that fat helps the singer's vocal production, that a rotund body gives the voice weight and substance, and that excess body mass helps to support the singer's voice.[15] This "rule" is, however, highly questionable. The loudest voice I ever heard came from the then-minuscule body of Renata Scotto, who blasted me against the wall even as I sat in the last row of the second balcony of the cavernous auditorium at Indiana University.[16] And why would fat be especially beneficial to female singers while male singers, as seems to be the general critical impression, can be of any girth they please (and, except for Pavarotti, we expect to be thin, to give visual credence to their heroic roles)?

The iconic image of the Fat Lady, rather than the evidence of reality, induces the belief that sopranos outweigh normal women. Opera certainly has its overweight sopranos (not to mention overweight mezzos, altos, tenors, baritones, and basses), perhaps more than its share. But for every Jessye Norman, Montserrat Caballé, or Sharon Sweet there is a Teresa Stratas, Agnes Baltsa, or Kathleen Battle who manages a stellar career with quite little body mass. And then there are the Maria Callases and Renata Scottos, who work both ends of the size spectrum. (Is there any opera fan who really wishes that Callas had stayed fat?) In the current opera market, the Brünnhildes of choice, the true Fat Lady standard-bearers, have been Hildegard Behrens and Waltraud Meier, both of whom are rather small. In fact, taking into account the rampant obesity in Western society, sopranos are probably much the same size as the rest of the upper-class population, and certainly none has ever matched the profound size of the iconic Fat Lady.

Still, we want to see the Fat Lady on stage; we want the reality to live up to the icon. And when the woman singing on the opera stage fails to meet our expectations, we can become disoriented, unable to interpret the spectacle. Audiences and critics have come to expect the Fat Lady's appearance, even to depend on it, especially when the opera offers us one of its notorious seductresses: Carmen, Dalila, Salome. We assume that the singer will not live up to the sexually charged ideal of the character she portrays; we are shocked, almost dismayed, when the paradox fails to appear, when Carmen really is attractive, when Salome drops her veils and reveals a slender figure. When Julia Migenes-Johnson portrayed a very attractive, svelte Carmen in Francesco Rosi's film version of the opera, the critics praised the realism of her performance but despaired of her ever performing the role live on stage.[17] Critic Peter G. Davis shows even greater discomfort with a slim soprano in his review of a video performance of the Dance of the Seven Veils from *Salome:* "Catherine Malfitano's go-for-broke, X-rated performance of the title role may drive you crazy. . . . This orgy of eye-rolling, twitching, and mugging culminates in a display of frontal nudity and necrophilia that comes dangerously close to pushing Strauss's 1905 shocker over the brink into camp comedy."[18]

Davis's attitude is revealing. His tone implies that Salome is not really supposed to be nude and that necrophilia and orgiastic revelry are somehow inappropriate to the role. But Salome *does* take off her veils, and she *does* make love to a severed head; that's the whole point of the opera's finale. If there is camp here, it is in the opera, not specifically in Malfitano's performance. Davis admits that the opera is a sexual shocker, but when this performance actually arouses and shocks him, he recoils and wants to laugh, seemingly as a defense mechanism. He expects a Fat Lady pretending to be nude, and he can't deal with a slim woman who is actually nude, even if only on video.

The characters portrayed by opera divas are, of course, not supposed to be fat. In the gender stereotypes that Clément traces, the characters of opera are the idealized women of nineteenth-century melodrama, erotic and alluring, or innocent and alluring, carrying with them all of the misogynist implications of the traditional patriarchal vision of desirable female appearance and behavior. The heroines are thin, weak, pretty, vulnerable, the seductresses voluptuous, erotic, alluring. The body of the large soprano represents a disjuncture of the real and the ideal. The large physical presence of the singer contradicts the stereotype of wraith-like fragility or svelte sexuality, just as the soprano's powerful voice contradicts the stereotype of feminine weakness. If the large body denies the implications of the narrative, it redoubles the impression of force of the soprano's vocal line. If a large voice does not require a large body, the two feel as if they go together.[19] The large soprano prevents us from accepting the stage spectacle as reality, even a theatricalized version of reality, but it provides a visual metaphor that allows us to believe in the potency of the singing body.

But opera thrives on this disjuncture, because it fits into the form's intense, insistent pattern of artifice. Opera plays by highly contrived conventions. All theater employs conventions; the stage is not reality. But the conventions of opera, particularly its defining assumption that a performer sings rather than speaks, push the limits of Coleridge's "willing suspension of disbelief." I need not believe what I see in opera, because opera insists so completely on its artifice. The psychological theories of audience identification and sympathy, which inform so much contemporary performance and film criticism and which depend so heavily on the assumption that the audience accepts the spectacle as reality, do not work neatly for opera. While spoken theater moves incessantly toward photographic realism as its visual and psychological norm (despite repeated assaults by the avant-garde, this norm remains intact), opera clings tenaciously to its artificiality. In spite of verismo, with its brief attempt to bring opera in line with theatrical realism, opera remains inherently nonrealistic, dependent on its overt theatrical conventions, happily so. I accept the Fat Lady, because a visually unbeliev-able soprano reinforces opera's paradox of plenitude and embarrassment.

If standard formulas for identity and desire do not apply to opera, how does an audience deal with the embarrassing excess of operatic spectacle? How do desire and identity (those twin pillars of popular psychology) func-tion differently in opera than in other kinds of theater? Do I see myself in the Fat Lady, this prodigy of non-nature at once appalling and fascinating, a spectacle to be marveled at and an unnatural whore put on display so that I may gawk and gasp in disapproval? Or do I see myself *as* her? Or, rather than identifying with her, is there some other relation of the audience to opera's excessiveness? I desire to see the image of the Fat Lady on stage, but beyond that, do I desire her more directly, crave her excess as an erotic ob-ject and, if so, how? How does desire deploy itself along the paths of opera's conflicted, craggy sexual landscape? The following chapters wrestle with these questions and test a range of theories explaining the ways in which the opera audience negotiates the problematic territory of physical desire.

Part Two

Opera and Desire

3

OPERA, SEDUCTION, AND DESIRE

Still, the fact alone that people of different sexes are brought together in a glamorous auditorium that's the last word in worldly luxury—and then the heathenish disguises, the painted faces, the footlights, the effeminate voices—it all can't help encouraging a certain licentiousness and inducing evil thoughts and impure temptations.

—Gustave Flaubert
Madame Bovary[1]

The Lure of Opera

I am in love with opera. I do not mean that I love opera; I *do* love opera, the way I love other kinds of great art, for rational reasons based on aesthetic judgment. But I am also passionately, irrationally in love with opera. Or perhaps "arationally" is a better term: My adoration for opera does not go against reason; it just has nothing to do with it. I live with my lover for entirely rational reasons: because he is kind, caring, funny, and intelligent; because he is a delightful conversationalist and a terrific cook; because we share interests and pleasures. But when it comes to the physical side of our relationship, reason fades into the background and impulse takes over. Similarly, I choose to spend my intellectual life with opera because of my academic interest in performance, because of opera's rich history and structural complexities, and because of the importance of opera as a performative and socioeconomic phenomenon. But when it comes to my physical relationship with opera, when I play a recording or go to the Met, intellectual interest wanes, and passion controls my thoughts. As with my lover, physical impulse first lured me to opera, and it continues to inform my immediate experience of opera in performance.

My arational passion for opera makes me indiscriminate. I love the great canonical operas, the Mozart and Verdi and Wagner masterpieces, but I also love not-so-great operas. I even love operas that I don't, on intellectual terms, much like, such as *La Gioconda* or *Samson et Dalila*. I have a burning passion to own a recording of every opera ever written, no matter how trivial (I even have Puccini's *Edgar,* as trivial a work as exists). I love recordings of bad performances and bad recordings of good performances. I find all opera houses thrillingly beautiful, even the most absurd post-World War II monstrosities (except perhaps the frigid lobby of the Opéra Bastille). I am especially seduced by the magnificent excesses of the Palais Garnier, or the ruins of the Arena di Verona. Half the time I can't even see the stage in these theaters, but no matter. The building alone, just being at the opera, is enough to arouse my desires. I am in love with everything about opera: Peter Allen's voice on a Saturday afternoon; the double staircase at the Met; the thrill of not knowing whether the top-billed singer will cancel; the inane purple, orange, and hot pink color scheme of the opera house at Indiana University, where I did my graduate study; the overpriced drinks and overdressed snobs at intermission. I even love opera without the expensive trappings. The most perfectly awful community opera production will literally make my heart race. Opera has seduced me, and so I suspend my judgmental faculties in the face of its lure, pardoning its faults, loving it all the more for its absurdities.

Opera's seductiveness is dangerous. Flaubert is right when, in *Madame Bovary,* he has Abbé Bournisien warn the innocent Charles Bovary against taking his wife to the opera. Emma Bovary, longing for something interesting in her dull rural life, immediately falls prey to opera's seduction. The very thought of going to the opera makes her vulnerable, the experience of it even more so. Opera puts her in a weakened moral state that makes her prey to seductions of a more carnal kind and ultimately leads to her destruction. Emma might have avoided her tragedy had it not been for the opera. Flaubert, in the epigraph that opens this chapter, puts in the conservative priest's mouth the whole range of tools that opera wields in its seduction: luxurious surroundings; masks and disguises; fame and notoriety; gender ambiguity; the defiance of accepted norms. Opera is a lure toward the illicit and atypical, toward all the things that "normal" life forbids. Opera seduces Emma the way Mephistopheles seduces Faust into selling his soul, by tempting her with every kind of physical, emotional, even intellectual excess.[2]

Because of opera's seductiveness, the air of immorality lingers over it. Anything so embarrassingly overdone must be a threat to the soul. Opera's seductive powers worry those in charge of public morals. The excesses of opera are not merely embarrassing—they threaten the established moral order. Opera's physical seductiveness lures the hapless public into a life of pure sensuality, away from their workaday duties. When the public craze for opera swept London in the early eighteenth century, the most vocal critics decried opera on moral grounds. They accused it of being excessive, effeminate, and representing a "decline in national virtue."[3] This "immoral" seductiveness is one reason why the upper classes have clung so tenaciously to opera. The people who make the rules never worry much about being lured away from them. But when the poor and the powerless get seduced by opera, those in power feel they have lost control; they fear that opera will make the general population stray from the narrow path, perhaps even make them forget the rest of the social strictures that keep them in their place. So the powerful must hold opera, like all luxuries, to themselves, forcing the lower classes out, or at least exiling them to the distant upper galleries, supposedly to protect the unwitting masses, but mostly to protect the privilege to be seduced.

But opera's air of immorality is not merely an illusion generated by the upper classes as a means of guarding their territory. Opera's seductive dangers are real. If opera presents itself as something for me to consume, at the same time it consumes me. Like the people interviewed by Michel Poizat at the beginning of *The Angel's Cry,* waiting in line all night at the Palais Garnier for tickets, it certainly consumes a great deal of my budget.[4] Opera tickets are expensive, and an academic salary does not justify the $200 I have spent for a ticket at La Scala. My driving need to own a recording of every opera ever written causes me to spend more money than I have, even if I will never listen to *Edgar* more than twice in my life. But more than draining my physical resources, opera consumes my mind, sometimes my entire consciousness. I define my relationships with friends and family in terms of opera. I walk around singing arias. I mark my calendar by opera seasons. Opera is a most demanding lover. Poizat sees opera as the eternal quest for a single moment of *jouissance,* the one great erotic high. But it takes inordinate amounts of time and energy to achieve that moment. Opera, in Poizat's terms, demands a lifetime of listening to capture a few fleeting instants of glory. But even if those moments never come, the thrill of the pursuit itself becomes a lure: the appeal of a life spent in the hypercharged atmosphere of operatic excess.

Seducing the Audience

If the external trappings of opera offer dangerous seductions—the vision of glamour often draws people to opera in the first place—then, more importantly, the live performance of opera itself seduces. First, and most directly, the music of opera engages the audience's erotic attention. I need only note here that music by itself is sensual and seductive, that it elicits the audience's emotions, manipulating them in powerful and often subconscious ways.[5] But the seduction of operatic performance goes beyond the powerful erotic allure of music alone; an opera performance has far greater seductive capacities than a symphony concert. Opera adds to the erotic impact of music the lure of physical presence, a range of bodily, theatrical means to arouse the audience's desire. The traditional performance practices of opera overtly aim to engage the audience's sexual interest.

When I go to a performance in a major opera house, the sheer massiveness of the staging seduces me. In art forms of more modest dimensions, seduction happens only at moments, after which the audience can stand back and contemplate the work from a distance. When I study a painting in a museum, I may momentarily be struck by it emotionally, but then I recover my senses and study it for its line, its form, its color, or its allegorical significance. When I go to a spoken play, I lose my critical stance only in selected emotional moments (the blinding of Oedipus, Lear's mad scene); the play's linear structure normally asks me to analyze while I watch and listen. But opera, by throwing at its audience a constant barrage of visual and auditory stimuli, overwhelms the senses and leaves little room for objective contemplation. The huge scenery, the lavish costumes, the powerful orchestra, the booming voices, the sheer number of other people in the auditorium overwhelm critical distance. The only time I have been seduced by a painting the same way I am seduced by opera was when I first saw Picasso's *Guernica,* a painting of operatic scale both in its size and its wrenching emotions.

More powerfully, opera uses the singers' bodies to seduce the audience. In the traditional stage conventions of opera, characters normally do not sing to other characters; they turn out to face the audience. Facing the audience is a long-standing practice in the theater. Actors of the eighteenth and early nineteenth centuries (and probably in earlier periods as well) spoke almost exclusively toward the audience.[6] The advent of modern realism ended this practice, and contemporary directors tell actors that they always must seem to address the other characters, even though they must "cheat out" so that the audience can see their faces. Acting teachers often disdain the archaic style of operatic acting, where facing directly forward seems a worn-out vestige of the more stylized acting methods of the periods when the standard repertory operas were written. But singing out is also a vital technical requirement, because of the greater demands of voice projection; if a singer does not aim directly toward the audience, then the voice may not carry over the orchestra. The faulty acting technique seems a necessary compromise to the demands of musical performance.

But if opera singers sing toward the audience for practical reasons, the upshot of this technique is that the audience gets the singer's full attention. The characters of opera do not sing to each other; at times the characters hardly seem to notice each other. Instead, they send their emotional energy out to the audience. I look at the opera characters on stage, and they return my gaze. Rather than pretending that the characters sing to each other, I can let myself believe that they sing to me, personally. When Carmen seduces Don José, she seduces me at the same time. When she sings the "Habañera," José soon fades out of the picture; I see only Carmen herself, dancing for me, singing for me. In the context of modern realistic performance, the static pose aimed straight out to the house may constitute bad acting, but it is a very effective sexual politic. This is precisely the way Flaubert describes Emma Bovary's reaction to the opera; as she listens to the Act I finale of *Lucia di Lammermoor*, she fantasizes that the tenor singing Edgardo is seducing her:

> The outraged lover brandished his naked sword; his lace collar rose and fell with the heaving of his chest; and he strode up and down, clanking the silver-gilt spurs on his soft, flaring boots. His love, she thought, must be inexhaustible, since he could pour it out in such great quantities on the crowd. Her resolution not to be taken in by the display of false sentiment was swept away by the impact of the singer's eloquence; the fiction that he was embodying drew her to his real life, and she tried to imagine what it was like—that glamorous, fabulous, marvelous life that she, too, might have lived had chance so willed it. They might have met! They might have loved! . . . and every night behind the gilded lattice of her box she might have sat open-mouthed, breathing in the outpourings of that divine creature who was singing for her alone: he would have gazed at her from the stage as he played his role. A mad idea seized her: he was gazing at her now! She was sure of it! She longed to rush into his arms and seek refuge in his strength as in the very incarnation of love; she longed to cry: "Ravish me! Carry me off! Away from here! All my passion and all my dreams are yours— yours alone!"
> The curtain fell.[7]

Emma initially tries to hold on to the belief that the opera is a fictional illusion, but the staging seduces her away from reality. The other singers vanish from her perception, as she lavishes her personal erotic fantasies on the body of the tenor singing in her direction.

This phenomenon works even more powerfully in the almost invariable stage arrangement for the climactic love duet that forms the centerpiece of most nineteenth-century operas. In a duet, both singers must, of course, sing outwardly while striking a pose that plausibly looks like romantic attachment. The typical staging solution to this problem places the singers side by side, bodies turned in slightly so they may clasp hands while faces turn out toward the audience (an occasional variation of this arrangement places the tenor behind the soprano, his head just above hers and to one side, his arms around her waist or on her shoulders). Although textually the two declare their love for each other, what I see and hear in this arrange-

ment is both singers declaring their love for me. This staging gives me the
option to focus on either the male or female object of desire—or both. The
visual image of the love duet becomes a pansexual fantasy, an orgy of indiscriminate lovemaking. Both tenor and soprano offer me their passion. And,
of course, I am perfectly willing to accept their offer. I can place myself in
the position of the singer with whom I most identify, imagine myself embraced by the object of my erotic interest. Or I may imagine both singing to
me in a mental ménage-à-trois. My desire is free to wander back and forth
or to engage with both singers at once. If a stage director makes the radical
decision to do something other than face the lovers directly toward me, as
happens sometimes in nontraditional stagings, I feel cheated. I have come
to depend on being seduced, especially in these duets; it is why I shell out
my hard-earned money.

This kind of seductive duet happens frequently in opera. But on occasion
opera offers a trio or larger ensemble where other voices unite with a pair
of lovers, creating a redoubled erotic energy. As in Emma's response to the
Lucia sextet, the audience in these situations can choose to focus on a single
member of the ensemble. But ensembles also permit a more transgressive
erotic reading, a phenomenon seen most powerfully in the trio at the end of
Strauss's *Der Rosenkavalier*. At the end of the opera, the Marschallin, a
married woman who has had an affair with the youthful Octavian, now
must abandon her young lover, because Octavian has fallen in love with the
more age-appropriate Sophie. In the trio, the Marschallin sings of her lost
love, Sophie of her new love, and Octavian of his bittersweet position in the
middle. All three singers turn outward; Hugo von Hofmannsthal's libretto
specifies that they sing "für sich," apart, lost in their private thoughts, typically arrayed with Octavian center stage and Sophie and the Marschallin to
either side. In performance, an anticipatory hush falls over the audience as
the orchestra plays the opening bars that lead into the trio; people stop
moving in their seats, they almost stop breathing, and all eyes gaze intently
at the stage. As the three lovers sing Strauss's intensely seductive music, the
erotic tension becomes increasingly palpable, until the tension breaks in an
orgasmic climax and the Marschallin departs, leaving the two young lovers
by themselves to end the opera.

Even more than in the standard love duet, in the *Rosenkavalier* trio the
singers' relationship to the audience supersedes the narrative relationship
among the characters. Everything that happens in the previous three hours,
that is, the entire plot of the opera, is a prelude to these last ten minutes.
There is no stage movement here, just three bodies singing to me, letting me
indulge in my fantasies. The sexual free-space of the love duet is even more
widely drawn in this trio, with its more varied possibilities of mix-and-
match erotic object choice. But there is something more here. Strauss's
music encourages me to blur the lines that divide these objects of desire, as

the vocal lines of the three singers grow ever closer in increasingly dense harmonies and orchestration. By the climax, it is virtually impossible to tell the three voices apart or the voices from the orchestra; the waves of sound, the three bodies visually separate but musically united, overwhelm me. The gender ambiguity of the "man" in the middle, Octavian, sung by a soprano in drag, heightens the erotic tension even further. All the societal rules of sexual object choice are off here. I may construct this moment any way I wish, place my erotic interest with any or all of the singers, sequentially or at once. Or, more transgressively, I can defiantly choose not to construct the moment at all and experience it as pure, unspecified eroticism. For me, these are the most dangerous ten minutes in opera—and the most beautiful.

Trick Mirrors

If theater, as Hamlet says, holds a mirror up to nature, then opera offers a fun house mirror. What an audience sees on the opera stage is not life as it is but life made into something that it never can be. No one lives a life as big as an operatic character, no human being has the capacity to live at the intensity of opera twenty-four hours a day. Opera was born during an era when art was bigger, when paintings occupied the halls of vast palaces and the ceilings of papal chapels, when all serious drama had to be written in elevated verse. When Shakespeare says that the actor holds the mirror up to nature, he presumes that the details will be amplified in the mirroring process. In the twentieth century, when film and television lead us to expect art to mirror life with the accuracy of a photograph, opera seems, by comparison, overlarge, distorted, entirely unreal in its characterizations.

The modern theory of theatrical psychology presumes that when I look at the stage I see elements of myself. I will, in theory, project myself into one of the characters on the stage, developing a sympathy for his plight (the subject figure presumably being male), and feeling for him as I might feel for myself in a similar situation, real or imagined. I must perceive that this character shares elements of my own life or, better yet, represents the universal situation of all humanity. If no one has ever murdered my father, I can still see in Hamlet the emotional turmoil of the human condition, and I can identify with him in my imagination. Further, I must like the person with whom I identify (or at least not find him entirely repulsive). Even a villain can garner my identification if the character also shows a certain nobility or desirable audacity. Most importantly, I must be able to narrow my identification down to a single figure. I can sympathize with Ophelia, but I have to see the play through Hamlet's eyes—at least so goes the psychological identification argument that forms the basis of modern mainstream theater criticism.

But this psychological process of audience identification becomes distorted in opera. First of all, since many audience members cannot follow the words of the libretto (either because they do not speak the language or because the technical requirements of singing or the volume of the orchestra blur the words), the familiar channels that present the discursive information necessary for identification function erratically. It is hard to know whether to identify with Giovanni or Ottavio if I don't know what they are saying. Next, the characters and situations of opera are normally too grandiose for me to see much of myself in them; the remote settings give me little room for identification beyond the most broadly based emotions. Opera also destabilizes the identification process in regard to gender; if, in *Carmen,* Don José is the logical choice as the male subject of the story, the hero to Carmen's villainess, I much more strongly desire to ally myself with the musically interesting Carmen, even if I find little in her to admire. Sometimes in opera I see myself in a male character, sometimes in a female character, and I regularly see myself in male characters portrayed by female singers.

This is not to say, of course, that identification cannot occur in opera. There are times when identification works with a vengeance, as when, identifying with Rodolfo, I break down in tears at Mimi's death at the end of *La Bohème,* no matter how many times I see it. The language barrier can be overcome, with productions in the vernacular, or with projected supertitles, or when I simply know the libretto by heart. Even without a word-by-word knowledge of the libretto, I normally know enough of the general narrative to distinguish between the heroes, the villains, and the victims. For audiences of earlier periods, the narratives were less historically remote than they seem today, and these spectators were better trained at seeing themselves in amplified representations. The problem is not that opera prevents identification but that it problematizes the process, especially for a twentieth-century audience trained in realism.

Most problematically, the presumed single-identity focus falls apart in opera. I want to identify with far too many characters, major and minor. I cannot see an opera through the eyes of a single character, only with a shifting focus. Opera seduces me into its realm and then refuses to give me a solid grounding for my identity. Wayne Koestenbaum muses on the strange and shifting identity games he plays with Puccini's *Madama Butterfly:*

> American Lieutenant Pinkerton, on duty in Nagasaki, has purchased a
> bride, Butterfly, who is about to enter, and whom I crave: I've bought a
> ticket, and I wait with horny Pinkerton for the purchased presence to
> appear. . . . I do not applaud Pinkerton's imperial system; I applaud the
> emotions released by Butterfly's voice, emotions to which no words in
> the libretto do justice. I rise above rapacious Pinkerton ("That fool
> doesn't understand Butterfly") and identify with the diva's exposure.

> ... Like Butterfly, if I enter the opera, I will die, so I linger on its border
> to prolong and never complete my moment of entrance. I long to re-
> main outside the frame of opera, immune to its dangerous charms, but
> I also feel narrative's seduction: I want to enter the story and I want the
> plot to proceed.[8]

In one way, Koestenbaum sees himself as Pinkerton, the heroic figure who
controls the narrative, who purchases Butterfly in much the same way that
the audience purchases the performance of *Butterfly*. But he also sees himself in (or as) Butterfly, the tragic victim and the emotional centerpiece. He
feels a need to resist identification, but the opera seduces him to identify, refusing to let him stand apart. He identifies with everyone and no one, seeing himself inside and outside the opera at once.

This confusion of identification is not the same thing as the disruption of
audience identification that Bertolt Brecht outlines in his theory of alienation, the *Verfremdungseffekt*.[9] Brecht sets out to upset the traditional
identification process of realism, to encourage the audience to stay outside
the narrative frame, so they may make a detached political judgment about
the story and its social implications. But opera does not set up such boundaries. Opera does not ask me to stay outside its narrative frame. Opera
fully expects me to enter its world, to identify with its central characters, all
of them; there is no Brechtian disengagement here, but rather excess engagement.

Opera problematizes identification because it offers too much with
which to identify. Standard repertory opera characters are meant to be
highly attractive. I feel drawn to them: beautifully dressed; singing exquis-
itely; framed in a highly romanticized image of some exotic world; performing heroic actions; living dangerous, impossible lives, either winning
their loves or dying admirably in the process. But once I get seduced into
this world, my values change. Brecht complains that traditional theater presents an audience with a mirror of itself and never challenges the beliefs
that the audience holds. But opera does more than just induce complacency.
It actively seduces me, draws me in by presenting alluring characters with
whom I might not otherwise identify. It creates a fantasy world, where I am
encouraged to role-play in the narrative. Opera makes me someone else, at
least for the duration of its performance.

By the rules of standard theatrical identification, it is hard to understand
why some opera characters appeal to me. It is not as if I would want to live
my life as one of these people. I have no desire to exist in a perpetual state
of near hysteria, suffering untold horrors, debilitating illnesses, and failed
love affairs. Characters in spoken theater at least lead a calmer life, and
they offer compensations for their difficult problems. I do not want to suffer Hamlet's fate, but I would love to have his mental agility and insight.

And, more importantly, Shakespeare never asks me to want to be Claudius or Polonius. I can stand apart from the villains and fools in spoken theater. But opera lures me into roles I do not want to play, even for a short time. I am not a tragic heroine, and do not want to be one. I don't like Pinkerton at all, and I do not want to identify with him. I feel deeply for Butterfly, but my common sense tells me that I should not see myself in her. Yet I, like Koestenbaum, see myself in both Pinkerton and Butterfly. Opera makes me want to embody someone I have no rational desire to be.

I would argue that the ways that I engage with opera characters are, ultimately, not really a form of identification at all. For example, I am entirely fascinated by Turandot, Puccini's ice princess, who asks impossible riddles of her suitors and slaughters those who fail to answer them. Like her doomed lovers, I am mesmerized by her presence. I cannot listen to this opera enough. But I do not identify with Turandot in the strict psychological sense of the word. I think she's awful, a twisted mind obsessed with revenge. I do not even admire her, except perhaps for her strength and defiance, and even that admiration disappears at the end of the opera when she abandons those qualities in exchange for a normal love life. And I certainly do not feel much sympathy toward her; she is a nasty person all around. I cannot imagine her as a tolerable figure in a serious spoken play (in Carlo Gozzi's original, she is comic and cartoonish). I identify with the self-sacrificing slave girl Liù and with the heroic Calaf far more than I do with Turandot. I can see some of my fantasies in Calaf, as the masculine figure who conquers his love object. I feel for Liù while she sings, though I forget her quickly once she dies. But my energy in the opera goes not to Liù or Calaf but to Turandot. She is the title character, and Puccini makes sure my attention fixes on her. Her presence, her power, engage me.

This power to engage underlies opera's seduction of the audience. Rather than identifying with the characters, what I feel more often toward them is a longing for their power. Opera does not seduce me into identifying with its characters; it seduces me into desiring them. The thrill of the voice, its ability to capture my attention and throw me into raptures: This is what I feel, much more consistently than I feel sympathy or identification. It really does not matter who is good or bad in opera, who is admirable and who is despicable. I feel desire toward, and under the spell of, whoever happens to be singing at the moment. The standard assumptions about narrative identification that I bring to spoken theater and film are overridden in opera by my desire for the singing character. As Catherine Clément argues, music's seductive powers supersede the facts of the narrative, making me long for the display of power inherent in the music in a process that she calls "risk-free identification."[10] I would suggest, instead, the term "risk-free desire" to describe opera's draw.

Risk-free desire for operatic characters explains why I can enjoy an opera performance even when I cannot follow its narrative. The details of the story are not necessary to my experience, because what I feel is not an identification with the character's traits or actions, but a desire for the power of the character's voice and physical presence. I can detest Turandot as a human being and reject everything she stands for; when she sings "In questa reggia" my feelings engage with her entirely. Risk-free desire also explains why I criticize a weak opera performance so much more intensely than a similarly weak performance on the spoken stage. A less than perfect opera performance indicates a weakness not only in the singer but in the character. If opera is not entirely thrilling, if a character lacks power, my erotic interest becomes disengaged, and there is often nothing to take its place.

Opera makes me desire its characters, but it also makes me think that I sympathize with them. I am not supposed to acknowledge my desire—it embarrasses me—so I tell myself instead that my desire is really sympathy or identification. Opera accomplishes this feat of transference mostly through its music. No matter which character in the story deserves to garner the most sympathy, the one I like most is the one with the best tunes. My response to a spectacular aria feels like sympathy. If I identify with a character, it is because I desperately want to be able to sing like that or, short of that, to possess that beautiful voice. Koestenbaum initially feels for the horrible Pinkerton because he is the character who sings first, and then he transfers his feelings to Butterfly, because she sings later and better. I cry at the end of *La Bohème,* not when Mimi exhibits signs of her mortal illness but when she sings the melodies from Act I. It is the music, more than the narrative, that engages. The power of musical desire to mimic sympathy is precisely the danger Clément warns against. Music obscures the narrative and my ability to judge its emotional effects, because my desire for the music overwhelms any feelings I might have about the narrative. I can forgive anything for a good tune.

Empty Mirrors

In the film *Moonstruck,* Loretta Castorini, unlucky in love, goes to the opera for the first time, escorted by Ronny Cammareri, a rather butch rendition of a heterosexual opera queen. The opera is *La Bohème* at the Met. In the third act, as Mimi bids Rodolfo good-bye without bitterness, "Addio senza rancor," we see tears run down Loretta's cheeks. The scene cuts to the end of the performance; as Ronny and Loretta leave the theater, she reveals her emotional response to the story:

> *Loretta:* That was so awful.
> *Ronny:* Awful?
> *Loretta:* Beautiful. Sad. She died.
> *Ronny:* Yeah.
> *Loretta:* I couldn't believe it. You know, I didn't think she was gonna
>   die. I knew she was sick, but—
> *Ronny:* She had TB.
> *Loretta:* I know. I mean, she was coughing her brains out, right, and
>   still she had to keep singing.[11]

For those of us in the know, Loretta's response is absurd. Of course Mimi is going to die; the consumptive soprano always dies. But her remark, and the fact that opera lovers see it as comic, raises a central issue. By the rules of Aristotelian narrative structure, Mimi need not die. Nothing in the story, other than the early references to her illness, requires her death. Mimi's death is entirely incidental to the love story, an unfortunate accident and nothing more. An audience member (especially one raised on the patterns of expectation of American television) seeing the piece for the first time has every right to expect that Mimi and Rodolfo will live happily ever after, to a ripe old age, singing gloriously until the end. Loretta wants to see herself in Mimi, as another troubled woman unlucky in love. She expects the stage to show her a mirror of her narrative expectations, of the way she wants her own life to turn out, and so she cannot accept the tragic ending. When she looks in the mirror, she fails to see herself.

If opera seduces a male spectator like me into thinking, against my will, that I identify with its tragic figures, it pulls a much more elegant trick in making a female spectator think she identifies with its fallen heroines. This question forms the center of Clément's argument: How can she, as a woman in the twentieth century, go to the opera and continue to be seduced by the characters, when the lives of the women she sees on the opera stage are such a constant denial of her own view of women's life in modern society?[12] Female characters in opera, relatively few in number and so often cast as victims, play for our sympathies more consistently than male characters. Puccini certainly throws our sympathies this way. It is much easier to like Butterfly than Pinkerton, Tosca gets the last word in her opera, Rodolfo and Des Grieux are ineffectual in saving Mimi and Manon, and even in *Turandot,* where the title character is far too powerful to be perceived as a victim and rather too unpleasant to be sympathetic, Puccini gives us Liù as a site for our sympathies. When Loretta refuses to accept Mimi's death, she is resisting Puccini's identity game. She declines to let her life become tragic and does not want to see Mimi give up on her life either.

As the title of her study, *Opera, or the Undoing of Women,* suggests, Clément argues that the destruction and victimization of female characters is inherent to opera, an exclusory and destructive pattern that she traces back to opera's origins.[13] Historically, however, this litany of death is a relatively new phenomenon. Operas with tragic endings do not appear consistently until the nineteenth century. Until then, virtually all opera libretti, both in comic opera and the more prevalent *opera seria,* ended with happy (or at least bloodless) resolutions. John Gay, in his parody of Handelian *opera seria, The Beggar's Opera,* has his narrator insist on an illogical happy ending for the narrative, because, he says, that's what the audience expects in an opera.[14] Clément is right in that these early operas, when they deal with female characters at all, do not grant them any real authority or autonomous voice. But the point remains that dead heroines are not *necessary* to opera. Our expectation of Mimi's death is a learned response. When the lifeless Bugs Bunny at the end of "What's Opera, Doc?" pops back alive at the last moment and says directly to the audience "What did you expect in an opera, a happy ending?" he simply echoes the enforced narrative structure that we have learned from Wagner, Verdi, and Puccini.

If we learn to expect death in opera, how does opera teach us to respond to its representations of women? In the July 1992 issue of *Opera News,* devoted to the subject of women in opera, Ralph P. Locke attempts to resuscitate opera's female characters from Clément's critical construction. In his essay "What Are These Women Doing in Opera?" he agrees that, on the whole, opera's female characters tend to fare badly and that opera usually reduces them to limiting stereotypes. He sympathizes that women might have a hard time seeing themselves in these roles. He argues, however, that in audience perception, these stereotypes serve a function beyond a one-to-one, audience-to-character identification. Opera's female characters, he argues, represent for the audience universal human feelings that, because of fears of lost machismo, they cannot associate comfortably with male characters: feelings of victimization, fear, loneliness, and similar "weaknesses." Female characters in opera become universals by transcending their gender, so that both men and women in the audience may identify with their tragic condition.[15]

Locke's argument may explain how primarily male audiences relate to these stereotypes and why female characters in opera, so few in number and so thoroughly deprived of power, still manage to command so much attention. But he does not address Clément's primary assertion that opera treats female characters as secondary objects. And he certainly does nothing to encourage a woman to see herself in one of these roles. In Locke's analysis, male characters in opera are universal precisely because they are male; the only way a female character can achieve universality is to "transcend her gender." Men can be men, but women have to be something more than women. Locke implies that a female character in opera can only become significant when she ceases to be a "real" woman. For a woman in the audience to identify with such a character, she must perform a double act of nonrecognition. She must forget that the character she sees on stage, though overtly female, does not really represent women, and she must forget that she herself is a woman being represented on stage in a negative light.

Opera assists this process of selective forgetting by turning its female characters into icons. The Fat Lady is not the only iconic woman of opera; she merely stands as the most visible representative of a whole range of female-gendered icons. Rather than the actual character of Carmen, the public recognizes the image of the Gypsy seductress, dancing with a rose between her teeth, the iconic figure to which the character of Carmen is reduced. We do not see Mimi and Violetta, the consumptive heroines of Puccini's *La Bohème* and Verdi's *La Traviata,* as individual personalities, but rather as iconic pretty young consumptives coughing themselves to death in run-down garrets. Plenty of people know the images of Carmen and Violetta/Mimi without ever having seen their operas, without knowing their names or situations. The stereotypes take on a life of their own.

Virtually all of opera's icons are female. There are a few male roles that might qualify for such iconic status: Giovanni, Figaro, or the generic Wagnerian Heldentenor. But here the icon is really the individual character rather than a character type. Figaro, in either Mozart's or Rossini's version, does not represent a larger group of clever itinerant barbers, or even one of clever servants. Figaro is Figaro and no one else. Giovanni is iconic because of the power of his singular character. Violetta and Mimi, however, are not individuals. They represent a general group of consumptive victims, even though they are really the only two examples of such roles in the active repertory, the same number as the available range of Figaros.[16] Men are allowed an individual personality; women become types. Even though in sheer numbers there are far fewer female leading roles than male leading roles on the operatic (or any other) stage, only women's roles become the focus of reductive icons.

These icons, then, become objects of audience desire rather than the individual characters. I do not need to sympathize or identify with an icon. In fact, I cannot identify with an icon. I desire it. Icons only need to represent something in a static manner and stand still for contemplation. I respond to an icon with a pleasure in its recognition and a satisfaction that the icon fulfills its iconic purpose, not with a feeling for its plight. I respond to an operatic icon the way I respond to a stereotypical sexy body in pornography. I do not respond sympathetically to characters in pornography, and I certainly do not see in them a reflection of my life situation or of my own less-than-iconic body. In opera, as in pornography, I see in the icon only an attractive image, and I desire that image. I want the icon to behave in a predictably iconic manner (by performing sexual acts or by dying), and I respond with appropriate emotions (arousal, tears) when the icon fulfills my expectation. Anything that deviates from the iconic behavior simply gets in the way of this erotic contemplation.

Locke wants female characters in opera to be universal, but they are only universal to the degree that they become archetypes, not individual examples of human existence. Men have been trained by society to see themselves in universal terms. I learn automatically to place myself in the subject position of any work of art and assume that everything on stage depicted in a positive light is about me.[17] Women, taught to see themselves as the other, the thing separate from the universal, have no way to see themselves in this psychological view of opera. They cannot see their lives in the male characters, and the female characters are normally too negative or too "universalized" to serve as objects for identification. As a man, opera lets me see myself in whoever is singing. Women can do the same only by complex processes of self-erasure. Opera offers women an empty mirror.

The female opera audience member, then, would seem to have only two spectatorial choices. On the one hand, she can perform the well-worn act of self-erasure that traditional western narrative demands, abandoning her own subject position and trying to look at the spectacle through male eyes. But, on the other hand, if opera denies to women any kind of identificatory outlets, it (unlike most film or spoken theater) offers an alternative: the option of giving up identification altogether in favor of a more direct erotic experience, the abandonment to opera's seduction. Emma Bovary feels no need to identify with Lucia; she quickly bypasses the soprano and directs her gaze onto the tenor. When there is no temptation to read the spectacle as reality (or when, as in Clément's model, the female spectator is actively discouraged from doing so), opera's flexible eroticism provides a viable option for audience engagement. Loretta's mistake is in trying to see reality on the opera stage. For a woman to achieve spectatorial pleasure from opera, she can much more easily disengage entirely from the identity/sympathy game, which narrative art normally expects us to play, and indulge instead in erotic fantasy.

For that matter, the male spectator can also profit from the same process. As Koestenbaum's response to *Butterfly* demonstrates, even for the male spectator, within the options of sympathy and identification, opera presents problems. Opera, through its physical excesses, music, and staging devices, actively encourages me to respond erotically to the spectacle rather than to read the narrative in psychological terms. As an alternative to chasing after elusive and shifting identities, the pleasures of erotic abandonment are much more attractive.

But this kind of oblivion is also hazardous. When I give myself over entirely to opera's pleasures, it seduces me into the most dangerous realm of all, the place where I forget my critical faculties and stop examining what I see on stage. I listen to the music, watch the spectacle, and forget the social implications of what I see and hear. Opera sings the song of the Lotus-Eaters, seducing me into forgetfulness and mental lethargy. It lulls me into an indiscriminate state of desire, where everything that floats across my ear and eye momentarily satisfies my erotic needs and immediately leaves me craving for more. I could easily, despite Clément's insistent warnings, lose myself in opera's realm of undifferentiated desire. Eventually, though, reality comes back to disturb my reverie. The opera ends, the bill for the opera tickets arrives, I have to go back to work to pay for my addiction. Between performances I can contemplate the nature of my desire, the strange ways in which I project myself into opera, how I get lost in its seduction. And in those pauses, perhaps I can eventually learn to bring my knowledge back to opera, to find ways to understand the destructive parts of my desire without losing my erotic pleasure.

4

DESIRE AND THE SINGER'S BODY

Claude: ... And then I went to see Behrens for the first time, in The Flying Dutchman*. I had seen it on TV and—this might sound stupid, but I found this woman extremely ugly. And so I went to the opera with preconceptions. I don't know why. She started to sing and from that moment on, I realized that on the stage, she became incredibly beautiful, physically beautiful. My first reaction when I heard her sing wasn't "She sings well" but "She's beautiful!" Strange! That was the decisive moment, the one that won me over.*

—Michel Poizat
The Angel's Cry[1]

Selling Three Tenors

On July 7, 1990, Luciano Pavarotti, Placido Domingo, and José Carreras (the latter recently recovered from leukemia) gave a joint recital at the Baths of Caracalla in Rome to celebrate the final round of the World Cup. They sang a variety of their best-known arias, along with songs from the popular repertory, separately in rotation and then together at the end of the concert. The event was billed as the opera concert of the decade, if not the century, the first time all three of the world's greatest tenors had ever sung together. The response to the concert was overwhelming. The fans in the audience cheered wildly, and the adulation resonated long after the concert ended. The concert was released as a sound recording and a videotape, and the first Three Tenors album broke international sales records for classical music. It captured popular attention for longer than any other recent event in "serious" music and has continued to appear regularly on public television, most often when stations solicit contributions from viewers. Four years later, the whole affair was repeated, this time at Dodger Stadium in Los Angeles. The second concert threw all pretense of artistic taste to the wind. Tenors Redux turned into a shameless display of Hollywood hype and profiteering, set against a ridiculous scenic display of tropical foliage, waterfalls, and faux-classical columns, with the lowest ticket price set at several hundred dollars, the highest over a thousand, many times the standard rates at Europe's most expensive opera houses.[2]

I hardly need to describe the concerts here. If you are reading this book, you likely already know about them. They were among the great media events of recent years. But why did these concerts create such a furor? It certainly was not the singing. Neither performance could make a claim to musical distinction. The repertory was mundane, mostly trite verismo arias mixed with overinflated cheap pop tunes, and all three tenors were past the peaks of their careers (Carreras in particular, who wandered regularly off pitch, especially in the first concert). The stars didn't even bother to learn all of the music; during the medleys at the end of both concerts, they stared awkwardly at their music stands and stumbled over the words. And it certainly wasn't the singers' intimate, personal connection with the audience, nor the acoustics, no matter how good the sound systems. I suppose these concerts might have excited people not already familiar with the singers, but even a new wave of opera fans does not explain the degree of adulation (not to mention the degree of profit).

In fact, the furor began long before any of them opened their mouths. The public reaction came in response to the events, not to the music. Three Tenors succeeded because of the unique situation of bringing three great stars, three loci of operatic desire, onto a single stage at the same time, even more because of the way the event was packaged for sale. If we love one tenor, we will go crazy over three. The Three Tenors events were not concerts; they were public orgies, the first set with brilliant appropriateness within Roman ruins, the second less successfully, though equally aptly, in a sports arena. They were P. T. Barnum tricks of eroticized excess, and they worked like a charm. In the video versions the directors made sure everything looked big, from the panoramic shots of the double orchestra and vast scenery to the facial close-ups and low camera angles that made the singers look larger than life. These extravaganzas were not, of course, the first such public media events involving multiple singers. Megaperformances were commonplace during the nineteenth-century, staged under the supervision of Barnum or composer and impresario Louis Moreau Gottschalk. Sol Hurok and Tibor Rudas are merely the modern heirs to an old tradition. Star quality continues to be the ideal for public performance: "Live, for the first time on any stage!" the posters read, and we still buy into the fiction.

It is not enough, however, simply to look at lots of stars on display. To make the performance more of an event, we need tension between the stars, a rivalry for the affections of the public. We need to hear all of the backstage gossip, the battles for top billing, the threatened walkouts, the wrangling over repertory and order of appearance. If the Three Tenors concerts were musically lacking, they lacked nothing as a display of artistic rivalry. The story of competition among the singers was already well known before the first concert: Pavarotti, the flamboyant megastar and media darling; Domingo, less flashy but generally acknowledged by critics as the more talented and serious musician; and Carreras, the lesser light of the three, but elevated by his heroic battle with illness and triumphant return to the stage. All through Tenors I the camera made the rivals out as good sports, showing us their embraces and high fives. But their friendliness only highlighted the air of competition. To add to the tension, Tenors I was clearly Pavarotti's show; he was the Italian, on his home turf in Rome, sharing the stage with two Spaniards; he got the climactic third position in the rotation of the singers. Pavarotti was also the one most comfortable in front of the camera, and the first concert included two renditions each of "O sole mio" and "Nessun Dorma," his signature pieces.

The staged rivalries in Tenors I didn't really get going, however, until the encores, and the jousting was duly recorded by the all-seeing camera. There were two particularly electric moments. The first came during the first encore, the repeat of "O sole mio." Pavarotti began to sing and seemed about to hog the entire number. But Domingo cut in and took over; Pavarotti deferred with an evil glare. When Pavarotti's turn came up next, he showed off with an inordinately long and loud trill. Domingo and Carreras then consulted secretly behind his back, and in the next verse responded in unison with an equally long and clearly parodic rendition of Pavarotti's vocal display. Though they seemed to be having fun, the moment came alive with the implication of ugly competition. Rather than a real battle, though, this back-stabbing came across as a fictionalized narrative generated by the media, enacted for the benefit of the cameras, which were careful to include the whole story, including the plotting behind Pavarotti's back.

The combat narrative continued in the final encore, which was a collective performance of Pavarotti's signature aria, "Nessun Dorma." Pavarotti identifies himself with this piece, and he sings it to end all of his recitals. No longer a musical moment, the triple performance of the aria became a battle for dominance on Pavarotti's home territory. Each competitor sang lines from the aria sequentially; eventually Pavarotti tried to wrest control, cueing his colleagues and orchestrating their rotation. Toward the end there was some confusion as to who would take the final phrases; Pavarotti seized the opportunity and usurped the last stretch. Finally, Domingo and Carreras joined in at the last moment, so they could end the concert in unison. At this moment, the audience got one last bit of suspense: Who would hold the murderous climactic note the longest? It came out essentially as a draw, and the number ended triumphantly, with referee Zubin Mehta beaming at all the competitors. The battle had been played out, but no winner was declared, allowing all fans to claim victory.[3]

Tenors II failed entirely to maintain this battle narrative. It may have made a lot of money, but it flopped as entertainment. Tenors II depended on its presumptive status as a rematch of Tenors I. But since the first concert had no declared winner, the rematch was pointless. To compensate, the PBS broadcast of Tenors II constructed the concert overtly as a sporting event. Besides its setting in a ballfield, the Trojan Marching Band from the University of Southern California entertained waiting fans, and the concert began with the playing of "The Star Spangled Banner." And, rather than artsy introductions, the broadcast offered play-by-play and color commentary. Unfortunately, PBS chose as their announcers violinist Itzhak Perlman and someone named Willo Carey, both charming but untrained in sports banter. They tried, in stilted and embarrassing dialogue, desperately to generate some excitement: "This is almost like a sporting event here," they said. The tenors, in their first medley, scored a "triple play"; and before the encores, they declared that the concert was "going into overtime." They tried to make the tenors into sports heroes: not three competing stars, but members of a hero-class of tenors in general. They conflated the tenors' stage roles with their personalities: "On the operatic stage they play every sort of hero . . . but they are always the good guys, they always get the girl, and they always save the day." Instead of three rival stars going at each others' throats, we got three generic heroes with no enemies to fight. If Tenors I succeeded as a fun, if obviously fake, battle, Tenors II fell flat because the rivalries disappeared.[4]

Professional Wrestling

Opera demands hierarchies. In light of its excesses, we judge everything about opera in terms of the best, the greatest, the most. The public must always be at odds over who is the greatest tenor, who is the *prima donna assoluta*. Other art forms do not have the same fixation with hierarchies. A film fan may have an individual favorite star but will generally allow other fans to prefer other stars. The Academy Awards ceremonies supposedly reward the best film and actors, but no one really believes that the Oscar winner is actually the best (though, in our fascination with hierarchies, we watch the event religiously anyway). But not opera fans. A Domingo devotee will scoff at anyone who prefers Pavarotti and think less of someone with such base tastes; and the good lord help you if you dare breathe a syllable of praise for Renata Tebaldi within earshot of a Maria Callas fanatic. You are not a legitimate opera singer in the United States if you only sing at the New York City Opera, never moving across Lincoln Center Plaza to the Metropolitan; and you haven't *really* made it until you have sung at La Scala. We want casts that are made up only of international stars, and then we argue over whether they are really as good as they used to be. There is also the hierarchy of opera's economics; opera tickets cost more than any other kind of performance admission, and we divide ourselves in the opera house hierarchically by our ability to pay (though we can claim a kind of beggar's pride by subjecting ourselves to the cheap seats or, better yet, standing room, where the *real* opera fans are).

Why must we crown the *primo tenore* and, even more important for most fans, the *prima donna assoluta*? We need these hierarchies, because the battle for primacy constitutes a public display of desire. Just as the Three Tenors must do battle in public to demonstrate their power to draw audience desire, so I must demonstrate the intensity of my adulation to validate my own desire. (The most interesting part of the Three Tenors phenomenon is that, for the first time since the early twentieth century, the erotic interest of the opera public focused primarily on men rather than on women.) Choosing between singers is like choosing between lovers. In the end, the choice is fairly arbitrary; good singers, like good lovers, all have their good points and their failings. But once I make my choice, I must prove to myself that it is the only choice, and I must legitimate my desire through impassioned argument.[5]

Of course, I am not supposed to fantasize about sleeping with opera singers (and, frankly, Pavarotti does nothing for me physically—Sam Ramey, yes, but not Luciano). In the earliest days of opera, as Anne Rice depicts in *Cry to Heaven*, wealthy fans might actually act on their erotic desire for opera singers and still can today, as Aristotle Onassis demonstrated with Maria Callas. But my income precludes such direct wish-fulfillment. Like a teenage fan of a rock star, I can only fulfill my sexual desire with my operatic lovers in my imagination. But even that admission causes excess embarrassment, especially within the high-art trappings of opera. So I must find other names for my desire, other outlets to release the sexual tension generated by the performance, for instance, arguing over which tenor is best.

Theatrical presentation in all of its forms eroticizes the body of the performer; whether on the spoken stage, in a rock concert, or on film or television, the performing body, placed on a stage or screen for audience consumption, becomes an object of sexual desire.[6] And in all kinds of theatrical presentation, this desire normally hides under a mask, however thin, of social propriety. But opera, in its excessiveness, amplifies the intensity of the eroticized body, and so requires intensive means to hide its sexuality. Both functions arise from the one element that sets opera's eroticized bodies apart from most other kinds of performance: vocal music. Music in opera both inflames and displaces my desire. It intensifies the erotic presence of the singing body and, at the same time, masks the nature of performance as commodified erotic exchange. The presence of music heightens the erotic stakes of performance, especially when that music is overtly orgasmic, as operatic music so often is. But the elevated realm of classical music, along with the elegant trappings of the opera house, makes me forget that I am buying an erotic experience. A high-class prostitute never seems as immoral as a cheap one. When I rave about opera, I can assume a stance of aesthetic chastity and cultural purity while getting my kicks.

A lot of people will become very upset when I suggest that opera is a kind of prostitution. How dare I defile opera so horribly? What kind of an opera fan am I? But as George Bernard Shaw argues in his exploration of the morality of prostitution, *Mrs. Warren's Profession,* all life in modern society demands that we sell ourselves one way or another. And when we are not selling ourselves, we are (if we have the means) buying others. A service- and labor-based economy depends on the sale of human bodies. Sexual desire and money are the two most powerful means of exchange that we have, and opera trades heavily in both. I do not think it degrades opera to acknowledge the desire I feel toward singers and my willingness to pay for the fulfillment of my desire. In an ideal world, I'd get all my fantasies for free, but until that happens I'll still buy my opera tickets. And if I can engage my sexual energies through magnificent art, all the better. I like my erotic exchanges a little better hidden than the Three Tenors concert, which embarrasses me for making its commercial display so blatant. But then, in opera, embarrassment itself is erotic. As long as I can forget for a moment that I have bought my fantasy, opera makes me happy.

Looking at Singers' Bodies

As a form of public display, opera lets me relate sexually not only to its characters in a fictional guise but also to the lives of its stars as public personalities, even more as sexualized bodies. Opera singers serve as sex symbols for an audience that is reluctant to admit its vulnerability to such base pandering in the more popular realms of film and television. Even theorists who actively acknowledge opera's sexual appeal refuse to admit the powerful attraction of the singer's body. Michel Poizat certainly sees opera as sexual, but he argues that the source of operatic *jouissance,* opera's erotic climax, comes exclusively through the voice of the singer. At opera's moments of intense erotic fulfillment, he argues, the singer becomes pure voice; the body, the scenery, everything other than the voice of the singer disappears from consciousness; and we in the audience become one with the ecstatic cry of the unmediated voice.[7] Poizat's argument makes for a powerful metaphor, but in practical reality the body of the singer does not disappear. The body becomes a physical manifestation of the voice, it is eroticized by the voice, but the body of the singer remains an integral part of opera's sexual display.[8]

The body on display on stage is public property. As Michel Foucault powerfully argues in his analysis, in *Discipline and Punish,* of public executions and torture, the act of putting a human body on public display turns that body into a commodity upon which figures of authority inscribe their power.[9] Similarly, in the theater, as recent performance scholarship has argued, the body displayed onstage also becomes a site for the public inscription of power, especially the conjunction between economic and erotic power. The performing body becomes the personal property of every member of the audience. I pay for the right to look at the body, and it is mine, at least for the duration of the performance. I look at the singer, and so maintain visual authority over the singer's body (even when it seems that the singer is looking back at me, I maintain possession by having initiated the gaze). I assert my ownership of the performer's body by looking at it; the stage becomes an elaborate peep show, where the gaze becomes the means of controlling desire. Limited-view seats cost less even in the opera house, because even though I can hear the music perfectly well, if I cannot look at the singer's body my erotic desire becomes thwarted.

We often forget the importance of looking in the opera house. Opera, because of its music, supposedly appeals more to the ear than the eye. It does not matter what the singer looks like, I hear, as long as the sound is beautiful. And sometimes the visual aspects of opera give me more offense than pleasure. If the singer falls too far short of the physical ideal of the character, if the acting is too awful, if the scenery is too silly, I am tempted simply to close my eyes and listen to the music, so as not to break the spell of the performance. These offenses happen more often than I care to admit. But I still keep my eyes open, no matter how painful the spectacle. I have to look at the singers, or else I lose my connection to them. Listening to opera recordings cannot completely substitute for live performance. Not even videos are enough. I have to have the singer's body there in the room with me, available to my gaze, there to be consumed by my hungry eyes.[10]

Claude, one of the opera fans interviewed by Poizat at the beginning of *The Angel's Cry,* experiences this erotic commodification of the singer's body in his changing opinion of Hildegard Behrens. On television, distanced by the camera, he experiences no physical desire for the soprano, and he perceives her as ugly. In the opera house, though, with the singer's live body placed on display before him, she suddenly, mysteriously becomes beautiful. Claude does not know why this transformation happens, and Poizat's explanation of desire for the abstracted pure voice does not sufficiently explain the process. Claude feels his sudden onrush of desire for Behrens because of her act of self-display, the offering by the singer of her body to the eroticizing gaze. A simple presentation of the body is not enough; the body must sing in order bring about the erotic transformation.

But the body's physical presence is the other necessary element of the formula.

This process can also work when the singer is momentarily silent. An English lithograph by R. J. Lane and A. E. Chalon, dated October 20, 1836, demonstrates the eroticized spectatorial nature of the singer-audience relationship (see Figure 4.1). This image, entitled "Spettatrice and Attrice" (Spectator and Actress), depicts on one side the soprano Maria Malibran in a performance, on 31 July 1830, at the King's Theatre, London, of the role of Fidalma in Cimarosa's comic opera *Il Matrimonio Segreto*. The other side shows Malibran viewing a performance from the audience in a sidebox. The inscription reads: "After playing Fidelma [sic] in Cimarosa's opera Il Matrimonio Segreto Malibran went into a Pit box to see the Ballet, or rather to afford the Public a better opportunity of appreciating her powers of transformation." In character, the illustration shows a decidedly unattractive vision of Malibran. Fidalma is a pathetic, love-sick, elderly matron, in the same school as Marcellina in *Le Nozze di Figaro*. The drawing of her character emphasizes her aggression (she wields a formidable fan, poised to strike) and her facial shortcomings (she seems to have a mustache). On the other side, however, we see the "real" Malibran, a striking figure in profile, the image of serene beauty and erotic appeal on which Malibran banked in her meteoric career.

This double image tells a powerful story about looking, in which Malibran first manipulates the audience's gaze and the artists then manipulate the desire of the operagoing public. In the performance at the King's Theatre that the drawing depicts, Malibran earns the astonished looks of the audience, who expect to see a beautiful singer and see instead a caricatured comic hag. But such an effective characterization (as well as its portrait, widely distributed to her public) could have proved detrimental to a singer noted for her beauty. Malibran could not afford to have her impersonation believed too thoroughly. So, after her performance, Malibran carefully displays her "true" self to the audience, poised at the edge of her box in a pose at once demure and statuesque, and this display is duly recorded by the artists. The audience here gets two performances for their admission price, that of Malibran the singer and the more important one of Malibran the beauty. The spectator may wonder at the skill of the performer in her ability to hide her beauty, more so at her miraculous act of restoration.

The lithograph plays an even more elaborate game of double vision than the performance itself. Both renditions of Malibran appear in profile, each facing the center of the page. We look at the singer in her two guises, and the singer looks at herself, reflecting on her own mutability. The "real" Malibran looks at her strangely transformed body, serenely confident in her control over her sexual allure; but because I look at the picture, I therefore own her self-reflexive gaze. I possess Malibran in all her transformations—

Figure 4.1 Madame Malibran as Fidalma in The Secret Marriage *and watching the ballet from a box; lithograph after A. E. Chalon, 1803, plate 8 of Chalon's Operatic Recollections 1836. From the collections of the Theatre Museum. By courtesy of the Board of Trustees of the Victoria and Albert Museum, London.*

almost. The illustration shows Fidalma in full costume, displaying the whole body of the singer hiding her sexual allure beneath the unattractive characterization and dowdy clothes. But when Malibran appears in her box, only her head, neck, and one seemingly bare arm are visible. The picture teases my desire, refusing to show me the full body of the attractive Malibran. Notably, in the picture the "real" Malibran appears on the left, so that I first see the beautiful, partly hidden singer, and only then the caricatured performance, a reversal of the sequence in the theater. If I am to own Malibran, she will make sure that my first and most powerful impression is the one she wants me to remember.

Applause, Applause

Most singers these days do not make appearances out of costume in the sideboxes. But I do get a chance to view the singer's body at the end of each performance, during the curtain call. Like Malibran in the box, the curtain call pulls the singer's body out of the context of the opera's narrative. The scenery disappears, the lights come on full, and I can see the sweaty, exhausted body of the singer as it is, without the mask of illusion. The singers emerge from behind the heavy drapery and into the harsh lights of the forestage, stripped of their roles, in their own personas, where I can give them my audible adoration. The fictional context vanishes. After the performance, in which the characters have declared their love for me, I get my chance to perform a reciprocal act of lovemaking to the body of the star.

During the curtain call the audience members perform back to the singers, acknowledging their acceptance of the seduction that had been offered them throughout the evening. Opera audiences applaud louder and longer than audiences for any other kind of theatrical performance, not to mention more often, usually after every major aria and at the end of each act. The audience at a Broadway play will normally only applaud with vigor after the last act, and the actors only take bows at that time, receiving two or three curtain calls, four in extraordinary circumstances. But four curtain calls are nothing in opera, where sometimes the numbers rise into the dozens. In this extended response, the audience expresses its erotic engagement with the performance and also prolongs that engagement in an effort to keep the thrill alive. Applause also offers the audience the sensual gratification that the distant bodies of the singers cannot fulfill; the violent act of banging hands together until they hurt provides tangible release from erotic tension. The curtain call becomes a part of the performance itself, and its excessiveness mirrors the excesses of the more "official" part of the performance. When I applaud, I answer opera's seductive call, shouting back enthusiastically that I am perfectly willing to be seduced. Unfortunately, when I finish applauding, the opera goes away. Opera only cares to seduce me until I acknowledge my capitulation, when, like a fickle lover, it immediately disappears, waiting for me to come back to the opera house, begging to be seduced again.

Some people cannot rest content with the anonymity of undifferentiated group applause. They must compete with other viewers for the erotic interest of the singers. They shout "bravo" or "brava" so as to be heard above the crowd, to show that they love the singer more than anyone else. They stand up, sometimes on their seats. (Is a standing ovation a kind of audience erection?) They throw flowers; if they are truly audacious, they bring the flowers to the edge of the stage, approaching the actual body of the singer. I have rarely engaged in such activities; I embarrass too easily. But I have played out this spectacle backstage at the Met, standing in the long line of adoring fans waiting patiently for the singer to emerge from the dressing room, so that I may catch a glimpse of the star, mumble a few words of tongue-tied adoration, and get my program autographed. But these moments are always awkward. I have nothing to say to the singer; I mutter a few clichéd phrases of praise, get my autograph, and leave feeling unfulfilled. The star does not look as big or as beautiful close up as on the stage. The lovemaking that happens between opera singer and audience cannot stand proximity; it can only happen at a distance, and it shatters when I cross the boundary of the proscenium into the realm of human contact.

In the curtain call, the singers, knowing full well the importance of this erotic display, carefully acknowledge it with an equivalent display of their own. They throw kisses to the audience, as if directly to me as an individual. The standard opera bow tangibly heightens the erotic interplay. In a Broadway play, the actors bow with a quick, stiff, almost mechanical motion, a polite acknowledgment of polite applause. The opera singer bows slowly and deeply, a seductive prostration, a physical offering of the body by the singer to the audience, as if to say, "I give my entire self to you, body and soul." The singer performs the bow through a mask of humility, accompanied by a silent, mouthed "thank you." And I believe entirely in this performance, far more than I do in the one prior to the curtain call; in return, I cheer all the louder, my libido driven to a frenzy. The singers leave and come back, again and again, each time adding more erotic energy to the display. Opera audiences applaud more than any other kind of audience, because the curtain call is itself part of opera's erotic display of the singer's body, perhaps its most important part.

The opera critics of the New York press regularly berate Metropolitan Opera audiences for being indiscriminate in their applause. How, they ask in disbelief, can these audiences cheer wildly for every performance they attend, no matter how mediocre the staging or indifferent the singing? Haven't these people been to the opera before? Can't they tell good from bad?[11] What these critics fail to realize, however, is that opera applause has little to do with an objective evaluation of the quality of the performance. The amount of applause that follows an aria or an entire opera does not reflect the abilities of the singers in performance. It *is* the performance, the climax of the opera's true narrative, the one that enacts the engagement between the singer and the audience. Underneath opera's fictional narrative lies another story, the principle characters of which are my body and the bodies of the singers on stage. And unlike the often tragic surface narrative, over which I have no control, I can always give my personal opera story a happy ending, a consummation of erotic desire, through my hyperactive applause.

Hysterical Fans

The erotic release of the opera curtain call can seem like a kind of hysteria, especially to those who have no particular erotic engagement with the performance. The only other art form that elicits a similar intensity of response from its audience is rock music, but rock audiences have the mitigating factors of youth, rebelliousness, mob psychology, and, not infrequently, mind-altering drugs to justify their behavior. Opera audiences—adult, conservative, and well-dressed (perhaps a little tipsy, but rarely stoned)—have nothing to blame but ourselves for our extreme behavior. Opera makes me do things I would not otherwise do in public, and it induces me to demand insane and extravagant spectacles on the stage. The era of the castrati represents one long, international exercise in public hysteria; rational people would not demand such a sacrifice for the sake of the voice. We no longer demand singers to be castrated to satisfy our hysteria, but we do want a whole range of other irrational displays for our pleasure, we will pay irrational amounts of money to get them, and we respond to them with an equal level of irrationality.

A brilliant performance throws me into hysterical ecstasy, an uncontrollable display of affection. Conversely, when a singer fails to please, or at least when a singer's faults are too blatant to ignore, I become more vicious than when I see any other kind of faulty performance. Most modern-day audiences maintain a quiet decorum in the face of the worst of performances. But only opera audiences greet obvious mistakes with physicalized displays of disapproval. As Poizat observes, when a singer misses a high note, it is as if a lover has betrayed me.[12] He states:

> This retribution for disgrace is always rather impressive, for it occurs
> with a violence, not to say shocking hatred, that is utterly dispropor-
> tionate, if observed from the outside, to what would seem to be at
> stake. After all, how important can it be that a singer should bungle a
> note that is supposed to last no longer than a few tenths of a second in

the course of a performance often more than three hours long? . . . It is as if the fan feels deprived of what he was awaiting with so much fervor: an instant of absolute ecstasy.[13]

A missed note is like coitus interruptus, a disruption of anticipated pleasure. And if we cannot release our hysteria in cheers, we will do so via boos and hisses.

Once, while I was in graduate school, I came home from a disappointing opera performance in a state of uncontrollable rage. I had not paid much for the performance, and I should not have expected much, but my fury knew no bounds. I don't even remember now what was so bad about the performance or even which opera it was; I only recall my outrage. I roamed the hallways of my dormitory, looking for someone on whom to vent my anger. I finally found a sympathetic soul to put up with my ravings, but it was not enough. I kept talking about the performance for days, until I worked my hysteria out of my system. The opera had aroused in me an irrational expectation, and my disappointment resulted in a subsequent irrational display of emotion.

Of course, I should not admit that I respond to opera hysterically. Hysteria is not a masculine ailment; as both Foucault and Elaine Showalter document, historically, hysteria is an ailment specifically ascribed to women, the disease of the wandering womb, a pseudoscientific excuse devised by the medical profession to "prove" the inferiority of women to men.[14] Anyone, male or female, who behaves hysterically becomes, by association, feminized and demeaned. Opera feminizes its audience, places it in the inactive sexual position. Opera seduces me, and so I become the passive partner in the sexual relationship, the partner being done to rather than doing. Perhaps I respond so actively to opera during the curtain call in order to counteract this passivity, to demonstrate to myself that I can also contribute actively to the relationship, that I can be butch as well as femme. (I notice that when I hear someone yell "bravo" at the opera, it is typically a male voice; women seem to feel less need to prove their masculinity in public.) But the effort is futile; in my attempt to demonstrate my masculine assertiveness, I only further demonstrate my hysteria. The more I cheer, the more hysterical I become, and the more I undermine my efforts to establish my masculinity.

This feminization of the hysterical male opera fan is captured in a drawing from 1835 by English satirist Robert Cruikshank (see Figure 4.2.). This illustration, entitled "A Dandy Fainting or—An Exquisite in Fits," shows a scene in a private box at the opera, during a performance by a castrato (though the performances of the castrati had, by this date, virtually disappeared from opera). Cruikshank shows only a glimpse of the stage; a vaguely drawn singer engages floridly in an aria. Five spindly legged young men occupy the box, all nattily dressed and wearing absurdly high collars. One of them has fainted; two of his friends prop him up, one applies a vial of eau de cologne to his nose, and the fifth dandy looks on in alarm. The friends comment about their comatose compatriot:

> *Onlooker [closing the box curtain]:* I must draw the curtain or his screams will alarm the House—You have no fello feeling my dear fellos, pray unlace the dear loves Stays and lay him on the couch.
> *First Upholder:* I am so frighten'd I can hardly stand!
> *Second Upholder:* Mind you don't soil the Dears linnen.
> *Man With Cologne:* I dread the consequence! that last air of Signeur *Nonballenas* has thrown him into such raptures, we must call in Doctor [name struck out] immediately!

Cruikshank clearly has no sympathy for any of the parties depicted in this vicious little drawing, neither his testicle-less singer, Signeur Nonballenas, nor the effeminate young men with their sexually charged language, who are thrown into such a tizzy by his singing. History shows how lingering was Cruikshank's venom against the castrati and their fans; Giovanni Velluti, the last major castrato to sing in London, had left the country in 1829, six years before this drawing. Cruikshank makes the singer a castrato specifically to link the young men to his patent lack of virility. Not only has the music of the singer thrown one of the men into hysterical raptures, in a state where he is in danger of "soil[ing] his linnen," these wispy, effeminized men are also forced, by the terror of the situation, to reveal their own attractions to each other, especially the one at the curtain, who calls his distressed friend "dear" and is so eager to have his clothes removed. (One can only imagine the sexual peccadillo implied by the deleted name of the doctor.) In Cruikshank's world, the fan's response to the singer has completely removed his masculinity as effectively as the surgeon's knife has removed Signor Nonballenas's. Opera has unmanned the audience.[15]

Cruikshank's drawing depicts a precursor of the stereotyped opera queen. As this drawing demonstrates, the connection between opera and sexual deviance long predates the formation of a modern gay-identified community, or even the medicalized conception of homosexuality, which does not emerge until nearly a half-century later. Effeminate men had already been linked to opera, and not in a kind manner. A truly "masculine" man, according to Cruikshank's morality, does not behave hysterically, toward opera or anything else. Excess pleasure in opera, especially when focused on the singing body of the opera star, becomes a kind of pathology. Later in the nineteenth century, English and German writers would begin to define a pathology of effeminate men and call it homosexuality.[16] Hysterical response to opera would become merely another symptom of this disease.[17]

55

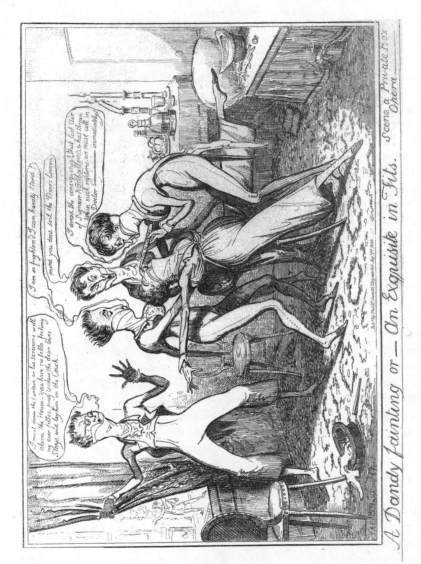

Figure 4.2 Robert Cruikshank (English, 1789–1856), "A Dandy Fainting or—An Exquisite in Fits," 1835. Hood Museum of Art, Dartmouth College, Hanover, N.H.; Gift of Mrs. E. A. Sherrard.

The modern iconic object of desire for the diseased, hysterical opera queen is, of course, Maria Callas. Callas has been made to embody opera as pathology, both in her own troubled life and early death, as well as in the remarkable, irrational devotion of her fans. In Tom Stoppard's play *The Real Thing*, Henry, the obtuse central character, recounts a scene from his youth: "I was taken once to Covent Garden to hear a woman called Callas in a sort of foreign musical with no dancing which people were donating kidneys to get tickets for."[18] Terrence McNally's *The Lisbon Traviata* centers around two gay men, with deeply troubled personal lives, desperately trying to use Callas as a way out of their problems and becoming even more desperate in the process. Callas is a drug, and Mendy and Stephen are addicts. And for Koestenbaum, Callas is the goddess of opera's gay cult of death: "She was Callas long before she died, but she would be a little less than Callas if she were still living. Ultimately death assists her legend and connects her to themes that have shadowed gay culture: premature mortality, evanescence, solitude."[19] Callas the voice, live and on record, has entranced several generations of opera fans, but the truly hysterical behavior is reserved for Callas the (dead) body.

Hysteria serves as a way to transcend pain, just as excess works as a means to neutralize abjection. If you can't avoid pathology, adopt it and embrace it. Even before the onset of AIDS, the gay community had a deep-seated need to find celebration in the midst of pain. AIDS has inevitably become the focal point for a more pervasive need for affirmation and celebration. Like all other minorities, forced to live daily with rejection and violence, we in the gay community need to find positive images, ways to transform pain into triumph. We look to people who have led hysterical lives, massive, flamboyant talents cut short by tragic early death. By our turning these figures—notably Judy Garland, Marilyn Monroe, and James Dean, along with Callas—into cultural icons, tragedy is turned to celebration; early death is hailed as the necessary ending to a life of passion, a passion too strong to permit a slow collapse into old age. It is the only way to ensure the perpetual attractiveness of the singer's body.[20] Death becomes a magnificent climax, expressed through beautiful music, surrounded by the wealthy trappings of the opera world, and culminating in the postclimactic afterlife of hysterical applause. Poizat's raw, untamed cry of *jouissance* turns into the scream of the hysteric. And it was—is—the voice of Maria Callas that most fully embodies this paradox of triumph and agony.

But if people outside opera regard hysterical audience response as a kind of disease, gay men have been able to find strength and community in this excessive behavior and even, recently, to reclaim this identity and turn its energies to positive value. Since Stonewall and the beginnings of the gay liberation movement, large-scale public displays of hysterical behavior have become the hallmark of gay identity. Refusing to become pathologized, embracing our embarrassing excess, we display our hysteria with pride and joy. We parade in the streets, we cross-dress (well, I don't, but some of us do), we sing and dance, we gather by the hundreds of thousands in the nation's urban centers. When I march in a gay-pride parade, I feel as if I am living in an opera. After four hours of walking in the hot sun down Fifth Avenue on the last Sunday in June, my reason blunted by thirst and sunburn, I turn the corner at Washington Square into the Village, with thousands of shameless queers cheering and dancing around me, and I feel like Radames marching in triumph into Thebes to the Grand March from *Aïda* (though the boom boxes around me are more likely to play Madonna's "Express Yourself" than "Gloria all'Egitto"). Only in these hysterical settings does my life take on the dimensions of opera. Only when I embrace hysteria can I live, however briefly, as do the bodies on the opera stage I so passionately desire. Only then will my body and the singer's body become one.

5

OPERA AND HOMOEROTIC DESIRE

Opera has always suited those who have failed at love. I entered sexuality assuming that I would fail at it and that it had failed me, that I, by virtue of my lust for men, was where sexuality broke down, where the system stopped working, where a mistake materialized.

—Wayne Koestenbaum
The Queen's Throat[1]

Surely nothing could be further from the life of a contemporary gay man than Wilde's Salomé. Haven't we outgrown the idea that opera and doomed heroines are our inevitable accessories?

—Neil Bartlett
Who Was That Man?[2]

Sad Stories of the Death of Queens

According to playwright Terrence McNally, we gay men who adore opera suffer from a fatal condition. In his play *The Lisbon Traviata* he depicts a hermetically sealed world inhabited by two lonely, dysfunctional men obsessed with opera: opera queens.[3] These sad men, Mendy and Stephen, lead lives apart from reality, hovering in a twilight world of spiritual death that leads, at the end of the play, to physical death. Mendy, the more obsessive and self-consciously tragic opera queen, spends his life surrounded by walls of opera recordings that form his fortress against reality. Safe within his enclave, he endlessly searches for the perfect operatic moment, the Maria Callas-induced musical orgasm, which, he thinks, will give his life form and fulfillment. He has no life, no lover other than Maria. He longs for real love with a real lover, but the world outside his cell terrifies him. The real world is cruel, but Maria, because she is dead, cannot hurt him; she becomes his substitute lover. Stephen, less flamboyant than Mendy, pretends to have a life outside of opera. He has a real lover, Mike, who should be perfect for him. But Mike refuses to compete with Callas for Stephen's attentions. Stephen's opera obsession destroys his personal life. As the play moves into the second act, Stephen becomes less and less able to separate his real relationship from opera. At the end of the play he actually turns his life into opera, specifically the finale of *Carmen;* he stabs Mike rather than letting him go off with another man.[4] Both Mendy and Stephen are emotional ciphers, empty shells of humanity, ravaged by the disease of opera just as much as the gay men outside their sanctuary are ravaged by the other "gay plague," AIDS.

Wayne Koestenbaum does not take a much brighter view of opera queens. Unlike McNally, Koestenbaum, in *The Queen's Throat,* himself claims the identity of opera queen. But, like McNally, Koestenbaum consistently portrays opera as a substitute for failed or absent love, a shadow land for gay men, a place of dusty memories and faded illusions. And even more powerfully than McNally, Koestenbaum links opera with the concepts of physical and spiritual death. We gay men love opera, he argues, because opera is dead and because it enacts death. For Koestenbaum, opera attracts gay men because it belongs to the past, a relic of an earlier, more idealized era. Gay men connect to opera in the same way that we connect to other dead icons of illicit passion and social transgression: Judy Garland, Marilyn Monroe, James Dean. Opera, he argues, appeals to gay men as a kind of sublimation, accomplished through the divine figure of the diva. But this substitute for true love is never complete. Failure and frustration always accompany the attempted erotic exchange. The opera queen remains doomed to wander forever, like the Dutchman, half-dead and half-alive, never able to arrive at his erotic destiny. We gay men need the perpetual frustration of pseudosex with opera, Koestenbaum argues, to embody the inadequacy of our own sexual lives and our sense of impending doom. At the end of his discourse on opera queens, he writes: "This person exists, outside my dream. He is real. He is the opera queen: my shy reflection, my flamboyant ghost. I've seen him at the local opera and around town. We pass each other on Grove Street, by the secret societies and the cemetery, and we never say hello."[5] For Koestenbaum, the great era of opera is dead, its heroines die on stage for us, and gay men flock to opera in a cult of death, a glorious but ultimately futile gesture of symbolic self-immolation in the face of a hostile society and impossible love.

Images of disease also pervade the stories gay men tell of opera queens. In these portrayals, opera queens are, in a word, sick. Koestenbaum explores the persistent depiction of diseased and disabled opera fans that he finds in early issues of *Opera News:* "the crippled, the infirm, the shut-in, and the pathetically lonely."[6] The bedridden opera fan is like the closeted gay man, he argues, in a construction in which opera, like homosexuality, becomes a metaphor for the shut-in's malady. For Koestenbaum, opera queens indulge in a diseased, dysfunctional relationship with opera, devoting themselves to an entirely one-sided love, where disdainful opera pays little heed to the adulation of its fans.

Ethan Mordden offers another powerful evocation of opera-as-disease in his history of the diva cult. Mordden, an openly gay author, does not write specifically about opera's relation to gay men, but his study is a virtual opera queen's handbook, filled with tales of the glories and downfalls of divas and their fans throughout opera history. He calls this book *Demented;* insanity is its central theme.[7] For Mordden, the cult of the diva is a form of mental illness. He titles his last three chapters "Rise," "Fall," and "Immortality": The diva climbs to madly dizzying heights, plummets irrationally like Tosca off the parapet, and only in death achieves her lasting though demented glory. Opera's cult of death is also a cult of madness (and we opera queens well know that a mad scene leads directly to the grave). If opera queens are not already dead, then we are seriously ill, well on our way to death.

Even when gay writers portray opera queens in a comic light, the shadows of death and disease persist. The deadly obsessions of the opera queen come to represent characteristics of all gay male culture, even for those gay men who spurn opera. If the opera queen lives in illusion, he is no different from all the other types of queens who populate gay society, each living in a self-contained fantasy disconnected from the real world. Opera provides a prettier illusion than most, but all gay fantasies are depicted as deadly. T. R. Witomski, in an essay entitled "How to Cruise the Met," places the opera queen in a broad realm of gay self-deprecation:

> Opera queens have gotten bad press. They are thought to be cruelly bitchy, horrendously petty, and extraordinarily demanding. And they *are.* But at the same time they aren't the sort who'll throw up on you at bars. . . . Opera queens are probably the closest approximations to responsible adults one is likely to encounter in one's journey through gay life.
>
> The negative image of the opera queen is largely due to the negative image of opera. Opera is thought to be a lot of fat people wandering around bizarre locales singing in foreign languages for many tedious hours. And it *is.* But, then again, a gay bar is a lot of drunk people wandering around bizarre locales either saying nothing or speaking in tongues for many tedious hours so it's not like going to the opera for the first time will be an entirely brand new experience for the typical cocksucker.[8]

These views of gay men and our passion for opera come right out of *The Boys in the Band.* They depict the gay man as a pathetic figure, desperately lonely, perpetually outcast from "normal" society, clinging fiercely to opera as a means to buffer the world's hatred, and even more as a means to fend off the hatred he feels for himself. Opera, like the picture of Dorian Gray, becomes merely an illusion that staves off inevitable death and dissolution. All of these writers buy into the stereotype of the tragic opera queen, or that image's comic counterpart, the bitchy opera queen. Like Canio in *I Pagliacci* (yet another simile—the discourse of the closet always depends on symbolic displacements), the opera queen presents a lively, entertaining face to the general public, concealing a tragic, weeping interior; brilliant bitchiness is the surest indication of internalized despair. This opera queen lives vicariously only through the unreal passions of opera; he is a failure at leading his own life. For these writers, the gay man's self-imposed sense of the tragic draws him to the strange and unreal world of opera.

When I read these passages, I feel depressed—not for myself, but for the authors. They love opera, but they don't seem to like themselves very much. And the picture they generate of opera and of gay men leaves a raft of lingering and troublesome questions: Is opera nothing but a sublimation for failed desire? If opera's appeal to abnormality and disease is so powerful, how does it appeal to the normal and the healthy—or does it? Is it possible to have a real, normal relationship (gay or straight) and still love opera? Can't we have *both* opera *and* true love? And why must we construct gay sexuality as deviant, diseased, tragic? Is self-deprecation our inevitable lot, or, as recent history suggests—and as I firmly believe—do we, by seeing ourselves as deathridden, uselessly internalize the hatred imposed by straight society? And if that is the case, will we have any place for opera in our lives once we finally drop this weighty psychological baggage?

Transcending Tragedy

I refuse to embrace this portrait of the tragic opera queen to explain my own passion for opera. My life is not tragic, and it never has been. I grew up in a stable, sheltered home, filled with loving, accepting, and open-minded people; they have not thrown me out for being gay, and they have embraced my lover as part of the family. It took me a while to deal with my sexuality, not out of shame but because I had such positive role models of heterosexuality around me. My love for opera grew out of no sense of tragedy but in imitation of the love for opera that I saw in my functional, largely heterosexual family. Koestenbaum's self-image does not apply to my life. I only failed at sexuality when I tried to be heterosexual; when I realized I was gay I experienced not sexual failure but sexual fulfillment. My passion for opera is as strong when I am in a stable relationship as it is when my sex life is more transient and less fulfilling, and my pleasure in opera only increases by sharing it with my lover.

And what of all those gay men whose lives truly feel tragic but who have no use for opera whatsoever? Alex Ross, reviewing Koestenbaum's book, argues, "Opera has nothing to do with the lives of most gay men, past or present. Conversely, most operagoers, fanatics included, are not gay in the least. Opera cannot serve as a synonym for homosexuality, because opera-going expresses no essential sexuality, gay or straight."[9] I find the last part of Ross's remark highly problematic; operagoing is intensely charged with sexuality, both gay and straight. But the point remains that, if the tragic opera queen presents a powerful image, it fails to account either for the lives of gay men or for the appeal of opera to its broader audience.

Reflecting on the second epigraph that opens this chapter, I sympathize fully with Neil Bartlett's frustration at the negative image of the opera queen in the post-Stonewall era of gay liberation. The figure of the tragic, self-immolating opera queen is a relic of the past, irrevocably tied to the painful codes of the closet. For the last century and a half the connection between opera and homosexuality has, like homosexuality itself, been a dirty little secret, something that everyone knows but no one is supposed to talk about. This secret has remained carefully hidden, only a little below the surface of public discourse but never allowed to break into the open. Because of this secrecy, gay men have used opera, as Koestenbaum so brilliantly portrays, as the site for complex encodings of hidden desire. When homosexuality refuses the closet, when gay men insist on claiming our identity in public, this system breaks apart. But, unlike Bartlett, I am not willing to throw out the baby with the bath water. I reject the identity of the tragic, closeted opera queen, but I do not reject opera. *Salome does* have a great deal to do with my life as a gay man, but not because I see my life as tragic. Koestenbaum errs in asserting that opera is both dead and a gay cult of death; opera is not dead, but perhaps the cult of the closeted opera queen is.[10]

Ironically, by writing successful plays and books about the closeted world of opera queens, McNally and Koestenbaum have shed light upon this world and helped to destroy the figure that they take such pains to evoke. Opera has come out of the closet. The opera queen is now a recognized type in popular discourse, along with the drag queen, the fashion queen, and the snap queen. Like the Fat Lady, the opera queen has become, even outside the gay community, a commodity in the media, subject to the whims and tastes of a broader and more fickle public. Gay men could always call each other opera queens in private, but now everyone else has caught on to the secret. And now that the stereotype of the closeted opera queen is a popular commodity, it will, ultimately, fade into the realm of nostalgia, the closet of our collective cultural trash, along with the rest of the ever-burgeoning refuse of media-generated popular culture.

The Lisbon Traviata and *The Queen's Throat* are, I believe, eulogies for the self-deprecating, pseudotragic opera queen of the stereotype. By revealing these sad figures, McNally and Koestenbaum have performed (intentionally or not) a powerful exorcism of evil spirits from the figure of the opera queen, leaving room for a healthier construction of the relation of opera to gay sexuality. The gay population still has a stake in opera, as a powerful means of embodying our desire. But we do not need to latch onto opera as a death cult to engage with this embodiment. Opera provides other avenues for sorely needed, positive public expressions of desire in the gay community.

The gay and lesbian population has no natural, demographically determined communities. Unlike racial or ethnic groups, lesbians and gay men are not born into exclusively gay families, and we do not grow up among large clusters of people like ourselves. We must form our own communities. Some of us find community by moving into heavily gay areas of major cities, some by dressing and talking in common patterns, some by forming societies and organizations, some by reading gay and lesbian publications, some by inhabiting particular social spaces. Just as important as these demographic communities, though, are cultural communities. Like any social group, we need our images, our heroines and heroes, our common languages. We need a variety of these communities, since not all cultural languages speak to everyone. Opera has been, and continues to be, one of these languages.

Eve Kosofsky Sedgwick, in *Epistemology of the Closet,* defines two opposing impulses in gay identity formation: the impulse to minoritize, and the impulse to universalize.[11] These impulses operate for any marginalized social group. The minoritizing impulse reflects a desire for separatism: We are different from the mainstream, we celebrate our difference proudly, and we wish to maintain that difference to preserve the identity of our community. The universalizing impulse, conversely, says that in spite of our differences we are really just people, who possess the same rights and privileges as all others. The minoritizing impulse speaks to our desires for a unique cultural identity and public recognition, whereas the universalizing impulse argues for inclusiveness, acceptance, and the protection of civil rights. Although these two strategies at times seem contradictory, both minoritizing and universalizing impulses (often represented in the African-American community, for example, by the contrasting figures of Malcolm X and Dr. Martin Luther King Jr.) are necessary to any marginalized population, and each impulse provides useful argumentational tools for achieving differing social and political goals.

Opera, in its glorious paradoxical tangle of undifferentiated desire, provides a fruitful outlet for both minoritizing and universalizing impulses. Opera, as I argue in Chapters 3 and 4, substitutes a broad and open-ended desire for the rigidly controlled identity formation of mainstream narrative art. Offering a field of unspecified desire, opera can speak to both of Sedgwick's opposing impulses at once. In the minoritizing mode, gay men can see in opera a world apart, a place that belongs to us alone (or with only a select few others admitted, mostly those with a lot of money or taste). Opera offers a world of unique emotional intensity, free from the rules and inhibitions of "normal" society. It is a world with an arcane code of names, dates, and foreign languages by which we can exclude the boorish lot who cannot appreciate opera's grandiose excesses. The illicit desire of opera, socially sanctioned by elite patronage and government subsidy, becomes a way, not to substitute for failed love, but instead to legitimate our "deviant" desire and to reinforce our brilliantly diverse and freewheeling sexual lives.

Simultaneously, opera allows the gay community to see itself as part of the mainstream. The all-embracing pansexuality of opera encourages us to feel as if our sexual passions are really the same as those of the straight world. Opera purports to tell archetypal stories of love and death, stories that claim universal status. Opera mythologizes these stories, abstracting them through music and exoticism, leaving room for spectators to fill in the details of their own lives. Through the romantic tribulations of operatic characters, gay men can find a parallel to the mainstream discourse of desire, connecting our feelings of love to those more familiar images of desire in a society that otherwise rejects us. The "high-art" status of opera and its association with the most powerful elements of society similarly bring us away from the margins and into the center of social discourse.

But if opera offers such an ideal realm for both minoritizing and universalizing impulses, why don't other minorities also flock to opera? And why does opera function as a locus of identity for only a segment of the gay male population and an even smaller portion of the lesbian community? It is not hard to understand why most other marginalized social groups do not go to the opera. For all its supposedly universalizing elements, opera only universalizes to the realm of the Caucasian, the European, the male, and the upper class.[12] It has appeal for those who aspire to this realm, but there is little in traditional opera that speaks to minority racial and ethnic groups. Women find little encouragement to see themselves in opera, in either universalizing or minoritizing terms. And, more directly, opera usually prices itself out of the community-formation market. Most members of marginalized groups who live in cities with opera companies cannot remotely afford the price of a ticket or even recordings of the music. These restrictions apply as well within the gay male community. Gay men come from all races and social classes, and not all of us can afford opera. But the popular construction of the "typical" gay man is white and affluent, the audience with access to opera. Thus opera, appealing to the perceived economic status of the gay male community rather than to its reality, serves as only one means of community formation. Opera will work as a social language only for some of us, at least until opera moves away from its strict limits of economic privilege.[13]

I suppose I should not disdain opera queens; people who hang around in glass closets shouldn't throw stones. I have certainly been known to engage in opera queen-identified behavior on frequent occasions. And though I do not own every recording made by Maria Callas, I have quite a few, and I too find myself endlessly fascinated with her strange, intensely theatrical voice. I have even made the pilgrimage to Père Lachaise Cemetery in Paris, placing a flower by the marker for Maria's ashes. (Père Lachaise is a Mecca for us sexual deviants; besides Callas, one must make obligatory visits to the huge, graffiti-laden, art-deco tomb of Oscar Wilde, the joint resting place of Gertrude Stein and Alice B. Toklas—though you have to look for Alice, demurely laid behind Gertrude—Jim Morrison, if one is of a less classical bent, and the graves of dozens of other artists, composers, authors, and well-known flamboyants.) I wear the badges of the Maria cult, but I do so only because I command sufficient resources to buy her recordings and fly to Paris on my vacations. Not all potential opera queens can afford to speak my language of desire.

Queer Desire

Opera's broad and ambiguous sexuality leaves me room to construct my nonmainstream erotic desires within its lush realm. In other words, to employ another of Sedgwick's terms, opera is queer: not gay per se, but standing in opposition to mainstream, normalized constructions of desire. For Sedgwick, anything is queer that refuses to conform to the imposed sexual mores of "normal" society. She writes:

> Think of all the elements that are condensed in the notion of sexual identity, something that the common sense of our time presents as a unitary category. . . . Normatively . . . it should be possible to deduce anybody's entire set of specs from the initial dictum of biological sex alone. . . . That's one of the things "queer" can refer to: the open mesh of possibilities, gaps, overlaps, dissonances and resonances, lapses and excesses of meaning when the constituent elements of anyone's gender, of anyone's sexuality aren't made (or *can't be* made) to signify monolithically.[14]

It is as queers, as rebels against normative sexuality, that Sedgwick and Michael Moon, in their essay "Divinity," locate the common ground between overweight women and gay men that energizes the image of the Fat Lady of the opera. And opera is nothing if not an "open mesh of possibilities" of sexual desire. Opera's sexuality exists apart from the norm; the majority of the population does not construct its own sexual life this way. To dwell in the world of opera is to engage in abnormal, excessive sexuality, a world distinct from mainstream desire. Operatic desire is bigger, more passionate, less controlled than "normal" sexuality. Operatic desire is shameless, brazen, refusing to hide its passion with proper modesty. Even more queerly, opera aims its desire ambiguously and indiscriminately, refusing to differentiate between acceptable and unacceptable, male and female, single or multiple objects of desire, merrily blurring the lines between the possibilities. As I argue in Chapter 3, when Alfredo and Violetta sing of their love for each other in *La Traviata,* they also encourage me to join with them in a queer threesome.

Opera's queerness, its undifferentiated sexual excess, makes it a channel for the expression of gay desire. For those of us with access to opera's hallowed halls, its ambiguous sexuality leaves space in which to read complex and multiple impulses of desire, buried not very deeply underneath a surface of more conventional desire. In opera's illicit passion, I feel a resonance with my own nonmainstream sexual desires, and I thrill at the way opera can flaunt its queer desire so openly. In opera's erotic excess I find room for my own desire and an implied license that allows me, at least for a time and within its protected space, to ignore the normative social rules that seek to restrict and delegitimize my feelings. It is possible, like Koestenbaum and McNally, to see opera as an unreal space in which to hide from the hatred of the world. I prefer to side with Sedgwick, seeing opera not as a protective closet but as a public playground for queerness. I refuse to buy into the assumption that the world of hatred and prejudice is the "real" one and the queer world of opera "illusory." I see opera not as a hiding place but as a public celebratory space of queer desire, a wedge driven into the cracks of "normal" desire that, slowly but powerfully, can help to break apart the normative assumptions that limit sexuality.

Opera does not restrict its queer breathing space to male desires, though the powerful icon of the opera queen seems to exclude the female spectator. Opera, in dislodging the normative rules of desire, permits female as well as male queer readings. Along these lines, Elizabeth Wood devises the term "Sapphonic" to refer to a lesbian erotics of opera. The Sapphonic voice sings opera's erotically charged, gender-ambiguous music, a melody in which Wood finds a space for her own desire:

> Like the writers who read Sappho of Lesbos as poetic precursor of modern lesbian identity, my act of naming claims Sappho the singer for a "lesbian continuum" of listening that itself engendered Sapphonic performances and Sapphonic operas. . . .
>
> I call this voice Sapphonic for its resonance in sonic space as lesbian difference and desire. Its sound is characteristically powerful and problematic, defiant and defective. Its flexible negotiation and integration of

an exceptional range of registers crosses boundaries among different voice types and their representations to challenge polarities of both gender and sexuality as they are socially—and vocally—constructed. Its refusal of categories and the transgressive risks it takes act seductively on a lesbian listener for whom the singer serves as messenger, her voice as vessel, of desire.[15]

Wood goes on to discuss how lesbian writers of fiction have used opera to communicate the desire felt by women in the audience toward women on the stage. If operatic queerness seems focused on the male body, that one-sidedness arises mainly from the systematic exclusion of women from the social discourse at large. If women have trouble identifying with opera's heroines, then opera's undifferentiated desire can instead leave an open space for a broad range of queerness.

Society has long suspected opera's queerness. Neil Bartlett, in his breath-taking evocation of the underground life of gay men in nineteenth-century London, *Who Was That Man? A Present for Mr Oscar Wilde*, lists a series of questions taken from *A Categoric Personal Analysis for the Reader*, which was published in 1899 by famed sexologist Dr. Magnus Hirschfeld. Hirschfeld designed the series of questions to determine whether a respondent had homosexual tendencies. The intensely stereotyped questions include references to physical traits (hairiness, softness of skin), upbringing (heavy maternal attention), behaviors and desires (interest in cross-dressing or aversion to raising children), and avocations. In this latter category, the survey turns to opera, asking if the respondent has a deep interest in the theater and acting, then goes on to ask if the person is "particularly fond of Wagner."[16] In the nineteenth century, Bartlett asserts, the name of Richard Wagner, and by metaphorical leap the entire German language (at least for the English-speaking world), became a code for homosexuality.

Why, of all opera composers, did Wagner in the nineteenth century become the focal point for operatic queerness? Arguably, Wagner invited this identification through his own excessive and illicit sexual dealings, as well as a certain ambiguity in them, especially his complex feelings toward his young, attractive gay patron, King Ludwig of Bavaria. Wagner's grandiose and self-inflated personality cult also had queer undercurrents, where even the most vague associations could become amplified into a secret sexual code. One can also argue that, if opera in general evokes marginal sexuality, then Wagner, the grandest of the composers of grand opera, the self-appointed peak of the operatic hierarchy, must necessarily represent the furthest reach of sexual marginalization.[17] Above all, it is Wagner's blatant evocation of sexual transgression in his music-dramas that labels his work as queer: Siegmund and Sieglinde's divine incest; the unrestricted sensuality of the Venusberg; the fatally intense passion of Tristan and Isolde. But more than any other work, it is the rampant sexual ambiguity of *Parsifal* that makes Wagner an inevitable locus of transgressive sexuality.[18]

Parsifal takes place in a world of men. It tells the story of an exclusively male society, the Knights of the Grail, whose leader, Amfortas, needs the services of an innocent male youth to heal the festering wound in his groin. That wound was made by the spear of the sorcerer Klingsor, who carries his own genital wound, a self-inflicted castration, the rejected symbol of his desire to enter the society of the Knights. The young Parsifal becomes the central object of the struggle between holy male bonding and illicit desire. Sexually, this is pretty heady stuff, especially in a work written specifically as a Christian religious ceremony. The only major female presence in this world is Kundry, a seductress in the power of Klingsor, who, along with the siren-like Flower Maidens, attempts to win Parsifal to the side of evil. Critics normally view Kundry and Parsifal within a strictly heterosexual formula: the experienced older woman seduces the innocent young man. Alex Ross, though, modifies this view slightly, seeing Kundry as a heterosexual substitute for Klingsor's impotent homoeroticism:

> Kundry, Parisfal's would-be seductress, is in the thrall of Klingsor, a grotesque magician who has castrated himself in the hope of joining the Grail brotherhood. . . . "Ah! He is beautiful, this boy!" Klingsor exclaims as Parsifal climbs the walls of his magic castle; a flotilla of Flower Maidens and, later, Kundry are deployed to attempt the seduction of Parsifal that Klingsor cannot manage himself. . . . After momentarily succumbing to temptation, Parsifal conjures this effeminate villain away with the sign of the cross. The "secret" of Kundry's kiss is that Klingsor looms behind it: the message is to renounce the sexual impulse that leads one astray.[19]

Ross's idea, though intriguing, problematically links gay men with effeminacy and castration. Wagner's narrative may, however, be read another way, as a deeply homoerotic exchange in which Parsifal rejects both female-embodied heterosexuality and incomplete male love in favor of a true homoeroticism. When Parsifal receives Klingsor's kiss via Kundry, he awakens immediately, and the first word on his lips is "Amfortas." At his moment of achieving sexual consciousness, Parsifal rejects the love both of the false woman and of the castrated man who desires him; he turns immediately to the father figure of Amfortas and to the society of "real men" who make up the brotherhood of the grail.

Parsifal, in other words, rejects the ambiguous and empty eroticism of Klingsor's world for the pure homoerotics of the Grail Knights. Kundry spends the opera being pushed to the margins of desire; she is the seductress, but there is no one for her to seduce. She has no erotic inroads into the fortified homoerotic world of the Knights, and Klingsor isn't interested in her. She makes one strenuous effort to win Parsifal, though in this effort she acts as a substitute for the castrated Klingsor, and when that fails, she has nothing left to do. She waits until the end of the opera to die, but in fact she dies symbolically when Parsifal rejects her love in favor of the love of men. Her death at the end is incidental, almost unnoticed, a piece of plot housekeeping (a fate shared by many of Wagner's other heroines). After her death, the opera ends with the triumphant assumption of Parsifal to the head of the holy brotherhood, an ecstatic climax that, unlike the death orgasm that ends *Tristan und Isolde,* in *Parsifal* is a life-orgasm, a swelling paean to the glories of true masculine love.

Of course, no one is supposed to mention this desire openly. Officially, Parsifal's love for his fellow knights is purely platonic, but it is no secret that love between men in Plato's time had physical as well as spiritual aspects. Like the Nazi culture that so admired Wagner, Wagner's world in *Parsifal* evokes on its surface a "normal" heterosexuality. But suppressed not very far beneath the surface is a deeply eroticized world of beautiful young men (the Wagnerian fantasy puts them in medieval armor, the Nazi fantasy in black leather), whose love for each other leaves women, the supposed objects of their desires, well out of the picture. It takes no great leap of the imagination for a gay man to read his own life into Wagner's glorious portrait of ecstatic male bonding, though we may well shy away from some of Wagner's less savory ideas about social construction. As the Nazis demonstrated, repressed homoerotic desire can respond to openly gay desire with remarkable violence.[20]

Duets for Tenor and Baritone

Opera's queerness rarely figures in analyses of tragic opera queens and gay male desire. In his extensive study of gay men's attraction to opera, Koestenbaum never addresses operas like *Parsifal,* which so clearly evoke images of a man's erotic desire for other men.[21] Koestenbaum speaks not of queer operas but only of queer moments in opera, isolated scenes in which a repressed gay sensibility finds special resonance. And of the many queer moments that he cites, only one involves an overt display of affection between two men, a scene in Bizet's obscure *Les Pêcheurs de Perles* in which he sees no particular erotic connection between the men, only a bonding over a heterosexual longing for an absent woman.[22] Not once in his book does Koestenbaum mention a situation in opera of attraction between two men, nor does he make the slightest reference to the best known of all gay opera composers, Benjamin Britten, or to any operatic works that even imply an erotic relationship between two men. In focusing only on female characters as objects of desire in opera, Koestenbaum omits a wide realm of opera's queer sexuality, one that requires no self-abasing displacement to generate images of desire. Scenes of male bonding are not limited to *Parsifal*; instances of male-to-male attachment pervade all of opera. As much as opera overtly shows the love between men and women, just as often it displays a not very deeply embedded desire between men.

Sedgwick defines this kind of same-sex desire, in her aptly titled study *Between Men,* as "homosocial" eroticism. Sedgwick argues that in nineteenth-century literary representation, homosocial bonding between male characters traces a powerful sexual narrative that underlies the more overt heterosexual narrative of the plot. She distinguishes between the homosocial and the homosexual or homoerotic; in a homosocial bond, two men form a union of deep affection, which implies an erotic attachment but which falls short of overtly expressing that desire. Instead, two men formalize a homosocial bond through the body of a woman; they first develop a close attachment of friendship and then, in order to perpetuate their relationship, one of the men marries the other's sister or forms some similar familial or legal bond. The woman in the process functions only as a commodity, the means of exchange that establishes the more significant bond between the two men.[23]

This kind of homosocial desire also underlies the frequent instances of intense male bonding in nineteenth-century opera. (Indeed, the kinds of narratives that Sedgwick traces in nineteenth-century literature often served as source materials for opera.) Verdi is very fond of these situations, where two strong male characters, usually a tenor and a baritone, bond either in friendship or, just as often, in a love-hate relationship. His most developed example of homosociality appears in *Don Carlos,* in the intimate friendship between Carlos and Rodrigo, Marquess of Posa. Carlos ostensibly loves Elisabetta, but he can't do much about it, because she is forced to marry his father instead. Rodrigo, meanwhile, follows Carlos throughout the opera, declaring his love and protecting him from harm. Elisabetta and Carlos share some magnificent duets, but Carlos and Posa get the scenes most commonly associated with lovers in romantic opera: the ecstatic affirmation of their mutual love in Act II, scene 1; and the moving death scene of Act IV, scene 2, in which the murdered Rodrigo expires in Carlos's arms.

Verdi offers a similar scene of ecstatic male bonding in Act III of *La Forza del Destino,* in which Don Carlo and Don Alvaro declare their undying love for each other, though soon after they realize they belong to feuding clans and become mortal enemies. Throughout their love-hate relationship, poor Leonora, Carlo's sister and Alvaro's betrothed, gets left mostly by herself. She never enjoys the romantic love scene that other heroines in Verdi do; instead she is separated from both her lover and her brother early in the plot, and she becomes a religious recluse until the final act, when the revenge-obsessed Carlo sees her and immediately stabs her. Her climactic aria, "Pace, pace, mio Dio," is as much as anything else a lament about being ignored by both of the men in her life while they are off conducting the romantic plot of the opera.

Verdi and his later librettist, Arrigo Boito, create a rather different erotically charged homosocial relationship in *Otello* between the title character and Iago. Boito's libretto eliminates some of the more overt suggestions of homoerotic desire between the Moor and his lieutenant in Shakespeare's original; the opera's Iago is more jealous of losing power than of losing Otello's love to Desdemona. But the opera still exudes a suppressed erotic passion: Iago, the lover scorned, and his desire for revenge. The finale of Act II, "Si, pel ciel," presents a potent image of two men joined together to destroy the woman who stands between them, a sharp contrast to the normative heterosexual love duet between Otello and Desdemona that closes the previous act. The end of Act III carries the progression even further, with Iago standing triumphantly over the collapsed body of Otello. Iago's quest for vengeance against Otello maps an erotic shift of sexual position, from submission to physical domination.

This kind of love-hate relationship between men proliferates in standard repertory opera. It appears again in Verdi in the rivalry between Manrico and his unknown brother, the Count di Luna, over Leonora in *Il Trovatore;* in the rivalry for the love of Amelia between Riccardo and Renato in *Un Ballo in Maschera;* and there are also hints of conflicted male bonding in the father-son relationships in *La Traviata* and *Don Carlos.* Outside Verdi, the homosocial relationships in standard repertory opera are generally less violent but no less frequent. In Mozart, we get the jocular interplay between Tamino and Papageno in *The Magic Flute,* and the rather more sinister relationship between Giovanni and Leporello in *Don Giovanni,* as well as the sexual rivalries between Ferrando and Guglielmo in *Così fan tutte* and between Figaro and Count Almaviva (and Figaro and Bartolo, and Figaro and Cherubino) in *Le Nozze di Figaro.* Wagner gives us the pairing of Tristan and Kurwenal, and Tristan's rivalry with Marke, and the all-male communities of (besides the Knights of the Grail) Tannhäuser and the Minnesingers and Hans Sachs and the Meistersingers. Charles Gounod, along with many others, offers Faust and Mephistopheles; Puccini depicts the male ménage à quatre of Rodolfo, Marcello, Schaunard, and Colline in *La Bohème,* not to mention the almost exclusively male world of the gold miners in *La Fanciulla del West.*

Less frequent, but still present, are situations of female homosocial bonding in opera. Women, more acted upon than acting, have fewer opportunities for making connections, but when they do happen the resulting scenes can challenge sexual norms just as strongly. In a twist on Sedgwick's pattern, in which two men bond through the desire for the same woman, Turandot's love for Calaf can be read as a displacement of her desire for the suicidal Liù; only when Liù dies to save Calaf does Turandot shift her love onto the man (one could also cite Turandot as a stereotyped example of the man-hating lesbian, who just needs "one good lay" to bring her around to "normality").[24] Duets for women appear with some frequency in opera. As in the duet between Lakmé and her slave, Mallika, in Delibes's *Lakmé,* in which the two women prepare to bathe together and sing of the sensual pleasures of their surroundings, these scenes often have heavy erotic over-tones. Koestenbaum suggests a similar repressed desire between the rivals Eboli and Elisabetta in Verdi's *Don Carlos.*[25] Each of the Mozart-Da Ponte operas features a central female friendship trio: the sisters Dorabella and Fiordiligi and the maid Despina in *Così,* Anna, Elvira, and Zerlina in *Giovanni,* and Susanna, the Countess and (cross-dressed) Cherubino in *Nozze.* In each case the women bond together to challenge the sexual domination of the men. The case of Cherubino illustrates the implied female homoso-cial relationships in the many operas that employ female-to-male cross-dressing; Richard Strauss certainly sees such implications in the all-female triad in *Der Rosenkavalier,* and he also has Zerbinetta try to seduce the cross-dressed composer in *Ariadne auf Naxos.*[26]

These erotically charged, same-sex pairings only rarely receive the official sanction of a heterosexual love duet. But, in the free play of the operagoer's erotic gaze, it takes a much less elaborate process for these duets to take on sexual meaning than, for example, the one a woman in the audience must undertake in order to establish psychological identification with a victim-ized female character. For a straight spectator, opera provides an opportu-nity to experience a less restrictive eroticism while still offering an overt heterosexual anchor to latch onto. For gay or lesbian spectators, condi-tioned by society to read between the lines of cultural texts for signs of af-firmation (or even for an acknowledgment of our existence), opera fairly bursts with instances of same-sex desire.

Persistent Closets

Still, opera's homosocial duets require a little digging in order to discover their homoeroticism. But what about open examples of same-sex love in opera? Not surprisingly, the standard opera repertory offers only a few ex-amples of overt same-sex attraction. The taboos of society afflict opera just as much as any other form of expression, and open and positive lesbian and gay male activity has remained a largely prohibited area. As in mainstream society, and in the literature from which opera takes its stories, opera rele-gates the representation of gay eroticism to the realm of suggestion, innu-endo, and deep repression. Benjamin Britten could lead a relatively open gay life with his lover, tenor Peter Pears, but he could only write about sex-

ual attraction between men through the violence of *Billy Budd* or the gnaw-
ing inner torment of *Death in Venice.*

Even the fairly obvious homoeroticism in Britten has only recently
formed a topic of discussion in critical literature, especially in the writings
of Philip Brett.[27] Britten is probably the first openly gay opera composer, or
at least the first whose sexuality was general public knowledge. He wrote
most of his leading male roles specifically to be performed by his lover (or,
as most press accounts during his life put it, his "very close friend"). Britten
walked a careful line in his work between hidden and overt gay desire,
waiting until his final opera, *Death in Venice,* to express these emotions
with any directness. And even in this stunning opera, so clearly homoerotic
from start to finish, critics have been reluctant to admit that such a "base"
sensibility could ever pervade the work of England's greatest modern composer.[28] Only with the advent of gay and lesbian studies as an academic discipline have critics felt capable of discussing the sexual sensibility of Britten's work openly.[29]

A few paragraphs cannot do justice to the complex and conflicted gay
sensibility found in Britten's operas; that is the subject for another book.
But Britten, in his many works for the opera stage, pursues a consistent
theme of male-male erotic relationships, most specifically the attraction of
older men to younger men. *Peter Grimes* centers around such a tale, but it
took some forty years and Brett's analysis to reveal the open secret of this
opera's intergenerational gay desire.[30] In *Billy Budd* the repressed homoeroticism erupts as violence rather than love, and the character who desires
Billy, Claggart, also causes his downfall. (The libretto for *Billy Budd* traces
a time-honored tradition of repressed homosexual desire in the literature of
the English language; the story is Herman Melville's, and the libretto was
written by E. M. Forster.) Britten similarly evokes an older man's desire for
a beautiful youth in *The Turn of the Screw* and plays up the sexual ambiguity in Shakespeare's *A Midsummer Night's Dream.* But only with *Death in
Venice* does Britten, in Gustav von Aschenbach, create the first overtly gay
male character in opera, or at least the first character to express erotic desire for another man in a manner too powerful to ignore.

In the field of overt gay expression in opera, women have a very slight
lead on men. There is at least one open and recognizable lesbian on the established operatic stage: the Countess Geschwitz in Alban Berg's *Lulu,* an
interesting if somewhat shadowy character. Critics cannot pretend that her
desire for Lulu is anything but sexual (though they have done a relatively
thorough job of ignoring her altogether in comments on the work).[31] But
even Geschwitz hardly offers a model for gay liberation. She does not apol-
ogize for her sexuality, but her presence must be read within the larger picture of the opera's story. In Geschwitz, Berg (drawing on Frank Wedekind's
original drama) does not depict a lesbian love relationship per se but in-

stead shows another facet of Lulu's all-encompassing and destructive sexual energy, a demonstration of the range of her fatal allure. Geschwitz has no choice but to love Lulu, because Lulu draws everyone in the opera into sexual deviance—not a very encouraging image for positive role-modeling.

Few composers since Britten and Berg have attempted to follow suit in depicting gay desire, even in an ambiguous light, and those few experiments rarely have lasted in the public arena. Leonard Bernstein, always more successful on Broadway, finished only one full-length opera, *A Quiet Place,* with decidedly mixed results. The piece has a lot of problems, not the least of which is the highly conflicted depiction of an openly gay male character. The picture is hardly encouraging. Junior is a psychologically disturbed basket case (with a silly name), whose sister marries his French-Canadian former lover. Junior can barely bring himself to talk about his family, let alone his homosexuality. His sexual turmoil seems to embody Bernstein's own inability to deal with same-sex desire in his work and, arguably, in himself as well.[32] With all its overt and covert sexual transgressions, opera seems unable to cross this one line.

Even openly gay composers and librettists have shied away from engaging gay issues in opera. In a recent interview, gay composer Lowell Liebermann talks about his opera version of that centerpiece of queer literature, *The Picture of Dorian Gray.* When asked about the gay content of the piece, he states: "It's not even about being gay. It goes beyond that—it's about much deeper moral issues."[33] This kind of reasoning, so familiar in antigay rhetoric, implies that gay subjects are not important enough or "universal" enough for art or that a straight audience could not possibly find "deeper moral issues" in a gay-themed opera. Note also the recent premiere at the Metropolitan Opera of *The Ghosts of Versailles,* the first new American opera staged at the Met in decades. *Ghosts* was written by composer John Corigliano and librettist William M. Hoffman, both of whom are openly gay and had previously presented works on gay themes. Hoffman edited the first major anthology in the United States of gay drama and wrote the highly successful AIDS play *As Is;* Corigliano gained fame for his striking first symphony, composed as a memorial to those who have died from AIDS. Who more likely, then, to bring a work dealing with overtly gay themes to contemporary opera? But for their Met debut, they chose instead a historical fantasy on the French revolution, centering around a heterosexual relationship between Marie Antoinette and the playwright Pierre-Augustin Beaumarchais. Arguably, this was a much safer choice for them, given the rocky history of new operas at the Met. But it does not bode well for the future of gay-themed opera. If Corigliano and Hoffman won't write an opera about the lives of gay men, who will?[34]

There may, however, be hope. The 1995 premiere of *Harvey Milk* by Stewart Wallace and Michael Korie, coproduced by New York City Opera,

Houston Grand Opera, and San Francisco Opera, about the life and assassination of openly gay San Francisco supervisor Harvey Milk, demonstrates that a gay story can make for a successful opera. I saw the opera in New York, and it has things I like very much and things I could live without. The production team planned to make a number of revisions, which may determine whether the opera will have a life beyond its initial performances. But whether or not *Harvey Milk* enters the repertory, there is no doubt that, at least for a moment, it captured the public imagination and made for a vivid evening in the theater. Opera, as usual, lags behind the other narrative arts in exploring new territory (and the relative dearth of new operas does not help this situation at all). Opera draws its stories from other realms of narrative: spoken theater, prose fiction, occasionally film, even the nightly news. With the increasing visibility of lesbians and gay men in all of these media in recent years, perhaps other composers and librettists will eventually follow Wallace and Korie's suit, depicting differing sexualities in more than a token manner. But this change will only happen with audience support. Those of us who love opera as a sexual free-space must help it to outgrow the closet, as we ourselves must break away from the self-imposed tragic personas that needlessly hinder our lives and loves. We must embrace positive images of our desires in all forms of public expression, even in—especially in—opera.

Part Three

Opera and Sex

6

OPERATIC ORGASMS

I follow the singer toward her climax, I will it to happen, and feel myself "made" when she attains her note.

—Wayne Koestenbaum
The Queen's Throat[1]

Tristan and Isolde *is the most sustained tract ever mounted on stage in favor of the right to female ejaculation. It isn't enough that they come together seven times in the second act. No. She depletes the poor guy, then hangs around to demand one last orgasm of her own. Women are like that.*

—Virgil Thomson
quoted in Susan McClary's *Feminine Endings*[2]

Making Love in the Afternoon

Saturday, late in the afternoon, early fall. I am alone in my apartment; Craig is out running errands. The Met broadcasts haven't started yet, so I resort to my recordings. I'm listening to the end of *Der Rosenkavalier*, the Karajan recording, the first one (I own both). For the past three hours, I've been working while I listen, reading, cooking, rearranging papers in different piles to fool myself into thinking that I'm working on this book. I have not been paying much heed to the music. On occasion, I have paused my activities to give special attention to a favorite moment: the Italian tenor's aria; the end of the Marschallin's Act I monologue as she contemplates her passing years; Octavian and Sophie's meeting in Act II; Valzacchi and Annina's cry of "Ecco!" as they reveal the young lovers to Baron Ochs; Ochs's lumbering waltz on "Mit mir keine nacht dir zu lang." Mostly, though, I have gone about my business, barely noticing the music, just as, usually, I barely notice the prints that hang on my walls.

But a few minutes before the end of the recording my relationship to the music changes. I hear my cue: Ochs growls out "Leupold, wir geh'n!" and the children cry their last round of "Papa! Papa! Papa!" (the passage when the comic portion of the plot comes to its gyrating conclusion), and the mood softens as the love triangle of Octavian, Sophie, and the Marschallin returns to the foreground. This is my signal to drop what I'm doing and listen. The first thing I do is lie down. I do it without thinking, a reflex response. I take off my glasses, my watch, anything distracting. I close my eyes and settle into the sofa, adjusting my position to achieve maximum relaxation. I pray desperately that the cats will not decide to take this opportunity to leap on top of my stomach, not this time, not for the next ten minutes.

The whooping waltz that marks the Baron's exit dies down. I settle in a little further. The Marschallin, Octavian, and Sophie begin their negotiations, the two women deferring to each other, poor Octavian caught in embarrassment between his old infatuation and his new love. Their voices overlap one another in excitement, relief, jealousy. Their melodic lines intertwine for a few bars; I catch my breath as they peak for just a moment on a densely harmonized chord, a taste of what is to come. The moment passes. I resume breathing, and the negotiation continues. The music slows, and Strauss's lush orchestration reduces to single instruments, as the Marschallin relinquishes her sexual interest in favor of the young lovers. My shoulders tighten in anticipation. I try to relax. The words, the music disintegrate to nothing: a broken phrase here, a hint of melody there. Elisabeth Schwarzkopf's trembling voice brings the Marschallin's nothingness to rock bottom, whispering a barely audible "gar nix." I swallow, then I lie completely still.

The orchestra returns, a single bell tone and woodwinds. Christa Ludwig softly croons Octavian's "Marie Theres'" and the horns slip in beneath her plaintive voice. Schwartzkopf begins the achingly familiar melody, the one I've heard so often, climbing step-wise up the scale, unbearably beautiful. A lump rises in my throat, but I suppress it. I don't want to get too involved; not yet. Ludwig and Teresa Stich-Randall (singing Sophie) rescue me for the moment; I let go a bit as their voices blend with Schwarzkopf's, slightly out of focus, dissipating the tension, each soprano reaching up in pitch in her turn. Then the tension starts to build again; the orchestra swells; the three sopranos hit their first high notes together. There is a pause, and I catch my breath once more.

Now the three singers begin their inexorable climb up the scale to the tops of their registers. They hit high note after high note, dropping down a little in pitch after each new high, only to climb even higher in the next phrase, barely giving me time to recover between them. The ever-building music washes over me in closely harmonized waves, each one more intense than the last. Wave after wave, the harmonic tensions get denser, the orchestra louder, the instrumentation more dominated by the strings, until I can no longer separate strings from voices. The words are gone; the plot is gone; only the sound of voices blending with the orchestra remains. My heart beats faster. My stomach muscles contract, my buttocks tighten, my face contorts at each new harmonic tension. My head sways with the music; I conduct the opera with my prone body. The three sopranos reach the tops of their registers. They can sing no higher, but I'm not satisfied yet. The harmonies have not resolved; the music must still go up, up. The violins take over, carrying the melody over the top, beginning to resolve the hopelessly dense harmonies. Strings and voices strain against each other, cresting on each climactic note. My back arches; it no longer touches the sofa. It stays that way through the impossibly long climax; all my muscles are taut. Finally the complex harmonies slowly unravel themselves and find resolution. The melody begins to work its way down the scale; my muscles gradually relax, and I sink back down into the upholstery. Schwarzkopf calls down divine blessing on our collective consummation, our ménage-à-quatre: "In Gottes Namen." The music dies away into Octavian and Sophie's monotonal duet. I start to breathe normally again. If I smoked, I would light a cigarette. Instead, I lie still, waiting impatiently for my final taste of pleasure, Schwarzkopf's raspy "Ja, ja." Then I get up and resume my normal life, as the opera's final bars fade once again into the background.

I enact this ritual every time I listen to the trio. I never tire of it, however often I hear this music. And it is always the same. Other passages in opera I can listen to differently under different circumstances, but this passage always consumes me physically, totally. I want to be alone with this music, so that we may enact our erotic performance in private. When I attend a live performance of *Rosenkavalier* I can't quite repeat this act of lovemaking; my internal censor prevents me from lying down in the aisle and embodying the same level of physical ecstasy, lest I distract the other patrons and wrinkle my good suit. Still, my muscles go through the same motions in miniature, as I dig my fingernails into the armrests. I love the rest of the opera, but for me it is all a prelude, an elaborate foreplay building up to the climax of the last ten minutes. I cannot conceive how anyone could feel differently. Once at a performance of *Rosenkavalier* at the Met, I looked with horror as dozens of people got up to run for their taxis just before the start of the trio. I was angered at the distraction, but more at the insensitivity of these people, their ignorance of the upcoming erotic act. I know it's a long opera, but there are people who hang around in bars for years to catch a thrill comparable to the one I get from this music. Did these philistines not know what was coming? Or did they just not feel what I feel? I do not understand.

The Operatic Sex Act

Anne Rice understands what I feel when I listen to *Der Rosenkavalier.* She understands the physical sexuality of opera. Here is her description of Tonio, the young castrato hero of *Cry to Heaven,* as he makes his public debut, singing a duet with his patroness, the wealthy Contessa:

> Tonio began to sing. . . . It was as if he wanted the Contessa's voice, and she knew it, and when she answered him, he felt himself actually falling in love. With a surge of the strings he went into a stronger and faster aria to her, and it seemed even the lovely poetry he was singing to her was all of it perfectly true.
>
> His voice was seducing her voice, not merely for its answers but for that moment when the two would come together in one song. Even his softest, most languid notes told her that, and her slow passages so full of dark color echoed the same vibrant desire. . . . They plunged into the final duet.
>
> Her voice was wed to his voice. Her cheeks were flushed and her eyes had the gleam of tears. Her little body heaved with the fullness of her voice, his own winding up and out of his immense lungs and this languid slender frame that seemed the flesh left behind in stillness and grace as the voice went free.
>
> It was over.
> It was finished.
> The room shimmered.[3]

Rice uses the language of sexual pleasure to describe these two singing bodies: "surge"; "languid"; "come together"; "flushed"; "heaved." Even the structure of her language imitates a sexual climax, with its rising intensity, peak of tension, and descent into exhaustion. Rice depicts Tonio's vocal interaction with the Contessa's voice as physical consummation, a mingling of two sexual instruments in an act of lovemaking. The two voice-bodies join in a physical union, which climaxes as an orgasm and gives way to a shimmering afterglow of post-coital exhaustion and silence.

An opera performance is a sexual act. I do not mean that opera is metaphorical or vicarious sex, an intellectual reenactment or contemplation of pleasurable sensations. There is nothing vicarious about opera's sensuality. It is real, physical erotic stimulation of the audience by the performance. Opera's ability to provide erotic stimulation for its audience is the answer to the question I asked at the beginning of the book: Why does an opera performance feel so much like sex? Opera feels like a sexual act because it *is* a sexual act. That is the secret of opera's irrational appeal and of its overwhelming effect on an audience that gives itself over to opera's excesses. When I engage my desire with an operatic performance, I feel its stimuli in all the muscles of my body. If the body of the singer on the stage serves as an object for my desire, then that desire manifests itself as a visceral response in my own body when I give my libidinal attention to the operatic spectacle. When I am in the opera house, I have the singer's body and voice in front of me as the object of my desire, though I usually must pay for this immediacy by repressing my physical response until the end of the opera, at which point my sexual energies can finally burst out as enthusiastic applause. When I listen to a recording, although the body of the singer is absent, I can compensate for the lack of the singer's physical presence by indulging in a more immediate and overt bodily response, as I do when I listen to the ecstatic trio of *Der Rosenkavalier*. And if the relationship between the opera performance and my body is a sex act, the most intense and climactic moments of that act are operatic orgasms.

Toward the end of her provocative essay, "On a Lesbian Relationship with Music: A Serious Effort Not to Think Straight," Suzanne G. Cusick asks, "What if music IS sex?" She wonders: "If sex is free of the association with reproduction enforced by the so-called phallic economy . . . , if it is then *only* (only!) a means of negotiating power and intimacy through the circulation of pleasure, what's to prevent music from *being* sex, and thus an ancient, half-sanctioned form of escape from the constraints of the phallic economy?"[4] If music in general is sex, then music in the context of opera is even more so, with the extra physical trappings of theatrical production and the sexualized framework of the operatic narrative to give musical sex a solid point of reference for eroticized fantasy.

Arguably, my relationship to opera cannot justifiably be described as physical sex, because, on the one hand, opera is not another human being, and sex happens between human beings; and because, on the other hand, the climactic moments of opera do not actually induce in my genitals a physical orgasm accompanied by an ejaculation, and so operatic sex is actually imaginary, no matter how real it may seem. Neither assertion deters me from my belief that opera is real sex. To the first objection, I would point out that most human sexual interactions happen not between two people but between a person and a mentally generated object of desire. Our fantasies occupy far more of our sexual life than human contact. Even during the throes of lovemaking, our minds (as much as we hate to admit it) normally focus on a fantasy object rather than on the person with whom we are rolling around. Sexual interactions between a body and a mental image are just as real as those between two bodies rubbing against each other, they are just as necessary for most of us to attain sexual pleasure, and for some people they are just as (if not more) fulfilling, even when not accompanied by human contact.

And, more fundamental to the question of the reality of operatic sex, an opera performance, unlike a mental fantasy, is in fact a physical thing, demonstrably more tangible than a sexual fantasy, with a measurable effect on the listening body. My body makes contact with the plush upholstery of the seats; my eyes absorb the images of lavish scenery and costumes. Much more importantly, and even in the absence of these trappings, the physical vibrations of the music create immediate neural stimuli in my body. An erotic fantasy creates sexual sensations through internal imagination, but opera's stimulation is physical and external; operatic sex rises directly out of the tangible physical sensations that music induces in the listener's body. The dense harmonics of Strauss's music touch my body as fully as my lover touches my body when he caresses my skin, and the two touches produce similar responses of tension in my flesh. As Koestenbaum suggests, in the passage that opens this chapter and in the following image, opera turns the ear into an erogenous zone: "Nuns in the Middle Ages believed they were pregnant because Jesus had *thought* of them; no wonder, then, that opera queens, nuns of an unnamed order, believe that voices entering through the ear are forms of the Holy Ghost. . . . To hear is metaphorically to be impregnated—with thought, tone, and sensation."[5] In response, I would offer that opera does far more than engage the ear in metaphorical sex. In opera, it is not a question of sex through thought but rather through physical contact via sound. If, in reproductive terms, opera can only impregnate the ear metaphorically, its erotic stimulation of that organ is entirely tangible, and it is transmitted by the ear to the rest of the body. And, in spite of Koestenbaum's construction, opera's erotic stimuli are available to every ear in the audience, not just those ears attached to gay fans.

To the second objection, that operatic sex is not real because its orgasms are not ejaculatory, I would argue that it is an entirely false distinction to limit the definition of sex—or orgasms—only to acts that result in ejaculation. The attitude that sex is not valid unless someone emits semen assumes that a male body must be present for sex to be real, a limiting and culturally enforced attitude based on centuries of the phallic economy. Women have sex without ejaculation all the time, sometimes without orgasms and sometimes with more orgasms than we men care to think about. There is a lot more to sex than the simple act of coitus. The human mind, with its infinite sexual resources, can transform virtually any act or physical stimulus into sex, and the reality of human sexual experience ranges far beyond the rather limited and pedestrian act of depositing seminal fluid into a vagina.[6] In the queer realm of operatic sexuality, any stimulus that comes at me from the stage, visual or aural, physical or imagined, can be eroticized. Operatic performance engages me physically, and that engagement is very much a real sex act, resulting in real (if not conventionally ejaculatory) musical orgasms.

Even Koestenbaum is uncomfortable with the reality of operatic sex. He asserts categorically, "Opera doesn't arouse me (opera isn't an aphrodisiac)."[7] Yet throughout his book he speaks of opera in intensely sexual terms; he explains its appeal entirely through its eroticism. If Koestenbaum's response to opera cannot be called arousal, I do not know what can be. When he says that opera does not arouse him, he really means that opera does not give him an erection, the necessary prelude to ejaculation. But if opera fails to bring his penis to attention, it certainly arouses the rest of his body and psyche, as it does mine. The need to deny opera's sexual power closely parallels society's persistent denial of sexual content in virtually every other public forum. The human mind has remarkable powers of not-seeing, especially in the realm of sexuality. Freud explained this mechanism of repression a century ago, but that knowledge has not made us repress our sexual feelings any less. We seem to need to deny our physical engagement with opera, to keep it separate from our "real" sex lives. But for all our denial, opera's appeal to its audience remains intensely, physically erotic.

Of course, some people might find the very concept of opera as a sexual act (especially a sexual act performed in public) intensely distressing. Officially, opera is about love, not sex. High art, I am told, is not supposed to be about sex, and it is certainly not supposed to *be* sex. Only low and tawdry art, I am told, has anything to do with physical sex acts. For that matter, according to our great moral pundits, a work that deals with sex should not even be dignified with the name of art, and art that elicits erotic stimulation is nothing other than pornography. This shocking revelation of the obvious, that much of our pleasure in art is sexual, elicits remarkably vehement responses. A growing army of benighted congressional politicians, led by Jesse Helms, aims to eliminate the already pitifully small funding for the National Endowment for the Arts in the terrified panic that the government might possibly fund someone's pleasure. Such moral posing is nothing but hypocrisy in the face of the pervasive and demeaning sexuality in the mass media funded, in part, by the Helms-backed tobacco industry. (I think of Claude Rains, in the classic film *Casablanca,* shutting down Rick's Café, mugging, "I'm shocked, shocked to find that gambling is going on in here" and then collecting his winnings.) But, as Roland Barthes argues in his revolutionary *The Pleasure of the Text,* the basis for our emotional response to art, even art as "pure" and linear as narrative fiction, is physical, sexual pleasure, culminating in moments of *jouissance:* sexual climax.[8]

The Operatic Orgasm

Looking strictly at opera's libretti, orgasmic sexual acts are only supposed to happen offstage. Operatic narrative dishes out love scenes by the dozens, but the lovers never actually get to the sex act, or, like Siegmund and Sieglinde at the end of Act I of *Die Walküre,* they run off into the wings just before enacting the consummation of their love. If opera narrative has any orgasms, they happen only by implication, hinting at activities that take place in the story, but which we in the audience never get to see. Even *Carmen* buys into this fiction of offstage sex, most notably at the end of Act II, when Carmen successfully seduces José into the life of the vagabond.[9] But I'm not satisfied to say that romantic love in opera only implies orgasms, that I'm supposed to think that Carmen and José are making passionate love in the wings, or that Otello and Desdemona are wrangling away in their bedroom after their Act I duet while I sip my champagne at intermission and the stagehands change the scenery for the next act. Siegmund and Sieglinde have their incestuous orgasm while they sing, not after they leave the stage. Opera orgasms do not happen offstage; they don't even really happen between the characters. They happen during the performance, and they happen between the singers and the audience.

These orgasms punctuate the narrative of opera. The physical stimulation that opera offers to its audience itself takes the form of a narrative: a period of foreplay, followed by a section of building tension, leading to one or more climactic moments of orgasm, and then a repetition of the cycle. The linear progress of foreplay through to orgasm becomes another narrative, a story of seduction and fulfillment that supplements, and at times even substitutes for, the ostensible narrative of the opera. As much as my engagement with opera may depend on my involvement with the story line, it is this underlying story, the less overt orgasmic narrative, that keeps my interest and propels me through the performance. This secondary orgasmic narrative explains why people feel they can follow the story of an opera, even when they have no access to its language; the orgasmic musical narrative creates the sense of forward motion. It explains why operas with the most complicated or disjointed librettos, the *Il Trovatore*s and *La Gioconda*s, seem to make so much more narrative sense in performance than in a simple reading of the text. And it also explains why opera can thrive on such a limited repertory of works, why we can return again and again to the same few operas and never tire of their repetitive narratives. If the human mind can only tolerate hearing a fictional story so many times, we never tire of hearing that great fundamental narrative, the story of sexual climax, especially when we ourselves get to participate in its enactment.[10]

Or, at least, male bodies never tire of this story, for the operatic orgasmic narrative, though it claims universality, only tells the tale of male sexual fulfillment. As recent feminist literary criticism suggests, the traditional Western linear narrative imitates the structure of male orgasm. The narrative structural criteria set up by Aristotle in the *Poetics* find value only in stories with a single movement from beginning, through a process of heightened tension, to a climactic ending and unitary resolution. Men impose this linear structure on the world and on the fiction that represents it, because this is the way we have sex. Women's sexual narrative, less linear and less structured, is accorded little or no value when translated into fictional forms. Even the linearity of language itself embodies male sexuality.[11] Similarly, opera's orgasmic narrative is linear and climactic. Catherine Clément argues that the primary operatic narrative depicting selfless female martyrs and tubercular heroines aims to destroy the female characters who enter its dangerous realm; the secondary musical narrative of linear operatic orgasm erases the female voice with equal vigor.

Michel Poizat also argues that opera's sexual narrative aims at the male audience. Although approximately equal numbers of men and women attend opera, he observes, "as far as personal investment in opera is concerned, very few women, it seems, are so deeply invested in this quest [for operatic *jouissance*] as some men are."[12] The more committed the opera fan, that is, the more sexual fulfillment the fan finds in the performance, the more likely, according to Poizat, that fan will be male. Poizat extends this argument through heterosexual logic to suggest that only the soprano voice, embodying the female object of male sexual desire, truly embodies the orgasmic moments of operatic *jouissance*.[13] By an entirely different logical route, one of psychological displacement of gay male desire away from other male bodies, Koestenbaum also finds opera orgasms only in the female voice. Both Poizat and Koestenbaum locate the opera orgasm in the voice of the diva, the soprano-turned-goddess, placed aloft on the pedestal of sexual desire, from which she sings her thrilling high notes.

But this view of operatic orgasm is, to my mind, too limiting. Opera's sexuality is too broad, too all-encompassing, to admit such restrictions. Although the structure of operatic orgasm is undeniably masculine, its presence in operatic narrative, and its importance to audience response, pervade opera more than Poizat and Koestenbaum suggest. And while the soprano voice may provide the most thrilling individual notes, opera's orgasmic moments do not reside only in the female voice, nor is the (male) audience member bound to find sexual excitement only through female performers. Poizat sees operatic *jouissance* as a very rare thing, a fleeting moment that may or may not happen at any given performance. In this theory, the opera fan, dependent on these elusive moments for sexual fulfillment, spends hugely disproportionate amounts of time and money seeking the almost instantaneous gratification of the perfect climactic note from the singular throat of the diva. Poizat's explanation of operatic orgasms relates closely to the Freudian-Lacanian notion that all human action is motivated by the sense of loss suffered in childhood, the endless and ultimately futile quest for our youthful sexual innocence. Koestenbaum admits a wider range for operatic orgasms, but he too sees them as elusive and futile, a substitute for real sex rather than actual sexual engagement. But if operatic orgasms really originated in failure and loss, they could not create the effect they do on the audience. Opera's orgasms are not momentary and elusive, nor are they a failed sexuality. They are overt and frequent and, most of the time, entirely successful as sexual stimulation. Their appeal is not that they are so hard to come by but that, in opera's world of sexual excess, they are so readily available, such an easy means of pleasure, at least within the context of male sexuality.

Opera abounds with orgasms. Every climactic note, in an aria, in an ensemble, even in an overture, can feel like a sexual climax within the sensually heightened realm of the opera house. Opera's music penetrates my ear, works around my body as the opera progresses, and climaxes at regular intervals, usually at the ends of arias. The orgasm inhabits the music itself, and it also enters my body, sending me into sexual ecstasy at the same moment the music enacts its climax. That is the miracle of operatic sex: its orgasms are always simultaneous. I, the passive listener, experience the climax at the very moment that the active, penetrating voice and orchestra perform it. Operatic orgasms provide a perfection of sexual satisfaction that sex with another human body only rarely affords.

But if all climaxes in opera can take on the quality of an orgasm, then, just as in sex between bodies, some operatic orgasms are more effective than others. Any musical climax in opera is available for eroticizing, but certain climactic passages induce orgasms more consistently and are intended to do so by the composer. The most significant operatic orgasms, the ones that frame the sexual narrative, are not merely a function of my personal response to musical climaxes. The narrative operatic orgasm is a thing distinct, a specific structure that induces in me a sexual response at calculated moments. In opera's sexual narrative, most of the performance consists of foreplay, with only selected moments reserved for orgasm. As with sex between two bodies, you can't (or at least men can't) live in a perpetual state of climax. What, then, distinguishes a narrative orgasm from a more preliminary climactic moment? Greater intensity? Deeper harmonic density? Specific reference to sex in the libretto? How can I define an operatic orgasm?

In a way, that pursuit is foolish. Like a biological orgasm, I can't define an operatic orgasm; I can't even really describe one. (And I can only begin to approximate a description of a male orgasm, the female variety being personally inaccessible to me.) Words have nothing to do with orgasms. When I was twelve or so I read David Rubin's *Everything You Always Wanted to Know About Sex but Were Afraid to Ask* before I had had any actual experience of sexual climax. Fascinating as I found Rubin's descriptions, my reading did nothing to allay the shock of the actual experience when it happened the first time. You know an orgasm when you feel it; any further discussion is superfluous. Criticism of an experience so intimate and personal is doomed to frustration.

Roland Barthes argues that the sexual pleasure that we find in art, just as the physical pleasure we find in erotic stimulation, obviates objective criticism. In *The Pleasure of the Text,* Barthes discusses how he as a critic approaches a text (or a voice) that gives him sexual pleasure, and he concludes that rational judgment has no place in that relationship:

> If I agree to judge a text according to pleasure, I cannot go on to say: this one is good, that bad. No awards, no "critique," for this always implies a tactical aim, a social usage, and frequently an extenuating image-reservoir. I cannot apportion, imagine that the text is perfectible, ready to enter into a play of normative predicates: it is too much *this,* not enough *that;* the text (the same is true of the singing voice) can wring from me only this judgment, in no way adjectival: *that's it!* And further still: *that's it for me!*[14]

My experience of operatic orgasm is entirely personal, neither good nor bad, only more or less personally fulfilling. The failure of the philistines to find orgasmic satisfaction at the end of *Der Rosenkavalier* is not analyzable; it simply indicates that they do not share my sexual psyche. But if not everyone experiences an orgasm at the end of *Rosenkavalier,* then Strauss clearly intends that they should. If I cannot analyze my experience of the operatic orgasm, I can at least pinpoint where and how these moments become available to the eroticized ear, the technical means by which the creators of opera seek to induce orgasm.

Making Orgasms

In my late adolescence and early adulthood, my favorite piece of orgasmic music was Aaron Copland's essay for strings, trumpet, and English horn, "Quiet City." Whenever I felt overwhelmed by anxiety or overburdened by work or personal trauma in college, I would lie on my bed and put on this music, listening much the same way as I would later listen to the *Rosenkavalier* trio. Ten minutes later my tensions would be relaxed and I'd go on with my business. (I suppose my more prosaic male classmates simply masturbated at such times, but my mind has always had an aesthetic strain.) "Quiet City" is hardly an earth-shattering piece, but it encompasses a perfect little musical orgasm. Copland begins with a simple melody, almost a monotone. The harmonies in the strings are open and diatonic, the two solo instruments clear and distinct. The intensity of the piece builds in pitch, in harmonic tension, in volume, slowly and steadily, step-wise, to a climactic moment in which the now dense string harmonies surge under the erupting lines of the solo instruments. After this extended climax the music comes down rapidly from its high point to a quiet resolution, back to the open harmonies and simple melodies of the opening bars. If "Quiet City" boasts fewer musical and narrative complexities than the *Rosenkavalier* trio, it exhibits an almost identical orgasmic structure.

Tension and resolution form the building blocks for the musical orgasm. The composer, employing the available means for creating tension (especially harmony and melodic departure from the base tonality), builds to a high point and then releases the tension in a climactic moment or passage, followed by an extended resolution. A simple build in intensity is not enough; the music needs to develop deep musical tensions and then release them climactically. Only in this way can musical tension parallel the Aristotelian structure of the orgasmic narrative. For this reason Maurice Ravel's "Bolero" does not feel to me like a musical orgasm. "Bolero" builds in intensity, and its build involves me emotionally. The music makes me tap my feet with the rhythm, but it does not make my shoulders tighten. The endlessly repeated melody is too predictable; there is no great tension to resolve. The climax is loud and explosive, but the music cuts off at the instant of the climax, in precisely the way that orgasms do not. An orgasm releases tension; it lets you down after it builds you up. The afterglow is just as much a part of the orgasm as the climax. Orgasmic operatic arias never leave off at the moment of climax. There are always a few bars of vocal or orchestral music to resolve the tension, to bring the listener back to earth.

Susan McClary explicates the musical basis of the tension-resolution pattern of the operatic orgasm in the context of instrumental music:

> The tonality that underlies Western concert music is strongly informed by a specific sort of erotic imagery. . . . The principle innovation of seventeenth-century tonality is the ability to instill in the listener an intense longing for a given event: the cadence. It organizes time by creating an artificial need. . . . After that need is established (after the listener has been conditioned to experience the unbearable absence of some musical configuration) tonal procedures strive to postpone gratification of that need until finally delivering the payoff in what is technically called the "climax," which is quite clearly to be experienced as a metaphorical ejaculation.[15]

The standard structures of Western tonal music depend on the creation of desire in the listener. The seventeenth-century ostinato perpetuates desire by making each moment of potential closure also a new musical beginning. The sonata form and similar repetitive structures promise recapitulation of established melodies at regular intervals. Most important, tonality and classical harmony create tangible physical desires for the listener to hear specific sounds; I want the melody to return to its base note, the leading chord to resolve to its home key (like Mozart, who, it is said, got out of bed to resolve a chord when someone less sensitive had left it unresolved on the keyboard). The conventions of Western music teach me to demand linear completion and resolution and create intense tensions around my expectation of this resolution.[16]

The most typical tensions used in musical orgasm—the sounds that feel most like an orgasm to my modern ears—are melodic and harmonic. As Susan McClary notes, Western tonal music depends on harmonic tensions that resolve back to a central defining tone of the base key. In most cases, this resolution is not a big event, because the music does not stray very far from the base tone. But when the music sustains the tension, when the harmony feels as if it is going to resolve at any moment but instead keeps building in tension away from the base tone, the moment of resolution, when it finally comes, feels intensely climactic. Deep harmonic tension produces visceral feelings in the listener, often with negative connotations (dissonance and its metaphorical associations: personal strife, war, bad weather, demons, and the supernatural). The resolution of intense harmonic tension causes tangible physical relief.[17] In the heady context of the opera house, these moments of release become more than the fulfillment of desire. Abetted by the love story, the opulent surroundings, and especially by the eroticized body of the singer, a purely musical climax becomes a full-fledged sexual consummation.

Opera has included musical orgasms from its earliest days. But to modern ears, the adventurous nature of romantic and post-romantic music, with its lush orchestration and dense chromatic harmonies, have come to define the operatic orgasm. The emotional gush of Verdi and the harmonic tension of Wagner dominate the modern perception of opera's sexual landscape. Climaxes abound in prechromatic music, and they can be entirely orgasmic, but these climaxes have now become difficult to hear, because modern audiences do not know how to listen for them. The showpiece arias of the castrati ended with remarkable displays of florid vocalism, in which the singer improvised elaborate orgasms via trills, scale runs, and held notes. Mozart has Don Giovanni and Zerlina enact a musical orgasm in "La ci darem la mano," but it no longer feels orgasmic to us because the harmonic tensions are subdued and diatonic.[18] Post-romantic chromaticism has blunted our senses to all but the most thunderous of musical orgasms. We no longer even perceive mere harmonic tensions; we demand harmonic traumas in our climaxes, just as we demand obscene amounts of blood and violence in Hollywood action films to sate our jaded tastes.

No matter whether classically subdued or lushly chromatic, however, most operatic orgasms follow the same basic form. They begin with a foreplay period, which establishes the basic melodic and harmonic tensions, and then move into a section of more intense buildup, leading to the climax and then a short postcoital repose. Altogether, this process normally takes a composer anywhere from seven to ten minutes to accomplish, about the same time as a successful act of biological coitus (personal vicissitudes taken into account, of course, along with the fact that orgasms, biological and musical, tend to disengage the perception of time). Samuel Barber's "Adagio for Strings" (another favorite little orgasm of mine), takes about seven minutes; Copland's "Quiet City," with a longer foreplay period, runs about ten minutes. The champion for duration is probably the *Der Rosenkavalier* trio, with its loose foreplay section of about six minutes, then the more focused build to the orgasm of another six minutes or so.

By contrast, the comically literal depiction of the sex act that Strauss puts into the prelude of *Rosenkavalier* goes a good deal more rapidly, almost a premature ejaculation. Strauss, the master of program music, who claimed that he could depict a fork musically, sets out in the opera's orchestral prelude to describe literally in music, blow-by-blow, the sexual episode between Octavian and the Marschallin that opens the story, and which the curtain hides from us until the lovers are safely dressed. The brass fanfare that opens the prelude represents Octavian, and the strings that follow depict the Marschallin; the two lines of music intertwine with increasing speed, complexity, and intensity until the point of climax. There is no question here about the location of the musically depicted orgasm; it is blared out in the horns, for all to hear, in a series of brassy spurts. It is even possible to locate the point in the music when Octavian rolls off his lover and collapses in exhaustion. This passage is a parody of the operatic orgasm, a way to disarm us so we are all the more enthralled when the real thing comes along at the end of the opera.

But the *Rosenkavalier* prelude is not an operatic orgasm. The prelude is *about* sex, whereas the final trio *is* sex. In order for a moment of musical climax to be orgasmic, it must involve us, not cause us to stand apart with irony, as the comic tone of the prelude does. It must create that sense of engagement, fulfillment, and exhaustion that Aristotle calls catharsis. For all the oceans of ink spilled in trying to decipher Aristotle's cryptic concept of catharsis as the climax of a tragic plot, to me the notion is quite simple. Aristotle's catharsis is a dramatic orgasm, the moment when the tensions of the narrative find their release. This explanation accounts for the physical nature of catharsis (the term means "purgation" in Greek, and an orgasm is certainly a kind of purgation), and for its ability to produce simultaneous feelings of exhaustion and elation, tears and a sense of well-being, in the audience. It accounts for the ability of musical orgasms in opera to take on the burden of narrative, even when disengaged from the overt story line. And it also explains why so many operatic orgasms occur at climactic moments in the opera's story, very often at moments of death.

Opera, Sex, and Death

Operatic orgasms often accompany moments of death. They live in the space created by *Carmen*'s chilling pun between *l'amour* and *la mort,* love and death. Not always; very often operatic orgasms happen in ecstatic love duets, especially those written by Verdi, Wagner, and Puccini, but then the orgasmic ecstasy of the duet usually dooms one or both of the lovers to death. Sometimes the musical orgasm only threatens death, as in Turandot and Calaf's climactic ending of "In questa reggia," just before the fatal riddles. Sometimes, as in *Rosenkavalier,* love dies while the lovers live on. But if not all operatic orgasms are deadly, they regularly appear along with death, a final cry from the throats of Clément's dying swans. It is as if the intensity of the musical orgasm overcomes the singer's body. Like Jacques Offenbach's Antonia, the very act of singing leads to bodily dissolution. The more sexually charged the music, the greater the danger of the singer's demise.

The relationship between sex and death—the inevitable link between *eros* and *thanatos*—is by no means unique to opera. Death often unites metaphorically to sex and more specifically to male orgasm, the moment when all conscious thoughts are obliterated from the mind in a kind of living death. Orgasm is a momentary oblivion, the closest taste of death we have in life. The Elizabethans used the term "to die" as a euphemism for ejaculation (in *Much Ado About Nothing,* Benedick tells Beatrice "I will live in thy heart, die in thy lap, and be buried in thy eyes"), and the French call orgasm *la petit mort,* "the little death." Foucault, in the second volume of *The History of Sexuality,* traces this parallel back to the earliest Greek medical tracts; he points out that if one believes, as the Greeks did, that semen contains the stuff of life, then loss of semen during ejaculation means a diminishing of life, and, in the extreme case, death.[19]

Certainly, the experience of operatic orgasm for the audience can induce oblivion; in the sweep of opera's sexuality, it is quite possible to "lose oneself" in the performance, to forget the distance that holds our bodies apart from the stage. But within the operatic narrative, the terms of the Greek metaphor get turned around. Instead of orgasm leading to death, in opera death becomes a kind of orgasm, an ecstasy of expiration, the ultimate form of catharsis. At climactic moments, the secondary orgasmic narrative unites momentarily with the overt narrative that controls the fate of the fictional figures, and the oblivion of musical orgasm manifests itself in the death of the character. The body ejaculates out its life in the form of a climactic high note. And, though grand opera clearly remains squarely in the grip of the male gaze, in this case orgasmic death is not limited to the representation of the male body. Opera may force female characters to embody male orgasms, but at least they have them. In fact, the death ecstasy of opera may be, as Virgil Thomson points out in the passage that opens this chapter, the only time traditional theater allows women to have an orgasm of any kind, literally or metaphorically, onstage or anywhere else.[20]

The central example of this sexual death is, of course, the "Liebestod" at the end of Wagner's *Tristan und Isolde.* I have intentionally avoided mentioning the "Liebestod" until now. The whole concept of the operatic orgasm ties so squarely to this one piece of music that one can easily forget how pervasive operatic orgasms are beyond Wagner's iconic example and how many opera orgasms do not result in instant death. In Verdi and Puccini, orgasmic love duets tend to appear not at moments of death but early in the opera, when the lovers first discover their passion. In the end, though, the "Liebestod" remains the quintessential operatic orgasm, and all post-*Tristan und Isolde* orgasms necessarily refer back to it, directly or obliquely. Isolde's orgasm changed everything.

Isolde's death occurs at the moment of her musical climax. Wagner's highly chromatic music surges in increasingly intense and heavily scored waves, building to a climactic moment of several extremely tense high notes followed by descending scales, then slowly sinking into the complete exhaustion of postorgasmic death. Wagner's accompanying text, though secondary to the emotional effect, highlights the musical ecstasy; it resonates with sensual language and ends with the words "höchste Lust," highest physical pleasure. Wagner carries musical sexual discourse to the edge of literal expression, embodying the sexual act on stage disguised as death. The influence of the "Liebestod" on later operatic music is pervasive, both for Wagnerian and non-Wagnerian composers, in the nineteenth century and beyond. Since death ends so many post-Wagnerian operas, and because of the appealing intensity of Wagner's overtly sexual music, the music-as-sex-as-death pattern proliferates after Isolde showed the way to orgasmic death.

Romantic opera on the stage reinforces the orgasmic sex-as-death motif with several recurrent visual tropes. In these images once again the underlying sexual narrative of the operatic orgasm threatens to break into the surface story. The most familiar of these images is the one that ends so many popular operas: the body of the grief-stricken or dying tenor collapsing on the body of the lifeless (and thus passive) soprano. This final gesture of despair leaves the audience with an overt visual symbol of sexual intercourse. And unlike *Tristan und Isolde,* in most operas this sex occurs in the missionary position, with the man on top. This image figures into the endings of, to name only the most popular operas, *Tannhäuser, Lohengrin* (Elsa dies in her brother's arms, not her husband's, but the effect is the same) *Luisa Miller, Rigoletto* (here it's father and daughter), *La Traviata, Aïda, Otello, Roméo et Juliette, Carmen, Lakmé, La Gioconda, I Pagliacci* (two men, one living and one dead, over the female corpse), *Manon, Manon Lescaut, La Bohème, Madama Butterfly,* and potentially in all three acts of *Les Contes d'Hoffmann.* And Richard Strauss, who always has to do things bigger, has a whole regiment of soldiers fall on top of Salome.

As the *Salome* example suggests, if the visual image of a male lover falling on the lifeless female body represents a (supposedly) consensual sex act, a second motif, murder—usually by stabbing—represents rape. At the end of *Carmen*, José stabs his lover while the fate leitmotif (which had earlier served as a prelude to his orgasmic "Flower Song") surges in the background. Rather than ecstatic intercourse, here the musical death becomes rape, the knife a symbolic penis. Carmen's climactic death is a strange orgasm, since neither José nor Carmen sings in the musical rape-death; the orchestra carries the entire musical burden, and neither character participates in the fatal musical orgasm. Even worse, their musical passivity implicates the audience in the rape. As Susan McClary points out, the operatic orgasm makes us desire Carmen's death; we are not satisfied, musically or dramatically, until she is raped by José's knife.[21]

Again, this stabbing-as-rape motif recurs in many operas, notably in *I Pagliacci, Wozzeck,* offstage in *La Forza del Destino* and *Lulu,* and, in a displaced rape, in *Otello,* in which Otello strangles Desdemona and then stabs himself. Butterfly stabs herself, though Pinkerton is the cause; she performs the "honorable" act of suicide with her father's sword, an action fraught with Freudian implications. And in an interesting reversal, Tosca responds to an actual threat of rape by turning the symbolic penis against the rapist and stabs the evil Baron Scarpia when he tries to take her body, as he cries out his climactic "Tosca, finalmente!"

This erotic discourse of death can become dangerously alluring. Opera, like Hollywood films of the thirties and forties, makes death seem attractive. Opera seduces me, engages my body sexually, and then represents our combined sexual act as death. At these moments, I envy those who can die supported by the power of a musical orgasm, and I despair that my own life, in its lesser sexual intensity and in its (presumably) less theatrical demise, will never measure up to the model opera shows me. Koestenbaum muses:

> Opera has the power to warn you that you have wasted your life. You haven't acted on your desires. You've suffered a stunted, vicarious existence. You've silenced your passions. The volume, height, depth, lushness, and excess of operatic utterance reveal, by contrast, how small your gestures have been until now, how impoverished your physicality; you have only used a fraction of your bodily endowment, and your throat is closed.[22]

If Koestenbaum and others see in opera a world of illusion and sexual despair, rather than joy and celebration, I imagine their visions arise in part from opera's coercive link between sex and death. But opera provides a means of escape from this formula of despair in the always present, but not always obvious, disjunction between the surface narrative and the physical climax of operatic sex. The orgasm that I experience in my body when listening to opera, whether in the "Liebestod," "La ci darem la mano," the love duet in *Un Ballo in Maschera,* or the *Rosenkavalier* trio, is equally stimulating and life-affirming, no matter how different the fates of the characters who enact them. The experience of the operatic orgasm tells its own story and engages my sensibilities in a glorious moment of erotic fulfillment.

It is easy to believe that operatic orgasms are better than biological ones. They certainly have distinct practical and social advantages over the biological variety. Operatic sex can be thoroughly intoxicating, it normally prolongs both the pre- and postclimactic ecstasy, it wears the cloak of public respectability, and it involves a lot fewer negative repercussions. I also know that the orgasms produced by my genitalia can never live up to the ideal set by an operatic orgasm. Opera shames and represses my self-confidence in my merely human sexual capacities. I cannot possibly generate the intensity of passion that Wagner's hundred-piece orchestra can, yet what the "Liebestod" tells me is that, if I were *really* in love, I could raise a passion like Isolde's. Operatic orgasms are as much a partner of sexual repression as they are a release from it; they illustrate the inadequacy, the inferiority, and "abnormality" of my own less intense and less idealized human-to-human sexual practice. Without music, sex isn't real. Perhaps this is why, when I try to validate the intensity of my latest sexual experience to my lover, I feel a desire to say to him, "I heard music."

7

OPERA, SEX, AND POWER

And is there really a fundamental difference between the thrill that comes at the climax of the love duet in Act II of Tristan und Isolde *and the shudders of dread—experienced explicitly as such when Lulu screams her death cry under Jack the Ripper's knife—that unfailingly overcomes us no matter how familiar we are with this work, no matter how prepared we may be for that rending cry?*

—Michel Poizat
The Angel's Cry[1]

Turandot *is continually played out between tragedy and a minor mime show. . . . A girl refuses to marry and there is total darkness. . . . The mythical consequence will be that women have to bleed every month, marked by the sign of fertility and necessary union. That will teach them. You have to keep them under control, these women who are so close to chaos and so incapable of submitting to the slow, regular rhythm that men want.*

—Catherine Clément
Opera, or the Undoing of Women[2]

Sex Wars

Sex is a weapon. Despite the persistent illusion that sexual acts arise only from feelings of love, human beings regularly use sex to gain control over other human beings. Society does not want me to believe this obvious and distressing fact. The organs of public discourse, still firmly entrenched in Victorian romanticism, would rather have me believe that people use sex exclusively to express love (unless I listen to those moral pundits who claim the power of divine authority, who want me to believe that sex is only for making babies). Sexual passions can get intense, I am told, sometimes dangerously so, and some poor person might get burned in the heat of the

97

flames. Still, I am supposed to believe that only good intentions underlie normal sexual interactions, even when they get violent. Only a tiny minority of perverts use sex for power, I am told, sick people who need legal or medical restraint, so that the rest of us can go about our blissfully noncompetitive sex lives.

But this romantic fantasy shatters under the weight of social reality. The statistics on rape, childhood sexual abuse, battered wives, and sexual harassment are so horrifying that they seem unreal, just another shocking Hollywood drama. And these statistics merely represent the most obviously abusive kinds of sexual power play. The more typical and subtle varieties of sex wars, the erotic mind games to which we subject each other in our quest for dominance, never appear in statistical surveys. The 1993 incident in California, in which a group of teenage boys, calling themselves the "Spur Posse," in a "friendly" competition racked up points by seducing as many female classmates as possible, only represents an embarrassing public revelation of a disease endemic to all sexual discourse in our society.[3] The popular slang term for successful seduction, "scoring," does not imply an idealized romantic view of sex as a function of love. Sex is a war game, a game with real consequences, and whether we like it or not, we all spend much of our lives caught in the battle trenches.

Operatic narrative reflects society's pervasive sexual competitiveness. Sexual encounters in opera are rarely peaceful affairs. Even more than in other public discourses, operatic sex means struggle, though it remains heavily cloaked in the language of romantic love. There is always something to be overcome in opera, always some kind of obstacle that gets in the way of sexual consummation. Sometimes external forces hinder the sexual liaison between two willing partners: war; unpleasant older relatives; the past. Just as often, though, one of the potential partners in the sexual battle becomes the obstacle: Don José fights Carmen's seduction and wavers between her and Micaëla (or his mother—they amount to the same person); Zerlina wavers between her seducer Don Giovanni and her fiancée, Masetto; Samson wavers between Dalila and God; the ice princess Turandot has the audacity to refuse to waver at all. The success or failure of one partner to seduce the other often determines whether the opera is tragic or comic, but the seduction is always there, and it always entails a battle.

The rarified romanticism of French and Italian opera cloaks opera's sex battles in a guise of idealistic love. In Wagner's more violent Germanic romanticism, however, opera's sex wars rise to the surface. In his gentlest opera, *Die Meistersinger,* the battle entails no blood—there is merely a singing competition with the girl as the prize—but the competition is still overt and intense. In his more serious works, the heroes must literally take arms in the name of sexual conquest: *Lohengrin* begins with a trial by combat for the possession of Elsa's body; in *Tannhäuser* only the intervention of Hermann prevents a similar outbreak of violence; Tristan receives his mortal wound defending his claim to Isolde. And the entire *Ring* cycle revolves around a series of violent acts committed to gain or protect male sexual privilege over women, especially in *Die Walküre,* in which a full-fledged war breaks out, on earth and in the heavens, for the sexual rights to Sieglinde. Except for the homoerotic world of *Parsifal,* in Wagner, if you want a woman, you have to fight for her.

Onstage, sex only becomes interesting when it gets competitive. No one goes to the theater to see two people happily in love living in carefree domestic bliss. It may be a charming way to live your life, but, at least by traditional critical standards, it makes for exceptionally dull theater. In the overblown world of opera, the sexual competition that livens theater frequently rises to the level of violence. When we go to the opera, we expect to see a powerful lover battling to conquer a reluctant love object, two lovers striving against insurmountable odds to consummate their love, two rivals fighting for a single love object, anything as long as there is a fight. In a way, who wins or loses does not really matter; as in professional wrestling, the fictional battle is all. Whether serious or comic in tone, in the theater love (or more to the point, sex) is war. Opera heightens this Orwellian paradox, because its sex wars are so much larger, and louder, than those in nonmusical theater. Music raises the intensity of theatrical sex wars and, at the same time, makes sexual violence more palatable, because the beautiful music mitigates the violence.[4]

Opera and Rape

Opera's litany of violence against women is, of course, precisely the issue explored by Catherine Clément in *Opera, or the Undoing of Women.* The libretti of grand opera, she argues, stage acts of violence against women that the music of the opera lulls us into not seeing. But if opera treats its female characters so violently, then in the hypercharged pansexuality of opera, where virtually every object or act can become eroticized, this violence perpetrated against women is sexual violence. Opera coerces its female characters into sexual roles, then makes their eroticized bodies the victims of domination and murder. Opera proliferates images of sexual acts used for power rather than love; in other words, it enacts rape. Even when the doomed heroine seems a willing victim, when she submits cheerfully to the violence done to her, or even becomes complicit in the aggression by killing herself, she is still a victim of sexual violence. In the standard courtroom ploy used to defend a rapist, lawyers say that the victim "really wanted it." In opera, where women's creative voices have been largely silent, men can play out this fantasy of the submissive sexualized female victim in the guise of high art. We in the audience use opera's female characters for our sexual pleasure, then increase our pleasure by watching them suffer and die.

This notion, that opera enacts rape, is remarkably discomfiting, even on a symbolic level. The very mention of rape raises intense reactions and, for many men, paradoxical feelings arising from their conflicted societal views of both women and sex. As I write this analysis, I balk at the very concept of positing any connection between high art and sexual violence. How can anything so beautiful and thrilling as opera participate in any way with something so horrific as rape? But as contemporary scholarship on rape has demonstrated, sexual violence leaves its traces on a broad range of social discourse, especially public expression through the media.[5] The excessive world of opera amplifies these traces. With the power of a hundred-piece orchestra behind it, every seduction becomes an act of force, all too often accompanied by narrative acts of physical violence.

Of course, opera never literally puts acts of rape in view of the audience. It regularly teases us with acts of near-rape, but it always stops short of the actual event, at least on stage. The rules of Victorian propriety ensure that operatic narrative only rarely involves rape committed against its heroines, and when it does, the physical act remains hidden from view. Most often, when a character attempts sexual assault, someone thwarts the act at the last moment, as when Tosca stabs Baron Scarpia before he can perform his rape. Alternatively, the attempt can occur offstage, as when Giovanni attacks Zerlina during the ball at the end of Act I of *Don Giovanni,* or when the Duke of Mantua has Gilda in his private chambers in Act II of *Rigoletto.* The victim runs with a scream onstage, on one level assuring us that she is all right, but at the same time leaving us with a lurid curiosity as to whether the rapist has consummated the act or not. Even so shocking a work as Berg's *Lulu* keeps its sexual violence in the wings.

But images of coercive, violent sex lurk not very far beneath the surface of opera. As I argue in Chapter 6, in the narrative representation of orgasmic moments, romantic and post-romantic opera frequently employ visual images that suggest rape, either in the collapse of the tenor's body onto the lifeless form of the soprano or, more powerfully, by the murder of the soprano, especially by stabbing. If we never see men raping women, we often see passive, lifeless female bodies in positions of submission to active male bodies. Most importantly, what transforms Clément's view of operatic violence against women specifically into sexual violence are the intense musical climaxes that invariably accompany these acts, making them the most sexually charged moments in opera. Isolde's death as she sings the "Liebestod" does not, technically, result from an act of violence. She dies in an ecstasy of love, not from an external blow. But the "Liebestod" still performs a kind of rape: The agency of Isolde's death is sex, as performed on her body by Wagner's orgasmic music. If Isolde seems to experience the pleasure of the fatal orgasm herself, this image plays out the rapist's fantasy that the woman really enjoys the sexual violence perpetrated against her.

In its overt narrative, opera's coercive sexuality lingers in the corners. But in its secondary narrative, the sexual narrative of desire enacted between the operatic performance and the audience, opera's coercive sexuality takes on broader consequences. As opera draws the audience into its world through its sexual attractiveness, it forces us to participate in its acts of domination. In effect, as much as it commits acts of sexual violence against its female characters (making the audience complicit in those acts), opera also commits acts of coercive sex directly against its audience. We even speak of operatic performance in terms of rape; we say that a beautiful performance has "ravished" us. The aggressive eroticism of the operatic performance makes us feel sexually passive, as if we have abandoned our control of the situation. Opera seizes us, forces us into a sexual relationship. If opera does not literally rape its audience, it certainly exercises its sexual power over it in a manner so forceful that those—we—in the audience may lose our ability to maintain our own sexual identity.

I believe that opera is a sexual act played out between the performance and the audience. But if so, is operatic sex consensual? Do I submit willingly to opera's domination? Apparently so, because I initiate the relationship by choosing to go to the opera. But does this act of consent really count, given that opera has made me drunk with its intoxicating sensuality? If opera did not lure me in, if I was not under the influence of opera, would I give it so much of my sexual attention? Would I go at all? If the rape depicted in operatic narrative is of the stereotypical variety, in which a stranger leaps out from the darkness to seize his victim, then the audience's experience of opera is more like an ambiguous case of date rape: a powerful seduction under compromised circumstances, complicated by the influence of alcohol or drugs, maybe coerced and maybe not, and performed by an intimate friend. As in many cases of date rape, we cannot believe that opera forces itself on us, because opera is our friend, and friends do not force other friends into unwanted sex acts. If, as Koestenbaum argues, the air of disease hangs over our obsessive attachment to opera, one of the reasons is that opera, like a virus, seems to take us over against our will, overwhelming the natural defenses by which we might resist its allure. Opera is a domineering lover, one who not only coerces us into sexual acts but even coaxes us into believing we control the sexual situation.

More insidiously, opera, as Clément suggests, uses sex to coerce us into accepting its violent vision of sexuality. In a self-reinforcing cycle, the sexual violence we see on the stage becomes inextricably linked with the sexual coercion performed on us by the operatic orgasm. Opera eroticizes the depiction of sexual violence and conditions us to find erotic satisfaction only in images of violent catharsis. In a coercive act of hierarchization, romantic

opera teaches us that only tragedy—a work that ends in climactic sexual violence—is "grand opera," as opposed to the less important comic operas
with their less violent endings. We learn not to question the necessity of
sexual violence in opera, and we learn to find our greatest pleasure in
opera's moments of greatest violence. Opera makes sexualized violence
"feel right."

By way of illustration, I offer three very different stories, one from each
of the last three centuries. They exemplify the synergy between sex and
power in opera, in which a musical orgasm becomes not a means of expressing love but of exercising control, by one character over another and
by the opera over the audience: the seductive duet between Giovanni and
Zerlina from Mozart's *Don Giovanni*, "La ci darem la mano"; the duet in
which Dalila seduces Samson in Camille Saint-Saëns's *Samson et Dalia*,
"Mon coeur s'ouvre à ta voix"; and Turandot's declaration of her sexual
unavailability and Calaf's subsequent challenge to her frigidity, "In questa
reggia," from Puccini's *Turandot*. These three stories, in their own ways,
demonstrate how opera uses the orgasm as a weapon in the sex wars. They
tell how opera's characters employ sex, in particular sexually charged
music, to gain power over each other. Even more, they tell how opera ex-
erts power over me, how they make me submit to their irresistible power.
As in most wars, the victims most severely affected are not the direct partic-
ipants in the combat but those who stand nearby to watch the battle.

Operatic Sex Wars I: "La ci darem la mano"

Don Giovanni is the ultimate sex warrior. In the moral world of the three
Mozart-Da Ponte operatic collaborations, a man's value—or at least his
theatrical interest—is a direct function of his skill at sexual conquest. Don
Ottavio, Giovanni's rival for the sexual rights to Donna Anna, inspires little
audience attention, because he is as flaccid as Giovanni is potent.[6] In this
world of eighteenth-century, Enlightenment comedy, the presumed average
male makes only one or two sexual conquests in his lifetime, then gets
stuck with the consequences; the unfortunate reward for winning a woman
is that you have to keep her. Bartolo suffers this fate, as does Count Almaviva, in *Le Nozze di Figaro*. On the one hand, we laugh at the Count and
find his threats comic, not because he commits adultery but because he fails
in his adultery. On the other, we admire Figaro because he gets his wife and
makes all the other women in the opera desire him as well. In *Così fan
tutte*, Dorabella and Fiordiligi come off better than the two men who love
them because, even though the women waver in their affections, they maintain their powers of sexual allure while Guglielmo and Ferrando demonstrate only their inability to keep hold of their women.

But Giovanni is not an average male. He also does not keep hold of women, but not for lack of ability to acquire them; like a sport fisherman, he catches prey only for the fun of it, then throws it back to the water, slightly damaged, for someone else to fish out.[7] The character of Don Giovanni has achieved a mythical status through his powers of sexual conquest; he is the central symbol of opera's sexual excess.[8] He is also the character who most fascinates philosophers and scholars, from Kierkegaard to George Bernard Shaw, the latter of whom makes Giovanni the prototype of the Nietzschean *übermensch* in his philosophical play, *Man and Superman*.[9] But Mozart's Giovanni, unlike Shaw's, is no intellect; our fascination with him arises not from his great mind but exclusively from his superhuman abilities at sexual warfare. And we in the audience fall victim to him as much as the women on his list; the mythos of his power, and the potent music that Mozart gives him to sing, make us his victims as well. Ironically, of course, even though Leporello assures us that Giovanni has conquered thousands of women all over Europe, in the course of the opera he fails at every one of his forays, and he goes to hell with a full stomach but a highly frustrated sexual organ. In the opera, the only people Giovanni seduces successfully are those in the audience.

Da Ponte's libretto constructs *Don Giovanni* as a series of sexual battles: Giovanni battles the Commendatore for his daughter, Ottavio battles for the hand, not to say the attention, of Donna Anna, Elvira battles to foil Giovanni, Giovanni and Leporello battle for macho dominance, Giovanni battles the Statue for his soul, or, rather, for the right to continue making more conquests in this world. In each of these battles the stake is sexual power, the power—Giovanni would say freedom—to exercise sexual influence over someone else. *Don Giovanni* works episodically, as a series of battles for the hearts and, more importantly, the bodies of women (Giovanni senses a woman's presence by her smell). For most of the opera, Mozart does little to hide the violent nature of these battles, setting them to intensely aggressive music. But in the Act I duet between Giovanni and Zerlina, "La ci darem la mano," Mozart changes the battle tactic. Giovanni puts on a mask of sincerity, promises marriage and fidelity, and sings music of indescribable sweetness. But for all its beauty, "La ci darem la mano" is a rape as much as the offstage rape of Donna Anna that opens the opera. And, though in the narrative Donna Elvira saves Zerlina at the last minute from Giovanni's clutches, in the musical ravishing of the audience Giovanni succeeds triumphantly.

Joseph Kerman, discussing Mozart's use of music as dramatic structure, argues that this duet, "one of the simplest-sounding things in the score, is also one of the most carefully calculated, with its gradual bringing-together of the two voices, Zerlina's nervous checks, and Don Giovanni's increasing pressure."[10] The object of this pressure is sexual conquest; the melting beauty and simplicity of the music contrast sharply with the harshness of Giovanni's intent. Like Zerlina, the power of Giovanni's discourse both attracts me and frightens me; I marvel at the ability of this music to turn an act of domination into an object of crystalline, mathematical beauty. In the rest of the opera I can maintain a certain distance from Giovanni's seductiveness, because he wields his music so aggressively. But in this duet, so meltingly suave and caressing, I lose all my resistance. In the audience I, unlike Zerlina, have the advantage of dramatic irony, of knowing that Giovanni is lying through his teeth, that his seduction is mortally dangerous. But it does not matter; I fall anyway, along with Zerlina, with no Elvira there to come to my rescue.

How does this music enact its ravishment? The musical form of the duet, though measured and sedate, parallels structurally the act of seduction through to consummation. Giovanni begins the seduction in the first presentation of the melody and development, music of utter lyrical simplicity. Zerlina replies by singing a repetition, a direct musical confirmation of Giovanni's advances, though her words indicate doubt. These solo passages present a teasing musical foreplay; Zerlina affirms in music what she denies in her words. As the duet progresses, this pattern of exchanged parallel phrases continues; each repeated phrase becomes shorter and the exchanges more rapid, then overlapping, as Mozart punctuates the intertwining musical lines with Giovanni's insistently rising "vieni, vieni." After an abbreviated recapitulation of the opening melody with alternating lines, a brief return to the foreplay, the duet reaches a climax as Giovanni repeats "andiam" twice with increasing harmonic tension and rising pitch, which is resolved by Zerlina's falling and prolonged answer of "andiam," "let's go."

This orgasmic "andiam" is the moment of Zerlina's fall. From this point the duet rushes to its conclusion in unison, except for a playful exchange toward the end, as the two celebrate their "innocente amor." Zerlina accepts Giovanni in principle verbally, but more importantly, their singing completes their union in actuality. It does not matter that Da Ponte preserves public morality in the libretto by having Elvira save Zerlina at this moment; in the music the hapless innocent has already fallen. (In a curious paradox, though Zerlina's honor has officially been preserved, when she returns to Masetto, she behaves as if she had cheated on him. In her aria "Batti, batti" she invites Masetto to punish her physically for a sin that she, in the narrative, does not commit. Although she briefly asserts her innocence, the force of her invited punishment implies the actuality of her fall, as enacted in "La ci darem la mano.") As an audience member, I have been made witness to, and a participant in, this act of musical-sexual conquest.

"La ci darem la mano" may be the most subtle seduction in opera. Mozart and Da Ponte have coerced me into falling head over heels for a completely disreputable figure, a liar and a cheat. They have ravished my sensibilities, so I no longer know whether Giovanni is hero or villain, even whether this opera is a tragedy or comedy. But if Giovanni has snared me in his sexual net, then I am certainly in good company; these confusions have plagued critics since the opera first appeared.[11] No one knows how to categorize this opera; we only know its allure. Two centuries of operagoers have given themselves over to Giovanni's musical seduction, and so must I. Giovanni's seduction of Zerlina serves as a prototype for the way opera itself seduces me, through its intoxicating sexuality. I eagerly put myself in Zerlina's position, letting Giovanni caress me with his lyrical melody, holding my breath as he beckons me with his "vieni, vieni." And I have no choice but to answer "andiam."

Operatic Sex Wars II:
"Mon coeur s'ouvre à ta voix"

The subtle seduction that Mozart weaves in "La ci darem la mano" awes me with its artistry, but such subtlety is rare in standard repertory opera. Most of the time I know when I'm being seduced by the performance. When opera moves into the mid-nineteenth century and romanticism, its seductive tactics take on the quality of the Wagnerian orchestra, a barrage of heavy-duty ballistics rather than an elegant eighteenth-century field maneuver. The love duets become more ecstatic, more overtly orgasmic. Rather than drawing me slowly into the seduction, the opera bowls me over with waves of chromatic harmonies. As the moral prudishness of the Victorian era reduces the freedom of opera libretti to deal openly with issues of sexuality, opera's music does more and more to carry the burden of the sexual discourse. Da Ponte's libretto talks clearly about sex. Romantic opera cannot say that its characters perform sexual acts, so the music must do the seducing instead.[12]

I am not going to talk here about the most obvious case of seduction in nineteenth-century opera, Georges Bizet's mysterious Carmen, but rather about the era's other seductress, Saint-Saëns's more obvious and less skillful Dalila. Everybody talks about Carmen, and for good reason. It is easy to be seduced by Carmen. She does it so well. I would follow Carmen into the lowest ring of hell, because I adore everything about her. When she opens her mouth to sing, even when she is silent, she exudes seduction, and I follow her as relentlessly as does her other victim, Don José. Susan McClary offers an incisive analysis of Carmen's erotic power in all of her slippery, seductive chromaticism.[13] In Carmen's operatic sex war, there is really no contest. Carmen wins hands down, and if she gets murdered in the process, she is only one of a long line of heroines, operatic and otherwise, whose sexual triumph leads to their demise.[14]

But I have no desire to be seduced by Dalila. She's not my type. I resist her attempts at seduction, yet in one stunning instance in the opera, and only one, her erotic powers overtake me, and they do so entirely against my will. Like Carmen, she offers physical attractions, but I just don't like her; for that matter, I don't much like the opera. I am not alone. *The Definitive Kobbé's Opera Book* does not think *Samson et Dalila* worthy of any substantive commentary; it gives the work less space than any other standard repertory opera, providing only a sketchy plot summary, which is all one can do, given the sketchy nature of the plot.[15] There is not much nice to say about this clumsy opera. Calling Ferdinand Lemaire's libretto "wooden" is an insult to trees. The opening scenes with Samson and the Israelites have less stage action than the average oratorio, and except for the Bacchanale, Act III is entirely static until the last ten seconds, far too late to make me care whether Samson gets crushed or not. The changes that the libretto makes in the biblical story merely confuse the narrative (we never hear what Samson's weakness is or when he and Dalila had met before), nor do we get any background about the characters and their lives. The characterizations never get beyond one dimension; Samson is heroic, the High Priest evil, the Old Hebrew noble, period. There is little here to generate theatrical excitement or even interest.

The music is not much better. Saint-Saëns might have been a musical prodigy, but he has almost no sense of theater in his music, certainly not in contrast to contemporaries Wagner and Verdi. Musically, I have no idea why Samson falls in love with Dalila in the first place; the music of her entrance with the Philistine women, "Voici le printemps," sounds like the procession of a convent of nuns, not a pack of sirens. Dalila displays almost no musical sexuality, and in the face of this dull music, her hypocrisy is so obvious that surely even Samson must see it. Only in the few moments of theatrical excitement in the libretto does the score rise to any kind of musical interest, but these moments are few and far between. Overall, the score here fails to generate the erotic engagement upon which opera's seduction of its audience depends.

Even the seductive duet between Samson and Dalila, "Mon coeur s'ouvre à ta voix," starts out with little promise. The scene that leads up to the climactic seduction of Act II does little to grab my attention. First Dalila spills the beans about her evil plans, then Samson has a solo of righteous self-deprecation, neither of which does much to arouse my erotic interest. As the seduction approaches, Saint-Saëns adds lightning and thunder effects to the music to create a sense of impending doom, but these silly rumblings sound pale and ineffectual next to Verdi's storm scene at the end of *Rigoletto*. Even Dalila's opening melody has little to draw me into the seduction. It is pleasant enough, but it has nothing of the arresting qualities of Carmen's "Habañera" or "Seguidilla." Without the libretto in front of me, I find it hard to tell that Dalila is trying to seduce Samson at this point, except for Samson's periodic and very obvious declaration "Dalila, Dalila, je t'aime!"

But then, just when the opera's climax looks as if it will disintegrate in a whimper of musical and textual banality, Dalila begins a new melody. She sings "Ah! réponds à ma tendresse! Verse-moi, verse-moi l'ivresse!" and, instantly, everything changes. Suddenly, the lightning becomes real, not the earlier pale imitation. The strings swell, the music turns wildly chromatic as it slides up and down the scale, lingering on minor intervals, building in climactic intensity but leaving off before resolving harmonically. In this context, Samson's declaration "Dalila, Dalila, je t'aime!" takes on an entirely different character. What had been a musically disconnected phrase now becomes ecstatic and real; he picks up Dalila's melodic tension and teases it out over the long phrase, finally completing her cadence as he declares his love in a musical orgasm of melting beauty. Dalila never has to cut one strand of Samson's hair to crush his power; she does it with a single strand of music. Their voices intertwine in the repetition of the orgasm, and, for the moment, I am completely taken in.

But the ecstasy ends too soon. This one moment of musical orgasm has no parallels in the rest of the opera. Samson hits his last high note, the fake lightening returns with a thud, and the scene loses all of its erotic energy. What remains is merely a lovers' spat, hard-edged and mechanical. Perhaps Saint-Saëns wants to depict the real Dalila in this music, the harpy hiding within the siren. But he succeeds only in disengaging my interest. I fold my arms again, watch the biblical spectacle from a distance, and spend the rest of the act thinking how much I really dislike this opera. For those few minutes of the duet, however, I am caught, and I would sit through the entire opera so that I could lose myself in those blissful passages again.

I remember first hearing *Samson et Dalila* on a Saturday afternoon Met broadcast. I was listening passively; I'm not sure I even knew which opera was on, and the music coming out of the radio certainly did not engage my attention. But then the seductive passage came, and I stopped in my tracks. It sounded familiar; maybe I had heard it before, or maybe I merely recognized the seductive process, that familiar feeling of impending sexual climax. I listened intensely to the rest of the broadcast for another comparable moment, but in vain. There was no repetition of the orgasmic pleasure. This opera has fascinated and maddened me ever since.

I can easily understand how the brilliance of *Carmen* and *Giovanni* seduce me. But the momentary seductiveness of "Mon coeur s'ouvre à ta voix," amid the ineptitude of the rest of the opera, tells me much more about how opera conducts its sex wars. Carmen does not have to work very hard to seduce me. But if I can fall sway to Dalila's powers for those few minutes, even as I firmly resist her seductions, then I know that opera can draw me in against my will and that it performs this act of coercion through erotic, sensual stimulation. Opera does not seduce me with intellectual genius. It conquers me aggressively, sometimes against my will, by engaging me sexually. Opera overpowers me with raw sex, enacted through music.

Operatic Sex Wars III: "In questa reggia"

Of all the operas that seduce me, I think I fall prey to *Turandot* more readily than to any other. If I had to make the mythic choice of only one opera to take with me to a desert island, I might ultimately choose *Don Giovanni* for intellectual reasons, or *Carmen* for its seduction, or *Der Rosenkavalier* for its final trio, but I'd be sorely tempted to go with *Turandot*. I suppose I should be ashamed to admit it, but then *Turandot* is a shameless opera. Everything here goes for broke: the lush pseudo-oriental exoticism; the sharp juxtaposition of murderous melodrama, tear-jerking sentimentalism, and high-camp farce; Turandot's stratospheric tessitura; Puccini's own melodramatic death before he could finish the score, and Toscanini's even more melodramatic gesture of cutting short the opening night performance at the point where Puccini stopped writing. Zeffirelli's overblown Metropolitan Opera production merely reinforces the excesses already in the opera. *Turandot* is my ultimate operatic fantasy, with music of sufficient head-banging orgasmic intensity that I lose myself in it completely from beginning to end.

Puccini knows the art of the orgasm. Clément argues that the least popular Puccini operas, especially *La Fanciulla del West,* are those where the female lead does not die.[16] But I think a more compelling explanation is that the unpopular Puccini works are those with the fewest or weakest orgasms (though probably because happy endings provide no opportunity for climactic sex-as-death). *Fanciulla* and *La Rondine* lack great erotic climaxes, and so they languish at the edges of the repertory. But in each of the "big three"—*La Bohème, Madama Butterfly,* and *Tosca*—Act I centers around an orgasmic duet where the central pair of lovers consummate their relationship before our ears. And then Puccini keeps the climaxes coming, in regular succession, until the heroine dies, in effect, of sexual exhaustion. Some critics, notably Kerman, find this tactic a cheap way to pander to an audience's sensual desires. (Kerman also disdains the even more orgasmic music of Richard Strauss; sex embarrasses him.) But as a listener fully in the thrall of Puccini's technique, I prefer to think of this orgasmic music not as a cheap thrill but as a logical extension of opera's tactics of seduction.

Turandot goes all out in the sex wars. It is a battle in music, a fight for dominance between Calaf and Turandot. Calaf wants Turandot, and she does not want to be had. From the beginning, the opera presents his "love" in terms of conquest: He cries "vincero," "I will conquer." Turandot resists this conquest with all her powers, but I am much easier prey. I'm on Calaf's side all the way. The sympathetic slave girl Liù makes sure of that in the first act; she pours out her unconditional love for him, and anyone who deserves to be sung to as beautifully as she sings to Calaf must be worthy of my sympathy (that is, my desire). I'm so taken by Calaf that I'm even willing to forgive the senseless suicide of Liù in the final act just to make sure he gets what he wants. Puccini seduces me so successfully that I forget to think about where my sympathies in the battle might more justifiably fall, even whether I should sympathize with anyone at all in this nasty story.

Act I sets the terms of the battle, rather like the opening of a boxing match. We get Calaf, surrounded by his trainers (father, slave, ministers), vocal and expressive, playing the audience for our support. In the other corner we get Turandot, stoic, mysterious, appearing late to heighten the tension, refusing to acknowledge her opponent. She does not sing at all in the first act, the ultimate insult to an opera fan, but also the ultimate mystery—what will she sound like? Act II keeps us on the edge of our seats with a delaying tactic, a comic/romantic intermission with the ministers. But this scene is a distraction; we really just want to get down to the real battle, the confrontation of Turandot and Calaf. Finally in the second scene of Act II we get the first round of the fight. Turandot lands the first blow with her aria "In questa reggia"; Calaf counters by usurping her climax at the end of the aria, and the fight is on.

"In questa reggia" starts out as the opposite of a seductive aria. Turandot wants to make it a sexual climax for one, an exhausting masturbation fantasy in the musical stratosphere. By singing in an impossibly high range and at great length, she tries to keep Calaf out of the musical picture. But Calaf will have none of this self-indulgence. At the aria's deafening climax, at an astoundingly high pitch, Turandot attempts to finish the aria alone: "Gli enigmi sono tre, la morte una!" But Calaf bursts into the music, topping Turandot's orgasm with an even higher one of his own: "No, no! Gli enigmi sono tre, una è la vita!" Finally, the passage turns into an "anything-you-can-sing-I-can-sing-higher" contest in unison, as both singers scrape the tops of their ranges in a violent simultaneous climax; only the entrance of the chorus rescues them from musical suicide. In the libretto, Turandot rejects Calaf's sexual advances before he solves the deadly riddles and wins her body. But in the music their love is already consummated, assuring Turandot's eventual conversion on the narrative plane when the final curtain falls. In other words, the fight is rigged. The end of Act II looks like a draw, but only because Calaf takes a temporary fall. In reality, in the music, he has already won.

Like Turandot, I give in to Calaf at this climactic moment and stay in his sway for the rest of the opera. He, of course, gets another orgasm of his own in "Nessun dorma," at the top of Act III, which only reinforces his power. Liù claims my musical attention for a moment in her death aria, but Puccini gets her out of the way soon enough, leaving the two contestants alone in the ring. After the death of Liù, Turandot has no musical tricks left; she has exhausted her power in her one big aria, and Liù has cornered the pity market. She has no energy with which to challenge Calaf (though Puccini might have given her some more force had he lived to finish the opera), and so she succumbs. The climactic kiss between Calaf and Turandot, underscored by hammer blows in the orchestra, sounds more like murder than lovemaking. Her destruction is complete, the final triumph only a capitulation of everything that made her interesting. And yet Puccini has seduced me into believing that this bloody battle is a romantic comedy with a happy ending. (Or not so happy: One of my students, unfamiliar with opera and its conventions, responded during a first viewing of *Turandot* to the opera's ending, with the death of Liù and Turandot's subsequent conversion, with the indignant cry, "That sucks!" I envy his innocence and his innate sense of justice. Opera made me lose my innocence long ago.)

I know that opera seduces me. I know that opera makes me think things about sex on a gut level that I reject on an intellectual level. I know that I should not let myself be seduced this way. I've read Brecht's views on opera; he warns precisely against opera's power to make me abandon my reason.[17] I've read Clément, and I know how opera makes me participate in acts of sexual violence. I know that opera makes me lose my reason and my will, turns me into a passive, only partly willing participant in its sexual acts. That is opera's danger, but it is also one of its most powerful attractions. I love the illicit thrill of being seduced. I know I'm supposed to be an equal partner in sexual engagements, but that's not always the role I want to play. When I'm having sex, sometimes I like to control the situation, but very often I find a greater erotic pleasure in lying back and letting my partner make the moves. Abandoning sexual control is dangerous, but—at least if I trust my partner—it can also add excitement. This thrill, this danger, explains the power of opera's sexual discourse. I want to lose myself in opera. I want to be seduced away from my reason. I go to the opera, as so many have gone before me, to be seduced, to sacrifice my reason, a (partially) willing victim, just another in the long line of cheerful casualties in opera's sex wars.

8

SEXUAL TRANSGRESSION IN OPERA

Well one day, who should turn up but Siegmund, and he falls madly in love with Sieglinde, regardless of the fact that she's married to Hunding, which is immoral, and she's his own sister, which is illegal. But that's the beauty of grand opera. You can do anything, so long as you sing it.

—Anna Russell
"The Ring of the Niebelungs: An Analysis"[1]

The Value of Shock

In mapping out the sexual territory of opera, there is a vast amount of space to cover. As I argue in previous chapters, opera's sexuality proliferates in both volume and depth; its sexual engagements are frequent and extreme. But opera deploys its embarrassing sexual excess not only along the axes of quantity and intensity, but also along a third axis: variety. Opera, in its polymorphous perversity (to use Freud's and Foucault's phrase), does not only offer its audience a constant barrage of intense sexuality. It also seduces the audience with varied and illicit sexualities, sexual experiences that deviate, sometimes in extreme ways, from accepted societal norms. The opera house creates a protected space for the enactment of sexual perversion. Opera, unlike many other social organs, need not hide illicit sexuality; it is fueled by the energy of perversion. The inimitable comedienne and critic Anna Russell hits upon a great truth of opera in her analysis of Wagnerian adultery and incest: Opera not only allows any kind of sexual impropriety; it virtually demands every kind of sexual impropriety.

Such flagrant wallowing in taboo sexuality remains off limits to the mainstream spoken theater; without music, overt sexual perversion appears on stage only in the most marginal venues, notably in the Off-Off-Broadway experiments of the 1960s. And even if the open enactment of perversion breaks into mainstream theater, it usually meets with violent protest.

Opera, meanwhile, can depict the same or worse perversions with little fear of repercussion. Critics inside the London press, for example, reacted with physical revulsion to the merest hint that the central character in Ibsen's *Ghosts* suffers from syphilis, when the play first appeared there in 1891, though Ibsen never mentions the disease explicitly at any point in the script.[2] But London went into ecstasies over the much more overt depiction of incest in Wagner's *Die Walküre*, which premiered in London a decade before *Ghosts*. In *Opera: The Extravagant Art* Herbert Lindenberger argues that operatic music not only mitigates the effects of Wagner's sexual transgression; the transgression actually amplifies the audience's response to the opera. He observes:

> Middle class audiences witnessing the romance of brother and sister in Act I of *Die Walküre* have generally allowed themselves to be enraptured by the music; indeed, whatever consciousness they retain of the incest being enacted before their eyes doubtless enhances the rapture they feel. One need only imagine the text being spoken without music to note the difference.[3]

The paradoxical response to *Ghosts* and *Die Walküre* has many parallels. For example, at the turn of the century, Puccini's *La Bohème*, with its two fallen women, played to enthusiastic audiences all over Europe and America; however, George Bernard Shaw's *Mrs. Warren's Profession*, with only one, was, like *Ghosts*, being banned in England and shut down in New York. The difference is that Shaw's play, by letting his procuress, Mrs. Warren, survive the final curtain, overtly defies sexual norms and loudly declares its support for women's economic rights, whereas Puccini's opera preserves propriety with the obligatory death scene for at least one of its fallen women. But the point remains that opera gets away with sexual abnormalities that spoken theater could never embrace. People seem to blink at opera's looser morals, perhaps because of its great popularity among the "looser" upper classes (though, of course, the upper classes always view the lower classes as less moral than they are, and vice versa). There have always been certain limitations placed on the representation of sexual relations on the stage, but opera seems less prone to these strictures: Richard Strauss's *Salome* got into a lot less trouble with the censors than did Oscar Wilde's.[4]

In opera, censorship historically has focused more on political rather than moral issues. When the censors gave Verdi trouble with *Rigoletto*, they did not care that the tenor hero is a sexual libertine who ruins every stable family relationship in the opera; they only protested the revolutionary plot in which a member of the lower classes threatens the life of a monarch. Censors have suppressed or forced revisions on many operas due to the revolutionary political sentiments they contain, but rarely does a government sanction an opera because of excess sexual display.[5] Yet since the time of Verdi and Wagner, opera has ceased to have much political shock value. Mozart could upset the titled classes by setting Beaumarchais's banned *Marriage of Figaro* to music, and Verdi and Wagner could use the stories of their operas as thinly disguised expressions of nationalistic or socialistic revolutionary sentiments. But we are long past the time when "Va, pensiero" could become the theme song for the Italian Risorgimento. Today, opera sits squarely in the realm of the financial and aesthetic elite, not in the realm of those who would disrupt the social hierarchy. If opera has any shock value in the twentieth century, it is sexual, not political.

The rules that govern "proper" sexual behavior cease to function in the world of opera. Behind its conventional exterior of social respectability, opera depicts a realm where incest is a virtue, where adultery becomes attractive, and where unbridled lust motivates the action. Opera protects every kind of sexual excess, under its heavy drapery and its atmosphere of moral propriety. At the opera, I can get the thrill of the perverse without risking my social position. If opera seems passé to so many people in the twentieth century, it is partly because so many other popular media outlets have now embraced opera's panorama of sexual transgression, without the elegant surroundings. Opera has lost its place as the only realm of officially sanctioned vicarious perversion. Why should I keep my passions in the operatic closet when I can get kinky sex with Madonna out in the open, at a much lower price?

But even Madonna cannot rival opera in the full range and depth of sexual perversity. Ultimately, the sexual excesses of popular music and film are rather mundane, and they rapidly lose their impact through obviousness and numbing repetition. Like bad pornography, overt sex in the media becomes predictable, and so its prurient appeal quickly wanes. Even the most outrageous sex bores me if it is too obvious, and perversion placed on the surface merely repels me. The excesses of the hapless murderer in the film *The Silence of the Lambs,* who tortures women in a well and flays off their skin, frighten me momentarily, but my fear soon fades; but the perversity of Anthony Hopkins's character, Hannibal Lechter, lingers in effect, because he masks his evil under a surface of perfect elegance. Opera, by pretending to absolute moral purity, keeps its sexual transgressions endlessly fascinating. Because of the rich trappings and high tone, I can choose not to remember opera's perversity and be genuinely surprised every time it offers a sexual shocker. Madonna may try to pass herself off as Carmen, but Carmen will never become a second-rate Madonna. Carmen wins the sexual transgression contest hands down.

Of course, if all opera is sexually transgressive, some operas sin more than others. Many composers achieve fame by providing a steady stream of works that fulfill audience expectations, without pushing the bounds of propriety; like Meyerbeer, they often have huge popularity in their own day, but their works fade rapidly once the social mores of their era become passé. Others attract their public by being consistently a little naughty, teasing the audience with minor sexual transgressions, but never offering anything so shocking as to risk offensiveness or condemnation. Most of the standard repertory opera lives in this realm, dancing along the boundaries of sexual perversity but pulling back before plunging into really serious transgression. Puccini has Mimi and Rodolfo tease us with their bohemianism; but even if they have sex out of wedlock, I can only imagine them doing it in the missionary position.

But then there are the works that throw all propriety to the wind and bask in the full glory of perverse sexuality. Some of these works, like *Carmen,* currently mainstays of the standard repertory, were considered at their premieres to be unspeakably sexual, major threats to the public morality (which did not, of course, prevent people from flocking to the opera house). Even Saint-Saëns's much tamer Dalila raised some furor at first, though mostly because of the opera's biblical context. As usually happens with sexual shockers, in time the protest against these works dies down, but the perversion remains. Other works of extreme sexuality, however, have passed into the repertory without even a preliminary public censure. Wagner created such an international buildup for the opening of the *Ring* cycle that audiences seemed not to notice its almost complete lack of Victorian sexual propriety (except for the whiny Fricka, the least interesting figure in the epic). And some opera composers have staked their entire careers on works that break the bounds, using the firestorm of controversy to propel them into fame, notably Alban Berg and the early Richard Strauss.

But sexual transgression in opera does not affect its audience merely as shock. The publicity generated by shock may have the temporary effect of drawing an audience to the opera house, but in time gratuitous perversion merely repels and distances an audience. Opera does not employ sexual perversion for its own sake. Perverse, excessive sexuality is integral to the relationship between opera and its audience. The public performance of an operatic orgasm is itself a kind of perversion, an elaborate form of exhibitionistic group sex. Surrounding this central sexual excess, opera collects examples of every other type of sexual extremity, to multiply and reinforce the effects of its all-encompassing queerness on its audience.

The Lure of the Pervert

Despite the adamant protests of those who would uphold the public morality and slash federal funding for the arts, the audience for popular entertainment is not, and never has been, much interested in normal sexuality.

At a bare minimum, I want to see passions of unusual intensity or people who consummate their relationship with a love virtually indistinguishable from violence. Preferably, I want to see people who perform extreme acts in the name of love. Violent passion is the stuff of fantasy and romance; without it, there would be no daytime television. The nightly newscasts, and the television miniseries and docudramas that they inspire, are filled with stories of those who kill in the name of love or people criminally obsessed with a sexual partner, the idea of a sexual partner, or a body part. We demand a steady fodder of information about psychokillers, child molesters, incest perpetrators, and the like. The more lurid the story, the easier it is to sell to the public. And this situation is nothing new; the tragedies of the ancient Greeks and, especially, of Shakespeare and his Jacobean contemporaries rely squarely on deviance from sexual norms. Whether live on the stage, broadcast over the airwaves, immortalized on celluloid, or ennobled by grandiose music or blank verse, normal sexuality has only a passing interest; perversion endures through the ages.

It is not that I want to imitate this kind of behavior. The thrill dissipates as soon as the perversion gets too close or too real. I, along with most of my fellow denizens of twentieth century "high" civilization, have lost the instinct for getting pleasure from witnessing public executions. I strongly oppose capital punishment; but (I am embarrassed to admit) I do have a lurid fascination with executions when I read about them in the news, abstracted from the actual event. The distance makes the perverse act exciting.[6] In the same way, illicit sexuality portrayed in public provides a vicarious experience, held at a safe distance. The public performance of illicit acts draws me in because it goes beyond my limited daily experience, giving me a taste of a sexual experience that I would never dream of enacting. Well, I probably would dream about it, but I wouldn't do it. Art does more than hold a mirror up to life; it creates images in which I can play out my private fantasies.

But I want my perversions dressed up; I demand that these lurid tales come in a slick and pretty package. And this packaging is the great strength of opera. Opera can take the most sexually deviant behavior and make it aesthetically appealing, convert the stomach-turning into the ravishing. Joseph Kerman, paraphrasing George Bernard Shaw, calls *Tosca* "that shabby little shocker." But a hefty proportion of operatic narrative is of the same ilk. *Carmen* without the music is a sensational melodrama about the violent consequences of overactive libidos; *Carmen* with the music is—or at least feels like—high tragedy. When I hear the silken melody of Zerlina's "Batti, batti" in *Don Giovanni,* so admired by Kerman, I forget that she is asking her husband to beat her up. Or rather, I do not forget that she asks for spousal abuse; what I forget is that, in my nonoperatic existence, I object strenuously to domestic violence.

In other words, opera makes me enjoy perverse acts I would otherwise find intolerable. I applaud things that, in retrospect, my superego in other circumstances wants to repress. I am not altogether comfortable with this realization. I am much more at ease with Poizat's version of operatic psychology, where I can explain my love for opera as a search for the moment of *jouissance,* the quest for the ultimate orgasm. But I cannot deny my attraction to aberration. Along with opera's sexual pleasure comes its perversity, the violence that underlies the passion. This sexual violence includes the violence against women that Clément finds in operatic narrative, but it also encompasses a wide array of sexual perversities of other varieties. When set to music, these perversities make me swoon with pleasure rather than horror.

Because of its power to make me forget my revulsions, opera has great freedom to stage transgression. Opera lets me, for example, revel in repressed oedipal feelings, among other psychic baggage. Sophocles keeps Oedipus and his wife/mother at a safe distance apart and their actual transgressive act of incest well in the play's past. But when Wagner shows his mythic equivalent of the Oedipus tale, the conception of Siegfried via the incestuous infidelity of Siegmund and Sieglinde, I get to see everything but the actual act of consummation on stage. And even then, Wagner gives his incestuous pair an orgasmic musical climax that more than compensates for the absence of the actual act of coitus on stage. Rather than merely watching Siegmund and Sieglinde engage in incestuous sex, Wagner lets me enact the perverse sex act with them, through my erotic engagement with the music. Opera is sexual drama therapy, a role-playing game where I get to perform my deepest repressed impulses in remarkably romantic settings, and so work them out of my system.

There is an important difference, though, between the sexual stimulation that the opera performance offers its audience through musical orgasms and the perverse sexual acts depicted on the stage. The difference is the same as that between sexual fantasy and sexual reality. In our fantasies, we may freely explore any kind of sexual behavior, even those labeled as most socially deviant, without repercussion. In our physical sexual practices, though, even in private, society and our own internal censors put limits on our acts. Far more people fantasize about sadistic sex than actually engage in it. Similarly, the physical sexuality of the operatic orgasm as enacted in the performance inhabits the realm of sexual "normalcy," whereas opera's narrative perversions are more free to play along the edges of fantasy. When Siegmund and Sieglinde sing climactically about their incestuous love, the image of their perversion may fuel my sexual engagement during the musical orgasm, but the orgasmic moment that I experience in this scene is not in itself incestuous. Opera defines its protected space for deviant sexuality through this distinction between fantasy and reality. It allows its audience to taste fantasized, taboo sex while engaging in perfectly acceptable and "normal" sex acts via the music.

Although the incest between Wagner's siblings remains the most famous act of sexual perversion in opera (Freud was right about the power of the incest taboo), incest is not the most common form that sexual perversion takes in opera. Even in its sexual excess, opera can only handle just so much overt oedipal material. But other varieties of sexual deviance pop up much more frequently. So, while my superego is temporarily on leave, I want to enumerate some of the more common varieties of sexual deviance in opera—perhaps as just another way to work these antisocial impulses out of my system.

Cheaters Never Prosper

Undoubtedly, the most pervasive sexual transgression in opera is adultery. I am, however, a bit reluctant to include adultery in a discussion of sexual perversion. First, I presume that most adulterous affairs culminate in perfectly mundane sex. Adulterous sex belongs to a rather different category than necrophilia, incest, and similar abuses; adulterous sex acts do not necessarily deviate in kind from more socially acceptable sex acts. Second, the real objection to adultery, the reason it makes it into the Ten Commandments, is not its transgression against sexual propriety but its transgression against property rights. If a woman "cheats" on her husband, she violates her husband's legally protected right to sole possession of her body and to the knowledge that all her children are his biological heirs; if a husband cheats, the woman just has to deal with it. In our still oppressively patriarchal legal system, adultery has virtually nothing to do with actual sexual acts, except to the extent that they usurp a husband's prerogative to exclusive sexual possession of his wife.[7] So, in many ways, adultery is really not about sex at all.

On the other hand, sex gives adultery its entertainment value. If the public demands endless gossip about the infidelities of our famous movie and television stars, our politicians, and our friends and relations, it is not because of property issues but because gossip about adultery fuels our sexual fantasies. We imagine adulterous sex to be inherently more passionate than sex within wedlock, because it is forbidden. When Jimmy Carter admitted to the American public that he had committed adultery many times in his heart, that is, without sex, we all laughed. Without sex, adultery isn't serious. If the laws about adultery care comparatively little about the sex act, the general population cares about little else. And the media make sure we know just how much adultery is out there, in order to keep us watching television and buying more tabloid newspapers.

Adultery, because it is such a popular perversion, appears in opera more often than any other sexual deviation. When all else fails, a librettist can fall back on adultery, or the threat of adultery, or the mistaken impression of adultery, to enliven the opera's plot. Claudio Monteverdi, the first opera composer whose works survive, first wrote operas about marital fidelity, *Orfeo* and *Il Ritorno d'Ulisse in Patria,* but at the end of his career he discovered that adultery made for a much more interesting story, and so he wrote *L'Incoronazione di Poppea.* Take adultery (actual or threatened) out of the operatic scene and the standard repertory loses a remarkable number of its most famous works, serious and comic, throughout its history.[8] Adultery is everywhere in opera.

Though adultery appears consistently throughout opera's history, critics tend to associate it as a sexual perversion most prominently with the verismo movement. This association persists probably because verismo operas so often revolve exclusively around adultery, and because the characters in verismo take adultery so very seriously. When Count Almaviva in *Le Nozze di Figaro* tries to cheat on his wife, everybody gets indignant; but most everyone is horny in *Nozze,* and in the end the Countess magnanimously understands and forgives her husband's indiscretions (in part because, as she tells us, she misses him in bed). But in verismo, cross the line once and you get killed. Or perhaps I make the association between verismo and adultery because verismo comes from Italy, and in my knee-jerk cultural stereotyping I presume that Italians worry more about adultery than other people do. Mostly, though, I make this assumption because the two surviving remnants of verismo in the international repertory, *Cavalleria Rusticana* and *I Pagliacci,* both revolve around murders stemming from adultery.

Besides, verismo and adultery fit together like hand in glove. Verismo opera makes its mark by enacting the lurid, dark underside of society for wealthy, well-heeled patrons of opera. In particular, it depicts the lives of the lower classes who disdain the "proper" bourgeois sexual mores of the middle and upper classes. These lowly people, verismo implies, live like animals, wallowing in passion, and it is this raw emotion that makes verismo so appealing. The genteel classes can go to the opera and watch these creatures enact their animal passions behind the proscenium, just as one watches wild beasts at the zoo, safely separated by bars. These lower-class types, of course, cannot (so the argument goes) control their passions the way proper bourgeois citizens can, and so they must be prone to adulterous behavior. Verismo opera dutifully depicts this parade of adultery, and especially its bloody results, as a grand morality play. The elite opera audience can then return home, husbands and wives reassured that their spouses would never dare follow through with such an act, for fear of stooping to such a base social level—or for fear of getting killed.

In verismo, adultery always leads to death. Besides standing as a chastening warning for the audience, the bloody end of adultery provides an erotic release. The murderer gets revenge by having the last sex act. The wronged husband might get to kill his rival, in which case he ensures the end of the adulterous affair (though I have a hard time, in *Il Tabarro,* imagining Michele having enjoyable sex with his wife, Giorgetta, after he presents to her the body of her lover). Or, preferably, he gets to kill both the lover and his wife, in which case he gets a final sexual climax in doing away with her, the ultimate act of sexual possession: "If I can't have sex with her alone, then no one will." In operatic adultery, the act of sexual deviance is not the adulterous liaison itself; the perverse sexual act is the murder that follows. The opera hides the adulterous copulation from my eyes, but in its place I get a violent murder (as discussed previously, often a stabbing, with its phallic implications) to satisfy my desire for deviant sexuality on stage.

Endless Desire

After the adulterers, the next most prominent group of sexual perverts in opera are the nymphomaniacs, the characters driven entirely by their insatiable desire for sex. There are fewer nymphomaniacs than there are adulterers in opera, though most nymphomaniacs wind up as adulterers as well. But what they lack in numbers they make up in fascination; the nymphomaniacs draw attention to themselves because of their excessive and flamboyant personalities. They are few, but they are the stars of opera: Don Giovanni, Carmen, the Duke of Mantua in *Rigoletto,* Lulu, perhaps a few others (maybe Baron Scarpia, though he has only one object of desire, Tosca; Mozart's Cherubino might qualify, but I assume that he will get over his randiness by the time he grows up). But these few figures have attracted so much attention that they virtually represent opera for their respective periods, especially the iconic and eponymous Carmen and Giovanni.

Unlike adulterers, nymphomaniacs are identifiable perverts, in the model of nineteenth-century medicine that Foucault outlines in *The History of Sexuality.*[9] The nymphomaniac has specific symptoms that the audience can readily recognize: the perpetual fascination with sex; the twisting of all activities to secure more sex; the range and variety of sexual partners; and the compulsion to list and keep track of those partners. I know a nymphomaniac when I see one in opera. But when I look at these perverts more closely, I am left with a puzzling paradox: Nymphomaniacs never get much sex during the opera's narrative. In fact, most often they do not get any sex during the opera at all, and they certainly never have more than two partners, hardly within the medical definition of nymphomania. Don Giovanni tries to seduce three women but fails with all of them. Cherubino also makes passes at three women without success. Carmen has two lovers but has little chance to sleep with either of them.[10] The Duke of Mantua shows interest in three women but only gets physical with Gilda. And even Lulu, the nymphomaniac's nymphomaniac, who has everyone in the opera falling over her, generally keeps to one lover at a time and marries the most prominent ones; she only has multiple partners at the end, when reduced by impoverishment to working as a prostitute.

What, then, makes me believe that Carmen, Giovanni, and their like have an insatiable sexual desire? Mostly because they tell me so. In each case, the librettist makes sure that someone, either the nymphomaniac or a close associate, presents the identifying symptoms in the earliest scenes of the opera. Giovanni's servant Leporello has the list aria, in order to document the Don's endless desires. Cherubino sings breathlessly in Act I that he falls in love with every woman he sees. Carmen sings her "Habañera," declaring her own sexual dangers and her resolute conviction to stay with no one man. The Duke of Mantua opens *Rigoletto* with "Questa o quella" so that I know he does not care with whom he sleeps, as long as he sleeps with some woman. Nothing that happens in these operas after such a declaration can alter the label of nymphomaniac. Even if the character never touches another person through the rest of the story, I still believe in the reality of the perversion.

As with the adulterer, the sexual thrill for the audience in these operas comes not when the pervert exercises the perversion but when the perversion brings about the violent destruction of the pervert. Giovanni's only successful onstage coupling happens with the statue of the Commendatore; the only time Carmen is involved in a sex act is when José stabs her. These moments provide narrative climax; they also evoke the most intense music in the opera and the most sexually involving moments for the audience. Opera enacts an eye-for-an-eye justice by letting us punish its perverts through equally perverse acts of sexualized violence committed against them. In their narratives, these operas punish the pervert, but for the audience, we only become increasingly attracted to the deviant, and we return to the opera house to see Carmen and Giovanni playing out their nymphomania, so we can enact our perverse punishment of them again and again.

When an opera's story focuses on a nymphomaniac, then, the purpose of the narrative is not to reveal the perversion but to quell it violently. When the curtain opens, the nymphomaniac's days of sexual success are over. That is why we never get to see the nymphomaniac having much sex. Da Ponte calls *Don Giovanni* a *dramma giocosa,* a comedy and not a tragedy, because through its narrative the world is rid of a pervert. Similarly, *Carmen* is not really a tragedy; it is the noble tale of a hero, José, who sacrifices himself to rid the world of the murderous siren, the monster woman, and make the world free once again for masculine sexuality and for submissive women like Micaëla, who probably does not even know what sex is.

Oddly, within the opera's narrative Carmen is actually more perverse for refusing sex, not for engaging in an excess of it. She may throw José a flower, but that is about all she throws at him. If Carmen were a textbook Freudian nymphomaniac, she would leap at José, not spend the first two acts teasing him with the promise of sex. When they are alone in the second act, Carmen tries to continue the teasing by dancing for him. But José, tired of waiting, decides to go ahead and have sex by himself at her feet, in the orgasmic "Flower Song," while Carmen listens passively. In the standard operatic sexual discourse of the nineteenth century, Bizet should follow José's intensely sexual aria with a consummating duet; instead, at the end of his exquisite climax, Carmen responds with "Non, tu ne m'aimes pas!" sung in a flat, frigid monotone. The result is an image of coitus interruptus. Carmen gets in trouble not for having too much sex but for not having enough. José kills her because she refuses him sex, not because she gives it to him.

By this definition, Turandot, for all her purported iciness and protests of chastity, is one of opera's great nymphomaniacs. She gears her whole life to collecting sexual partners, not to sleep with them but to tease them with her riddles and then to deny them sex by killing them. It is dangerous to desire both Carmen and Turandot. Unlike Carmen, though, Turandot adds the extra perversion of wanting to be on top. In *Turandot* Puccini turns the *Carmen* formula upside down, with the heroic tenor setting out to seduce the fatal nymphomaniac. This reversal accounts for the opera's strange mix of the serious and the comic. *Carmen* begins like an *opéra comique* and ends in murder; *Turandot* flirts with tragedy until the end, when Turandot declares that her glory is over; at that moment the potential tragedy turns to triumph, at least for Calaf. He does not have to kill Turandot to rid the world of a nymphomaniac; like Otello, he kills her with a kiss.

In clinical terms, Lulu is opera's closest approximation to a true nymphomaniac. Whereas the sexually frustrated nymphomaniacs of previous opera emerge from the sensibilities of the eighteenth and early nineteenth centuries, Lulu is a product of the Freudian fin de siècle. Unlike her predecessors, Lulu spends the entire opera engaging in sex, hopping from one partner to another. Both Frank Wedekind, the playwright who created Lulu in his plays *Earth Spirit* and *Pandora's Box,* and his faithful adapter, Berg, set out to create a tragedy of sexual perversion using the newly developed psychological models. Lulu's godparents are the turn-of-the-century sexologists, such as Havelock Ellis and Magnus Hirschfeld, who set out to remove the stigma of sin from sexual deviance by finding medical explanations for aberrant behavior. *Lulu* then becomes opera's only true case study in nymphomania. She is made into an animal on display (quite literally in the opera's prologue; the wild animal tamer brings her onstage as a snake), someone to be viewed with horror and fascination, though with some pity as well.

Because of its new context, *Lulu* overturns the expected behavioral patterns for an operatic nymphomaniac. Like her ancestors, Lulu too is a kind of monster. But her monstrosity manifests itself not in what she does but in the way people respond to her. She lacks the predatory nature of Giovanni, Carmen, and Turandot. Rather than seeking sex, sex simply happens to her, because everyone who looks at her, of either sex, finds her attractive. Lulu's sexual excess leads (until the end) not to her own death but to the deaths of those who desire her. No normal hero like José or Calaf can arise to rid the world of Lulu by conquering her in murder or marriage. The only way to eliminate her is for an even greater pervert, Jack the Ripper, to kill her and take her place. The message is bleak: Freudian perversion can only be displaced by greater perversion, innocent nymphomania by mass rape/murder. Unlike *Carmen*, *Lulu* provides no assurance for the bourgeois operagoer that the sexual perversion has been kept in check. No wonder it took until the 1970s to get the complete opera on the stage.

Klingsor's Spear, Salome's Head, and Octavian's Sword

The last major category of operatic perverts are the fetishists: the characters who turn intense sexual energy toward an object rather than toward another character. These are the truly sick folk of opera, the obsessive types who spend the entire opera fixated on their fetish, never swaying from their obsession. Opera's fetishists have no sense of shame; they get so tied up with their obsession that they forget to show proper remorse for their behavior. Like other perverts, often the fetishists die at the end, but not always. Sometimes the fetish is so bizarre that society does not need to purge the character. As long as the fetish makes the character sufficiently marginal to ensure safe distance, the opera can dispense with the actual act of violent purgation.

Wagner is the master of the operatic fetish. All of Wagner's great works have an obsessive feel about them. In a sense, the whole concept of the leitmotif works as a kind of musical fetish, where Wagner takes a melody and turns it into a physical obsession, incessantly repeating it and playing with it until it reaches a climax at the end of the opera. More directly, Wagner often builds his operas around objects that take on powerful sexual significance: the ring, Wotan's spear, the sword Nothung, Tannhäuser's blooming staff, Lohengrin's transmogrified swan, Isolde's love potion, music itself in *Die Meistersinger*.

But Wagner saves his greatest use of fetish for his final work, *Parsifal*. Poizat gives a lengthy psychoanalytic reading of *Parsifal*, which he calls "The Quest for Illusion."[11] He offers an incisive statement of the fetishistic nature of the opera:

> What then is the Grail . . . ? It is *the* Thing, the lost Thing that sustains
> an endless Quest, because this Thing is inaccessible completeness.
> . . . For it is precisely this Thing that in a fundamental way arouses de-
> sire—the causal "objects" of desire are stand-ins for it, taking its place
> after the initial experience of lack, which is the locus of the Thing.[12]

The Thing (with its obvious phallic implications in Poizat's language) becomes a fetish because it cannot be possessed, and the desire for that unat-
tainable Thing propels the action of the opera, and it defines the fetish-dri-
ven characters of the story.

    Parsifal's quest for illusion actually centers around two Things, one holy,
one perverse. The grail is the good fetish, the center of phallic desire and
the outlet for sexual energy for the all-male society of knights. The knights
depend on their fetish, but Wagner spares them any sense of perversity. The
evil fetish is Klingsor's spear, the phallic substitute that causes Amfortas's
wound, and which Parsifal must appropriate and transform from an evil
fetish into a good fetish to bring the opera to its sacred climax. Klingsor is
not merely the evil sorcerer; he is the man who sacrifices his sexual organs,
by his own hand, to achieve admission to the inner circle of the Knights of
the Grail. When he is denied admission (because he dared to reveal the unspeakable secret, the fetishistic nature of the grail), he replaces his lost testicles with his magic, phallic spear, like a proper fetish now made lurid and
evil. A neophyte listener to *Parsifal* might be hard-pressed to pick up the
fact of Klingsor's self-castration, since the libretto offers little information
in dialogue, even less indication in the character himself. But Klingsor's lack
propels the obsessive desire that makes up his character and drives the action of the last two acts of the opera.

    The phallic imagery surrounding the Klingsor-Parsifal interaction is so
intense as to be almost parodic. Parisfal is the "real" man that Klingsor so
desperately wants to be, though Parsifal remains, of course, entirely innocent of this distinction (real men do not have to try to be real men).
Through the course of the second act, we see Parsifal losing his innocence
but also systematically stripping Klingsor of all the external trappings of his
pseudomasculinity, trappings that he has gathered around himself to replace his lost genitals. Klingsor has possession of Kundry, the ultimate
erotic woman (though what he does with her is something of a mystery).
He sends her to seduce Parsifal in order to destroy him, and she winds up
leaving Klingsor in favor of the holy knights. And, at the end of the act,
Klingsor tries to strike Parsifal with the phallic spear, the source of his
power, but Parsifal catches it in midair, wresting control of the symbolic
phallus and leaving Klingsor externally as well as internally impotent. Parsifal is then free (after ten years of wandering) to apply his acquired phallus
to Amfortas's crotch, heal the wound, and unite both fetish objects in tri-

umphant holy ceremony. Phallic masculinity is preserved in the arms of virtue and religion.

By comparison, the fetishes displayed in the early Strauss operas are rather obvious: Electra, with her obsessive desire for revenge, and especially Salome, with her lust for Jokanaan's head. Although this obviousness makes Strauss's notorious fetishists more famous for their perversions than Wagner's, they certainly owe their existence to Wagner. In the final scene of *Salome,* Strauss creates a logical extension of Isolde's "Liebestod," a sex-death where the male partner is already dead. The execution of Salome in the opera's final moment not only punishes her sin; it also represents the orgasmic climax of the violent sexual act that she initiates. In that way, she relates closely to the nymphomaniacs and their violent purgative deaths. *Salome* is not merely about the destruction of a woman with a fetish; it offers a compendium of operatic perversity: nymphomania, necrophilia, adultery, incest, not to mention the lingering shadow of Oscar Wilde and the public exposure of his homosexuality.[13]

Everybody knows that *Salome* is about sexual fetish, but *Der Rosenkavalier* hardly leaves the impression of being an opera about lurid sex. Still, Strauss carries over the fetish-laden atmosphere of his first two successes and transforms it into a much more subtle use of the sexually obsessive symbol. *Der Rosenkavalier* is an opera built around props. Most notable of these is, of course, the title prop, the silver rose that Octavian presents to Sophie on behalf of Baron Ochs and that precipitates the comic chaos of the marriage plot. Equally as prominent as the rose, however, is Octavian's sword. Although no one in the opera fondles the sword the way Salome makes love to the severed head, this symbolic phallus keeps popping up. In the context of the opera's gender-role reversal and cross-dressing, the sword becomes a pseudophallus, a comic fetish, and the visual objectification of Octavian's elusive masculinity.

In the opera's first scene, Octavian appears disarmed; he has removed his symbolic phallus to make love to the Marschallin. The audience first sees Octavian swordless, undeniably a soprano. Octavian leaves the phallus lying casually on the furniture (an uncouth act, for which the Marschallin berates him soundly), and when others appear, he must quickly hide the sword and get into women's clothing. Octavian's dual gender is an open secret, one that the audience may see, but the other characters (except the Marschallin) may not. Only at the end of the act, when he has left his lover's bed and his playful role as chambermaid, does Octavian appear in his "proper" masculine clothes, his sword firmly strapped, crotch-level, at his side and appearing on the surface, for the first time in the opera, as a "complete" man.

Like his Mozartean namesake, Octavian does not actually do much in the opera. Other than falling in love with Sophie, he has few purposive acts in the plot; he bounces around as a functionary of the schemes of the Marschallin, Ochs, and the conspirators, a willing participant, but not a very active one. The only assertive actions he takes are with his sword. This is especially the case in Act II, in his swordfight with Ochs, in which he scratches the Baron's arm. Unable to convince his rival of his masculine assertiveness, Octavian reverts to his fetish, the slightest touch of which is enough to reduce Ochs (whom I suspect of having little virility himself, despite his basso profundo) to a blabbering child. Octavian looks foolish wielding this oversized and misgendered phallus, but the fetish does its job.

If Strauss's operas seemed daring in their sexual irregularity eighty years ago, they hardly seem so now. Given the late-twentieth-century discourse of open sexuality, it is very hard for a modern opera to shock an audience sexually, even with the most overtly displayed perversions. Like Edward Albee, who had to rewrite *Who's Afraid of Virginia Woolf?* for its revival in the 1980s to reproduce the original impact of its dirty talk in the 1960s, the shockers of earlier eras can only be made shocking now by especially lurid stagings. These days, it takes a fully nude Salome to seem at all jarring, and then only because we don't expect it, not because we're shocked by nudity. Sex alone does not have much shock value, and sex with violence only becomes shocking when that violence reaches a sickening level, at which point most of opera's audience (at least those well-off patrons who finance opera in the United States) run screaming out of the theater.

But the point of sexual perversion in opera is not to make the audience gasp aloud or to leave audience members shaking their heads at the depths to which society has plummeted. Opera's perversion demands a double vision. We want our perversions to be visible and invisible at the same time. Opera's hermetically sealed world precludes the possibility of these perverts ever impacting real life, no matter how lurid their sins. I have nothing to fear from Carmen or from Salome or even from Lulu, for they are locked safely away in opera's elegant prison, and I am merely a visitor to their cell. Opera gives me power over these perverts because I can look at them and know them for what they are. But, just for a moment, I can let myself forget that I have that power. I can thrill to the suspense of not knowing whether Salome will really get away with her necrophilia, whether someone will come along to put the pervert in check, crush her under the shields. And when another bystander comes along to do the job for me I feel greatly unburdened, heaving a sigh of relief, not to mention sexual thrill, as Herodes shouts, "Man töte dieses Weib!"

Part Four

Means and Ends

9

THE CASTRATI AND THE EROTICS
OF VOCAL EXCESS

*Tonio Treschi was that half man, that less than man that arouses the
contempt of every whole man who looks upon it. Tonio Treschi was
that thing which women cannot leave alone and men find infinitely disturbing, frightening, pathetic, the butt of jokes and endless bullying, the
necessary evil of the church choirs and the opera stage which is, outside
that artifice and grace and soaring music, very simply monstrous.*

> —Anne Rice
> *Cry to Heaven*[1]

Evviva il coltello!
> —Italian opera cheer popular during the eighteenth century

A Pitched Battle

In the account of his musical travels to Italy during the 1720s, British com-
mentator Dr. Charles Burney relates the story of a notable musical battle.
Farinelli, the young castrato of growing fame,

> left [Naples] to go to Rome, where during the run of an opera, there
> was a struggle every night between him and a famous player on the
> trumpet, in a song accompanied by that instrument; this, at first,
> seemed amicable and merely sportive, till the audience began to interest
> themselves in the contest, and to take different sides: after severally
> swelling a note, in which each manifested the power of his lungs, and
> tried to rival the other in brilliancy and force, they had both a swell and
> shake together, by thirds, which was continued so long, while the audi-
> ence eagerly waited the event, that both seemed to be exhausted; and,
> in fact, the trumpeter, wholly spent gave it up, thinking, however, his

antagonist as much tired as himself, and that it would be a drawn battle; when Farinelli, with a smile on his countenance, shewing he had
only been sporting with him all the time, broke out all at once in the
same breath, with fresh vigour, and not only swelled and shook his
note, but ran the most rapid and difficult divisions, and was at last si-
lenced only by the acclamations of the audience.[2]

Burney's account of the battle between two sets of lungs holds a key to
understanding the frenzied popularity of the eighteenth-century Italianate
opera, and the public adulation lavished on its jewel-less jewels, the castrati. The baroque opera captured its audience by staging battles. On the
surface, it enacted the conflicts between the heroic combatants of its fictional narrative, with love, honor, or military glory as the stake. But more
importantly, the *opera seria* of the eighteenth century enacted battles between the musicians performing the opera: one castrato versus another, and
the castrati versus the other vocal and instrumental musicians in the performance. And they fought not for the conquest of some ancient Roman city
or the love of a high-born virgin but for the erotic attention of the audience.

Burney describes this musical competition in intensely sexual terms; the
two men have a "swell and a shake together," and after the trumpeter is
spent, the male soprano has another swell and shake on his own, with a triumphant smile on his face. Burney's language puts only the thinnest veil on
the erotics of this public display. Farinelli's voice becomes his phallus; it
swells, shakes, and leaves the less potent rival in its wake, until it reaches a
musical climax and induces in the audience a frenzy of applause. The two
musicians enacted a contest of virility, to see who could, in effect, keep it up
the longest. And this was no spur-of-the-moment face-off; it was a nightly
battle, in which the trumpeter could hardly have been surprised at his loss, as
the story implies. The battle became, as Burney notes, the center of the audience's attention, the main draw for them to come to the theater at all, far
more so than any theatrical interest in the narrative of the unnamed opera.

The curious paradox of this sexual battle is, of course, the castrato's ostensible lack of virility. As every member of Farinelli's audience was acutely
aware, the only way for a singer to acquire a vocal phallus like Farinelli's
was to lose the efficacy of his biological phallus, by being castrated. The audience could take the virility of a bass or a baritone singer for granted, but a
castrato had to fight to prove his sexual potency. Every time a castrato put
his body on display by walking out on stage, he placed his sexual efficacy in
doubt, through his identification with the public role of the castrato and the
audience's consequent knowledge of his incapacity. And every time he successfully negotiated a climactic aria, he won the battle to demonstrate his
potency, convincing his audience that his strangely constructed vocal phallus
wielded more power than his biological one, at least within the frame of the

stage.[3] The audience's ecstatic cry of "evviva il coltello," "long live the knife," in praise of the castrato, was both an affirmation of his successful sexual performance and a crushing reminder of its essential emptiness, of the lack that enabled and necessitated the battle in the first place.

The castrati stand at the intersection of the axes of opera's extreme sexuality outlined in Chapters 7 and 8: sexual competition and sexual transgression. No singers have embodied opera's sexual dynamic more fully than these strange figures. Their battles for phallic domination engaged the audience's fascination with sexual power plays more directly than the most seductive of nineteenth-century operatic sirens, even as the physical reality of their castration far outweighed even the most shocking sexual transgression in opera's fictional narrative. Anne Rice, in *Cry to Heaven,* depicts vividly (if not always with complete historical accuracy) both the competitive frenzy and monstrous transgressiveness that engulfed the world of the castrati. She outlines the high stakes of their battles: the control over the lucrative industry of baroque opera; the dominance over the factionalized audience; the access to the halls of power and influence over political and religious leaders.[4] She also explores the sexual power games played by the castrati, the way they used their erotic allure, in public and in private, to exercise social and political influence. In *Cry to Heaven, opera seria* is a closed, artificial world, where singers express their power through their sexual allure, toward the audience at a distance, and in close contact among each other and with "normal" people of both sexes.

Even more vividly, she explores the transgressive nature of the castrato's sexuality, both as pleasure and as pain. The act of castration, Rice asserts, both frees the singer and enslaves him. The castrated singer, his transgression permanently imprinted on his body, is released from the restrictive sexual norms of society, allowing him to take erotic pleasure from any and all sources, then to wield his transgressive freedom as a tool to fascinate his audience. Cut off from sexual normality, the castrato teases his audience, saying, "In my bold deviance, I have access to sexual secrets about which normal bodies can only dream." At the same time, Rice's castrati long desperately for normality. The castrato's lack haunts him as much as it empowers him. If the castrati enacted a normative sexuality on stage within the frame of the opera's narrative, it was only by an elaborate process of artistic and medical construction to create an image of the "natural."[5] To portray heroic and powerful sexuality, the singer had to become less than a man. If the audience desired the forbidden sexual secrets of the castrated body, it also rejected and ridiculed the monstrous sacrifice necessary to attain those secrets. The frenzied adoration went hand in hand with fear and loathing. For Rice, the castrato's impossibly powerful voice is a cry to heaven, at once the beautiful song of an angel and the scream of rage and despair aimed at the sky, arising from the body of the sexual siren condemned to the devil.[6]

The public response to the castrated body represents precisely the same excess-embarrassment pattern outlined by Sedgwick and Moon in relation to the fat female body today. Not only did the castrati wield voices of inhuman power; their bodies were often also excessive. The effects of the operation could make them either very tall or very obese, reinforcing the visibility of their excess. These physical excesses became the subject of satirical drawings, which depicted the castrati as abnormal, excessive monsters worthy of ridicule.[7] The same crowds who cried "evviva il coltello" in the theater, recognizing these bodies offstage, would gawk and laugh at them in the street. London society of the eighteenth century virtually worshipped the castrati, putting them at the center of public attention, both onstage and in private salons. But at the same time critics like Joseph Addison repudiated them with disgust, saving some of their sharpest vitriol for the male sopranos (feelings that the general public would share later, when the castrati lost their popularity).[8] The Catholic Church vehemently disavowed the practice of castrating boys to save their voices, yet simultaneously gave them the bulk of their employment. Since the decline of the castrati at the end of the eighteenth century, opera historians have perpetuated this embarrassment by developing a blind spot toward the castrati. There is remarkably little modern scholarship about them; opera critics, when they discuss the castrati at all, generally attribute their vast success to their brilliant voices alone. Modern popular discourse remains far too squeamish to talk about men without testicles, symptomatic of our much larger blind spot toward sexual irregularity in general.[9]

Nowhere is the embarrassment about the castrati more acute than around the topic of castration itself. There is a deafening silence about the transition from boy to castrato, the unspeakable sacrifice made to obtain the male soprano. No one in the eighteenth century ever disclosed the anatomical details of the procedure, whether the surgeon actually removed the testicles, or crushed them, or merely severed them from the blood supply.[10] Some of the castrati, in an attempt to reclaim their virility, argued they were not actually castrated but had the equivalent of a modern vasectomy (which in reality would not have the biological effect of preserving the soprano voice). Dr. Burney recounts his great difficulty in tracking down those who performed the deed or where it was done; he was sent from town to town in a fruitless chase.[11] The Pope vociferously banned the procedure, and the singers themselves at times fabricated tales of childhood accidents that required the operation for therapeutic purposes rather than admit to its being done for musical effects. Only Rice, from her modern perspective, gives a speculative description of Tonio's castration in full, bloody detail. The mystery of the operation is remarkably empowering. Its great potency, besides the stomach-sinking reaction of male listeners, lies in its unknowableness; without the mystery, the castrati become impotent medical curiosities. Mystery intact, they become vehicles of musical strength.

I understand this power when I listen to the only extant recordings, made in 1902 and 1904, of the last known castrato, the director of the Sistine Chapel choir, Alessandro Moreschi.[12] I do not love this recording the way I love other opera recordings. Aside from the marginal sound quality of the wax impressions, and Moreschi's less-than-stellar command of phrasing and pitch, I cannot give myself over to this eerie voice. It is too remote, too mannered, too distant to love. Yet I cannot stop listening to this recording, especially the opening notes of the "Domine salvum fac pontificem nostrum Leonem" and Rossini's "Crucifixus." I play it over and over with obsessive fascination. Like the strange eyes in Picasso's paintings that insistently stare back at me, this voice will not let me not listen to it. Moreschi's voice is not beautiful, but it carries great power. Even on these awful recordings, this voice, more than any other on record, evokes a physical presence, the image of a solitary, wounded body singing its glory and its pain from the depths of its absent vitals.

Power Plays

The stories of the *opera seria* that were written to frame the battles of the castrati both reinforced the competitive nature of their performances and masked the less-than-noble ego battles that arose between the star singers. These operas told stories of political conquest, the classical tales of heroes and demigods, and the clashes of mighty empires. Given the fierce competition between the singers, the stories of these operas were almost unnecessary, a conventional appendage to which the audience paid little heed. The audience could not have had much interest in the stories. These narratives often were far too complex to follow in detail, and the common practice of reusing the same libretti (especially those by Pietro Metastasio) by dozens of different composers also suggests a lack of interest in the narrative. But the competition enacted in the stories satisfied the rationalist impulses in the eighteenth-century audience by offering a logical setting for the battles between the singers. These narratives provided a gilded frame for erotic competition, serving to reinforce and heighten the sexual battles between the singers. As well as heightening the competition, the narratives of the *opera seria* also provided a serious and respectable cover for the often rather petty personal clashes between the singers, a way of hiding and justifying the embarrassing excess of the castrato competition.

Mozart's early work *Mitridate, re di Ponto* offers a vivid example of the contestative nature of eighteenth-century opera embodied in its dramatic narrative. The libretto, by Vittorio Amedeo Cigna Santi, based on a play by Jean Racine, depicts the battle between the two sons of King Mitridate, the good Sifare and the traitorous Farnace, for the throne of Mitridate and the love of the beautiful Aspasia. In it the fourteen-year-old Mozart created, in his first *opera seria,* a musical battle of wills. Employing the established conventions of eighteenth-century opera, Mozart staged a battle among the various singers, with music as the central weapon in the contest. The clash between good and evil here becomes a battle of musical skill: who can sing higher and more brilliantly, and who gets the arias most likely to win over the audience.

The musical conventions of the *opera seria* insist that it be read as hand-to-hand combat. *Mitridate,* like virtually every other opera of the period, consists almost entirely of solo singing; there is no chorus and only two ensemble pieces, a love duet between Sifare and Aspasia at the end of Act II and a brief final quintet. The rest of the opera consists of solo arias strung together by *secco recitativo,* highlighting the contrast between the characters and showcasing them in their solo turns. Mozart places the vocal music entirely in the treble range; of the seven characters, there are no basses or baritones, and only two "natural" male tenors: Mitridate himself and the small role of the Roman Tribune Marzio. There are two female sopranos, Aspasia and Ismene, and the other three roles are written for castrati.[13] In their musical battle, the contestants start from virtually the same gate, pitch-wise, and small differences in tessitura thus take on exaggerated importance. Most notably, within this field Mozart creates a clear split in tessitura between the two brothers, both castrati; Sifare, the noble and manly brother, is a high soprano, whereas Farnace, the unnatural traitor, is an alto. Before the opera begins, good has an upper hand over evil.

The libretto sets up Act I to display the vocal abilities of the central characters, to frame the competition. After a brief recitative, we first hear the "natural" female soprano of Aspasia, in a set piece filled with complex vocal display, to show off the singer's vocal agility. Mozart follows this spectacular aria by an even more spectacular one for Sifare, higher in range and a good deal more complex in its runs and leaps. In his aria, Sifare vows to conquer Aspasia's heart, but in fact he conquers her musically, with a higher, more elaborate, and more highly ornamented showpiece. The castrato defeats the female soprano, because Sifare is superior in virtue to Aspasia, but even more because Pietro Benedetti, for whom the role was written, would not have accepted his opening aria had it been less spectacular than that written for Antonia Bernasconi, the first Aspasia. Star singers at the time had the right to refuse an aria written for them, or to substitute one of their own favorite arias from another opera, if they felt the music did not show off their voice to advantage.[14]

Of particular note in this vocal battle are the number and position of the arias allotted to each singer. Conventionally in the *opera seria,* each major character must sing at least one aria per act, so any deviation from this pattern becomes significant. In this opera, Mozart provides in Act I a generous two arias apiece for most of the major characters, one each for the minor characters. But the evil Farnace, certainly a central character, gets only one aria in this act, and he must wait until both Sifare and Aspasia have sung their two before he gets his moment of power, in a much lower range than his competitors. Acts II and III even out the aria allotment, though in Act II Farnace's two arias are placed weakly, and they cannot compete with the impact of the act-ending duet for Sifare and Aspasia. Only at the end of Act III, when, calling on nature, Farnace renounces his evil and repents, do his musical fortunes turn around, and the opera gives him the final, climactic aria. The narrative battle between brothers resolves as their unified voices sing the opera's finale; the audience is left to judge the winner of the singing competition.

The solo turns that characterize *Mitridate* are suspended at the happy end of the opera and at one other moment, the remarkable love duet between Sifare and Aspasia, "Se viver non degg'io," which ends the second act. This duet is arguably the most electric moment in the opera. Musically it is stunning, allowing both singers complex trills and runs, separately and in unison. Because it is the first time in the opera when two voices sing together, even the simple harmonies generated by the two voices create powerful erotic tension.[15] The words of the duet describe their desire to die together if they cannot live together. But the narrative expression of harmony between the two singers contrasts sharply with the rivalry that underlies the entire opera. If the duet symbolizes Sifare's and Aspasia's love, it also provides the only chance for true head-to-head competition between two performers, for a male and a female singer (or two castrati, or two women) in the same soprano range. In the first act, Sifare has dominated Aspasia, but the duet gives her one last chance to win dominance back. Mozart uses the fiction of love to raise the stakes of the musical battle, in a war game that would be played over and over again in the elegant frame of the *opera seria*'s combative narrative.

The *opera seria* separates the fictional battle between characters and the actual battle between singers by only the narrowest of margins. These battles persist today in the ego-laden bouts over who is the world's greatest tenor or diva, but the narrative devices of the romantic repertory mask rather than enhance this competition. In the eighteenth century, new works written for specific theaters and, more notably, specific singers foregrounded the competitors and their rivalries much more intensely than later romantic operas. The stories of the *opera seria*, formulaic and extremely complex by the standards of romantic opera, elevate these rivalries, recasting the petty ego squabbles between singers and the competition for the audience's erotic attention into epic struggles between classical heroes. Through the musical competition, the castrato could take his wounded body and turn it into an image of sexual power, in spite of—or because of—his sexual incapacity outside the frame of the narrative.

The Castrated Body

As Joseph Roach observes, sexual lack defined and marked the public perception of the body of the castrato in the eighteenth century. The castrato, of course, necessarily hid the actual site of absence in his groin from public view, but that very act of hiding generated a popular fascination that marked the body of the castrato even more powerfully than a more overt display of transgression. Roach argues that the body of the castrato, thus marked, became a site for the display of sexual ambiguity and free play. The sexual power of the castrati, Roach states, arose from their marginality as neither male nor female and from their defiance of traditional sexual categories.[16] Citing Roland Barthes's analysis of the castrato La Zambinella (a character in Balzac's story "Sarrasine") in *S/Z*, Roach emphasizes the open erotic space created by the sexual ambiguity of the castrato's body:

> Liminality intensifies signification. . . . For Barthes, La Zambinella performs as an unstable signifier, a gap, a hollowness, a blank space wherein Sarrasine will inscribe his own urgent meanings. The castrato is the neutral surface upon which the spectator projects his fantasies, not unlike the automata in pornographic films, who are purposively neutralized to invite the imaginative participation of the beholders.[17]

By dwelling on the margin between the masculine and the feminine, the castrated male body permitted its audience to generate sexual desires otherwise forbidden in normal social discourse. This erotic free space was further heightened when (as was often the case in Rome, where women were forbidden from the stage) the castrati took on female roles in drag. At the same time, the castrati were just as famous for their leading male roles, the classical heroes of the *opera seria*. The castrato body enacted both the male and the female while occupying neither sexual space. The castrated body, Roach asserts, "physically contains sexuality within a being whose essence is defined by what it does not have, whose actions are predicated by what it cannot do, whose most powerful presence exists as an absence."[18]

But was the castrated body really a neutral, absent space? It was certainly an ambiguous space and difficult to place within standard sexual categories. But it is, I think, problematic to characterize the frenzied sexual engagement of the eighteenth-century audience with the castrati primarily as a response to neutrality. Joke Dame, in "Unveiled Voices: Sexual Difference and the Castrato," argues that the central problem with Barthes's (and, by implication, Roach's) configuration of the castrato as a neutral body or androgyne is that it denies the gendered reality of the castrati. Although the castrated body made feints at the feminine, and may even have stood at the margin between the masculine and the feminine, that body was still permanently marked as male. Even though the castrati sang in the female range, even though they often performed female roles in drag (onstage and, at times, even in public), the audience always retained the perception of the castrato's maleness, if not his masculinity. Dame cites the diaries of Casanova, also quoted by Roach, in which the notorious libertine muses on the sexual attractiveness of a certain castrato, Giovanni Osti, in female guise. Casanova remarks on Osti's feminine beauty, then observes (in a line that Roach omits from his quotation), "It was obvious that he hoped to inspire the love of those who liked him as a man, and probably would not have done so as a woman."[19]

Dame argues that rather than creating ambiguous desire the castrati appealed to a specifically homoerotic desire. The baroque opera placed male bodies, some in masculine roles and some in feminine roles, on the stage declaring their love for each other, a display in which the audience members (for example, Casanova) could read their own homoerotic desires. Dame calls the performance of the castrati "aural homosexuality."[20] In this argument, the castrated body represents the feminization of the submissive partner in a homosexual relationship, and male audience members could engage their desires through the display of an already conquered and feminized male body. Anne Rice's depiction of the castrati reinforces Dame's argument; the most sexually charged moments in *Cry to Heaven* are those that place the castrati in homoerotic situations, sometimes with each other, at other times between castrati and "normal" male bodies (in the latter case, the castrato always playing the receptive, "feminine" role).

But Dame's argument also does not account fully for the audience response to the castrati in the eighteenth century. Women in the audience engaged just as enthusiastically with the castrated bodies as did men, and their sexual idolization of the castrati was considerably more overt. As Roach observes, if men played out their homoerotic sexual fantasies privately, many women very publicly displayed their affections for the virtuosi, some ladies of quality even leaving their husbands to pursue favorite singers around Europe. Many castrati constructed elaborate fictions about their virility. Some claimed to have fathered children, and they were frequently at the center of lurid sexual scandals involving the wives of notable figures.[21] If the castrati engaged a homoerotic desire in some members of their audience, they also played on a clearly defined, if sometimes fictionalized, heterosexual attractiveness in their public personas. In Rice's narrative, the castrati keep their homosexual affairs private but flaunt their heterosexual liaisons openly.

Rather than a neutral space, or a specifically homoerotic space, I would argue that the castrato's body presents an excessive space, an overdetermined signifier, one that provides not an absence but an overabundance of sexual meanings for the audience.[22] The castrati did not offer a blank canvas for sexual interpretation; they bombarded audiences with sexual enticements of every variety. Roach likens the castrato to the neutralized body of a porn star. But the body of a porn star is neutralized and distanced by the medium of still or moving photography. The body of the castrato, however, did not stand passively on the stage, waiting for the audience to imbue it with images, nor was his physical presence distanced by an abstracting medium like film. The castrato, tangibly present on stage and in society, had to work actively for the audience's attention. Passivity and neutrality, as represented by the absence of sexual organs, were images *actively* employed by the castrati in their battle for the audience's erotic engagement. Roach argues that the act of castration represents a kind of public discipline of the body, in the same way that, as Foucault outlines, military drills, public tortures, and executions enacted submissiveness on the bodies of soldiers and criminals.[23] Yet unlike these victims of public control, if the castrato's body was subjected to an act of discipline, he could, subsequently, turn that discipline toward the audience and employ his subjected body as a weapon for subjecting the audience. The power of the castrati lay in their ability to wield both masculinity and femininity, same-sex and opposite-sex desires, centrality and marginality, as conveyed through their subtly trained bodies and voices.

The Mask of Heterosexuality

But if the castrati used both same-sex and opposite-sex desires to conquer their audience, in public they employed heterosexual images far more often than homosexual ones. If men felt private desire toward these bodies, in popular discourse women were seen as the chief source of the public frenzy surrounding the singers. This dichotomy is especially prominent in England, where sodomy was still a matter for violent suppression and where, at the time of the appearance of the castrati in England, a complex homosexual subculture was developing along the most lurid margins of London society.[24] In the satirical drawings of the period, when cartoonists wished to depict the overwhelming sexual power wielded by the castrati, they did so in a heterosexual context. Only later, when the popularity of the castrati declined and they had become objects of ridicule, did these satirical drawings shift focus and depict the erotic frenzy surrounding the castrati as a function of same-sex rather than opposite-sex desire.

Popular drawings and verses of the time frequently depict women in love with castrati. Roach cites a verse by T. J. Walsh meant to demonstrate the devotion of women to the castrato Nicolini, entitled "The Signior in Fashion: or the Fair Maid's Conveniency."[25] In the poem, the female spectator is overcome with desire at the manly and heroic feats that the castrato enacts on the stage, especially in the taming of a lion. A more complex version of the heterosexualized castrato can been seen in a satirical song sheet published by George Bickham around 1738, entitled "The Ladies Lamentation for ye Loss of Senesino," depicting the sorrows expressed by London's female population at the departure from the city of the beloved castrato (see Figure 9.1). The lyrics of the song, if less than inspiring as poetry, clearly relate Bickham's attitude toward the castrati, as expressed by his narrator: his awe at the irrational sexual appeal of the singers to women, and his inability as a "normal" man to perceive the reason for this attraction:

As musing I rang'd in the Meads all alone,
A beautiful Creature was making her Moan,
Oh! the Tears they did trickle full soft from her Eyes.
And she peirc'd both the Air and my Heart with her cries.

I gently requested the cause of her Moan,
She told me her sweet Senisino [sic] was flown,
And in that sad posture she'd ever remain,
Unless the dear Charmer wou'd come back again.

Why who is this Mortal so cruel said I,
That draws such a stream from so Lovely an Eye,
To Beauty so blooming, what Man can be blind,
To Passion so tender, what Monster unkind.

Tis neither for Man, nor for Woman said she,
That thus in lamenting I water the Lee,
My Warbler Caelestial Sweet Darling of fame,
Is a shadow of something, a Sex without Name.

Perhaps 'tis some Linnet, some Blackbird, said I,
Perhaps 'tis your Lark, that has soar'd to the sky;
Come dry up your Tears, and abandon your grief,
I'll bring you another, to give you relief.

No Linnet, no Blackbird, no Skylark, said she,
But one much more tunefull, by far than all three,
My sweet Senisino for whom thus I cry,
Is sweeter than all the wing'd Songster's that fly.

Adieu Farinelli, Cuzzoni, Likewise,
Whom stars, and whom Garters, extol to the skies,
Adieu to the Opera, adieu to the Ball,
My darling is gone, and a fig for them all.

Figure 9.1 George Bickham, "The Ladies Lamentation for ye Loss of Senesino." Satirical song sheet, c. 1738. Etching. From the collections of the Theatre Museum. By courtesy of the Board of Trustees of the Victoria and Albert Museum, London.

By the time this song sheet appeared, the initial frenzy in London over the castrati and Handel's Italian opera had begun to wane, though the castrati would continue to sing in London to loud acclaim until the end of the century. Bickham demonstrates this continuing popularity in the face of increasing public disdain for the castrati in his paradoxical verse. His distraught woman is clearly in love with Senesino, but she admits that he is neither man nor woman, "a shadow of something, a sex without name." Bickham projects onto his subject his own inability to fathom women's attachment to this strange object of desire. The castrato is a monster, a shadow, a thing without a name, yet the focus of women's all-consuming passion. Bickham also ridicules the ephemeral nature of these attractions, and their dependence on the fashion of the moment. The weeping woman has no attachment to the opera per se, which she rejects in the final verse, nor to Senesino's rival, Farinelli, nor to the female soprano Cuzzoni; she will only weep for her love, and once he is gone, she will presumably find another entirely different object for her passion.

More than Bickham's own disdain for the castrati (an attitude he shared with many other commentators in the London press), this song demonstrates the power of the castrato's heterosexualized public stance. Bickham's male narrator, and so presumably Bickham himself, is entirely discomfited by the ability of this "half-man" to conquer women's desire while "real men" failed to attract a remotely comparable level of interest. If Bickham shows disdain for the castrati, it is largely out of jealousy. He is disgusted by the idea of the castrati, but he grudgingly must admit their potency, at least in garnering the attention of female spectators. This satire, though mocking, validates the construction of heterosexuality wielded by the castrati.

By the beginning of the nineteenth century, this situation had completely changed. The popularity of the castrati was heavily in decline. And now, rather than validating their virility, the satirical images of the castrati emphasize their femininity, and especially their castratedness. In these cartoons, women no longer find them attractive. Two unattributed drawings appeared in London around 1825, during the visit of the castrato Giovanni Velluti. Velluti was the first castrato to appear in London in twenty-five years, and his appearances, though they initially attracted attention, soon lost the public's interest and became more a topic for ridicule than for admiration.[26] Again, the satirist frames the public reaction to the castrato primarily through the eyes of female spectators. And here, what had been a relatively mild lampoon of the singer's physiological condition in the eighteenth century becomes the central focus of the satire in the nineteenth.

In one drawing, entitled "SOME-THING!! peeping at NO-THING," a large matron sitting in a box at the opera peers through a glass watching Velluti perform in Meyerbeer's *Il Crociato in Egitto* (see Figure 9.2). She remarks, "Really I can see *no*thing to admire about the Creature. He will never prove a load*stone* of Attraction, for he is *not* perfect in his *parts!!*" The drawing makes Velluti look entirely ridiculous, with an over-large, obviously fake mustache, armor perched on spindly legs, and a tunic that looks like a woman's skirt, emphasized by his graceless, off-balance, splay-legged stance. Velluti appears anything but virile in his silly armor, and the woman's emphatic lack of erotic engagement with him arises from the ridiculous spectacle of a feminized male body attempting to enact virility. Even more important is the double entendre about Velluti's imperfect parts and his lack of a loaded stone with which to entice her. Where Senesino could enthrall women in spite of his sexual impairment, this woman has no interest in someone not perfect in his parts, no matter how well he sings.

A second print shows Velluti singing in a drawing room. This time the artist depicts him much more kindly; he seems quite handsome, but his clothes are out of the fashion of the period, and he looks even more feminine than in the first drawing, more like a female singer in male drag than a proper man. The drawing is entitled "An Italian Singer, *cut out* for English Amusement. or, Signor Veluti [sic] Displaying his *parts*" (see Figure 9.3). As he sings, the various listeners in the room comment:

> *Gentleman:* Do you not think he's a well made man!
> *Lady:* Why y-e-s, but not exactly the *thing!*
> *Another Lady:* La! how delicious [words crossed out] he strains, it's
>   enough to melt the heart of a Stone!
> *Another Gentleman:* He is quite perfect in his *Parts!*
> *Yet Another Lady:* Not quite!

Here the drawing goes much further in homosexualizing the castrato. Velluti, as the title indicates, puts his absent parts on display, but only the men in the crowd think he is attractive, well-made, and perfect in his parts. Two thirds of the women know better and reject his sexual imperfection (the third finds him delicious, though she associates him with a melted stone). In these satires—along with the drawing depicting the "Exquisite in Fits" discussed in Chapter 4, with its highly feminized dandies fainting in the opera box at the sight of the castrato—the castrato has ceased to be perceived even as a singer; unlike the song about Senesino, here Velluti's vocal performance is entirely secondary to his image as a display of non-masculinity. The castrato is now seen as attractive only to men, and the persistent harping on parts, stones, and things reveals that the public's attention has shifted almost entirely to the singer's absence of sexual organs and that this ambiguity of gender no longer appears virile. Without the ability to wield his overdetermined, excessive sexuality, the castrato became

Figure 9.2 Anonymous, "SOME-THING!! peeping at NO-THING." Satirical drawing, c. 1825. By courtesy of the Board of Trustees of the Victoria and Albert Museum, London.

144

Figure 9.3 *Anonymous, "An Italian Singer cut out for English Amusement. or, Signor Veluti displaying his parts." Satirical drawing, c. 1825. By courtesy of the Board of Trustees of the Victoria and Albert Museum, London.*

merely a bizarre anomaly, with heavy implications of the sodomite, and so lost the audience's erotic attention.

In the end, the castrati were to lose the battle for the operatic stage. Late in the eighteenth century, largely due to Mozart's comic operas written in collaboration with Da Ponte, the formal *opera seria* gave way to the looser structures of the *opera buffa* and its more recognizable and gender-normalized vocal patterns, featuring tenors and baritones rather than male sopranos. Nineteenth-century audiences, fascinated as they were with the grotesque, were unwilling to afford to these unnatural wonders the power of the masculine heroes of opera. Masculine desire transferred instead to the tenor voice, high but not too high; more importantly, the female soprano entered the equation of operatic sexuality in a significant way for the first time. The erotic tension of nineteenth-century opera lay not in the solo soprano voice but in the tenor-soprano duet and its overt representation of the heterosexual sex act. The remaining castrati reverted to the churches, and the works of the *opera seria* rapidly dropped out of the repertoire, not to be revived regularly until the late twentieth century. The current revival of interest in the castrati is propelled, perhaps, by our historicism, perhaps even more by our current fascination with public sexual transgression—as long as we have female sopranos and countertenors singing the castrato roles. We want to make sure that the sexual terror of the castrati never gets any closer to our reality than the scratchy recorded voice of Alessandro Moreschi.

10

WOMEN-AS-MEN IN OPERA

One of the most consistent and effective functions of the transvestite in culture is to indicate the place of what I call "category crisis," disrupting and calling attention to cultural, social, or aesthetic dissonances. . . . The binarism male/female . . . is itself put in question or under erasure in transvestism, and a transvestite figure, or a transvestite mode, will always function as a sign of overdetermination—a mechanism of displacement from one blurred boundary to another.

—Marjorie Garber
Vested Interests[1]

Cross-Purposes

While a graduate theater student at Indiana University, that bastion of operatic tradition, I took a friend, another theater student who knew very little about opera, to a performance, in translation, of *Le Nozze di Figaro.* She was a freshman, an aspiring actress, already well versed in the conventions of realistic acting. I took her to the performance as a noble deed, intending to instruct her in the joys of opera (it was also ostensibly a date, one of my last desperate and doomed flings at normative heterosexuality). As the curtain closed on the first act, I prepared, in my best high-toned graduate student mode, to deliver my enlightened observations on the theatrical merits of Figaro's act-closing aria, "Non più andrai." But my friend stopped me in mid-oration and asked, in a very puzzled tone, "Was that supposed to be a man? The woman who sang the number about being in love with every woman she meets. The one who is going to be a soldier. I think it was a woman—wasn't it?" I was taken aback. "Of course," I replied, after I realized she meant Cherubino. "Cherubino is a breeches role. They happen all the time in opera. It's sung by a woman, but it's supposed to be a man." "Oh. Well, now it makes sense. I couldn't figure out what was going on. How are you supposed to know?"

How indeed? Opera puts women in men's roles so often that the strangeness of their cross-dressing virtually disappears for the regular operagoer. In contemporary social discourse, transvestism is usually made visible by its anomaly; we find someone in the clothes of the opposite gender inappropriate, or comic, or frightening, or unsettling. But not in opera. To opera's faithful audience, pants roles are a familiar part of the landscape, as much an element of operatic convention as taking an excessive number of curtain calls. But opera provides very few clues to let a first-timer in on the drag secret. Women singing male roles neither look nor sound much like men, in defiance of twentieth-century expectations of theatrical realism. Yet drag performance in opera generally lacks the self-conscious, self-referential framing, the camp attitude or overt transgressiveness that normally signals a drag performance for a contemporary audience. Mozart, employing the conventions of his own time, simply expects the audience to know Cherubino's sex, as well as that of the singer portraying him, and to negotiate the difference. My college friend, not yet in tune with the mysteries of operatic transvestism, had no basis for reading its gender signals.

Attempts to describe the phenomenon of cross-dressing in opera to those uninitiated in the convention often do more to reinforce this confusion than to alleviate it. Anne Rice, elucidating for her popular audience the practice of operatic cross-dressing in eighteenth-century Rome, where women were banned by Papal decree from the stage, observes:

> [In Rome] the Church had never relented its ban on performing women, that prohibition which had once dominated the stages of all Europe. And these audiences simply never saw a female creature before the footlights, never witnessed the spectacle of womanly flesh magnified by the cheers and clapping of thousands packed in a dark hall. . . . [W]hen the woman is taken out of an entire realm of life that must needs imitate the world itself, then some substitute for that woman is inevitable.
>
> Something must rise to take the place of what is feminine. Something must rise to *be* feminine. And the castrati were not mere singers, players, anomalies; they had become woman herself.[2]

Rice's slippery language undergoes a problematic terminology shift in this passage. She configures the cross-dressed body of the castrato first as a substitute for the feminine, then as the female body itself. In Rice's formulation, the absence of "real" women requires the castrato in drag to assume the role of a woman, and then to become an actual woman, or all women at once: both the signifier and the signified.

Rice confuses the representation with the embodiment and conflates the terms "feminine" and "woman," but the trouble with this configuration runs even deeper, for it belies the function of cross-dressing in opera. The cross-dressed castrati did not merely substitute for female performers in eighteenth-century performance. (Rice errs in her history; other than in Rome, women played a significant role on the stage, operatic and spoken, throughout continental Europe.) And they certainly did not become women. As Marjorie Garber argues in *Vested Interests,* her sweeping analysis of transvestism as a cultural phenomenon, cross-dressing offers to the spectator not a substitute of one gender for another, nor even an image of one gender presented by another, but an entirely different representation that defies such unambiguous either/or categories of gender. Rather than a simple substitution or representation, the cross-dressed figure, Garber asserts, puts the traditional binary constructions of gender that we take for granted into crisis, in the process generating transgressive desires unavailable in more familiar gender frameworks. The desire that the cross-dressed singer generates in a male audience member is not that of a man toward a woman, nor of a man toward a man, but of a man toward an overdetermined gender image, specifically in this case a castrated male body in the clothes of a woman.

Garber locates in the transvestite figure a site of representational overflow: "Excess, that which overflows a boundary, is the space of the transvestite."[3] The transvestite transgresses against societal norms not by switching from one gender category to another but by occupying multiple spaces of representation, providing an excess of gender information that breaks apart the comforting binarisms of normative categories and precludes a simple and unambiguous reading of the performer's gender. This representational overflow draws in the spectator who, unable to translate the gender signals emerging from the cross-dressed body, is seduced by the excess. "The transvestite . . . is both terrifying and seductive precisely because s/he incarnates and emblematizes the disruptive element that intervenes, signaling not just another category crisis, but—much more disquietingly—a crisis of 'category' itself."[4] That crisis can induce terror, but it more often induces sexual fascination. Like the overdetermined body of the castrato, the cross-dressed body attracts and amplifies undefined and transgressive erotic engagement. "The transvestite," Garber asserts, "is the space of desire."[5]

Cross-dressing is, of course, not the only space of desire in theatrical representation, and especially not in opera, that transforms every element of its physical presence into a potential space of desire. But given its overtly transgressive nature (and in the absence in modern times of the even more transgressive presence of the castrati), cross-dressing becomes a particularly fertile site for opera's sexual free play. Transvestism fits squarely into opera's dynamic of erotic transgression and embarrassing excess. Like the body of the castrato, the drag figure is embarrassing because of its excessiveness, and that embarrassment becomes its source of power. (Rice depicts with particular astuteness Tonio's embarrassed reluctance to appear on stage dressed as a woman and then configures the story so that Tonio can use his shame-ridden power to assume a female identity in order to triumph at the end of the novel.) Like the body of the castrato, the cross-dressed body on the opera stage offers more erotic data than will fit into normative constructs of desire. Transvestism thus becomes one focal element of opera's queerness, a cornerstone of its systematic refusal to submit to sexual binaries. Opera has embraced drag since its earliest days, and drag has remained a central element of operatic performance ever since.[6]

But if the drag hero represents the most obvious successor to the transgressive sexual space left open by the decline of the castrati, the desire generated by the drag hero functions in fundamentally different ways from that created by the male soprano. First, the castrati always maintained an intense visibility on stage as sexual anomalies, and the opera conventions of the eighteenth century worked to foreground their sexual abnormality. The drag figure in opera, on the other hand, has become increasingly less visible, especially since the early nineteenth century, when (as I will discuss later in the chapter) audiences began to expect cross-dressed figures in certain conventional roles. Drag figures have also assumed a steadily smaller percentage of opera roles over time. Castrati occupied almost all the leading parts in the *opera seria;* cross-dressed singers since that time have been relegated mostly to smaller and supporting roles. More fundamentally, even though the audience's desire for the castrati centered on the male body (in male or female clothing), the desire generated by operatic cross-dressing has, since the beginning of the nineteenth century, focused almost exclusively on the female body dressed as a man or, more importantly, as a boy. In order to understand the space of desire opened by cross-dressing in opera, then, we must look for a different set of rules than those that governed the performer-audience interaction in the castrato-dominated eighteenth century.

Girls Will Be Boys

If, as Garber asserts, transvestism throws binary categories of gender into crisis, generating seductiveness and, most of all, visibility for the drag figure, then operatic cross-dressing presents a problematic issue: How does the transgressive, visibility-generating act of cross-dressing become so invisible, so normative, in opera? Garber barely mentions operatic cross-dressing in her exhaustive study, and what little she says is almost entirely in the context of the castrati; for opera after the beginning of the nineteenth century, she simply observes that at one time, "Operatic 'trouser roles' had achieved a considerable popularity."[7] This is, to put it mildly, something of an understatement, and it does not begin to address the continuing pervasiveness of these roles, especially in the standard romantic repertory. If transvestism puts gender roles in crisis, then opera audiences have done a thorough job of embracing that crisis and assimilating it into their normative perception of opera. The wealthy New York opera patron who looks at a Greenwich Village drag queen with horror and disdain will raise no protests that the soprano singing Octavian at the Met is similarly dressed in the wrong clothes and is, furthermore, making love to another woman.

The normalization of operatic drag can be explained, in part, by the same mechanisms that hide all of opera's other sexual transgressions so effectively: the elegant surroundings; the fiction of musical "purity"; the intense emotionality of the music itself. The pretty atmosphere mitigates the transgression. Operatic drag also fails to attract attention partly because, though drag roles occur frequently in opera, they tend to be secondary and marginal parts, whereas the central roles (at least from the nineteenth century on) remain predominantly gender-normalized. Moreover, the conventional nature of operatic drag, and the repetition of the convention in similar roles, tend to hide the anomaly.[8] But for a contemporary audience, other factors come into play to allow the audience to assimilate operatic drag.

Centrally, opera inverts the images most commonly associated with transgressive drag in the modern consciousness. For most casual observers today, drag means male-to-female drag, but opera almost exclusively employs female-to-male cross-dressing. Other than the fans of old Garbo and Dietrich films and people who frequent performance spaces in the East Village, few today have much chance to see women taking on male roles in spoken performance (lesbian chic notwithstanding). Whether a performance by British pantomime dames or the Monte Python troupe, Milton Berle or Flip Wilson or Tony Curtis and Jack Lemmon or Dustin Hoffman, Divine or Harvey Fierstein or RuPaul, drag means men in dresses. The drag queen is a familiar commodity in popular culture, but there is no equivalent "drag king" category to account for women dressed as men. Modern society has no popular terminology to explain the phenomenon of female-to-male drag, and the lack of terminology reinforces invisibility.[9] If my college friend at the opera had a hard time reading the character of Cherubino, it was because the performance she saw bore no relationship to any context of cross-dressing that she brought with her to the opera house.

In the same vein, drag today typically means farce, especially an attitude of self-ridicule taken on by the drag performer. Popular sensibility uses comedy to relegate drag to the margins, something silly, meant for community talent shows, college pranks, and gay bars, but not a serious vehicle for artistic or social expression. Just as there is no social category to account for women dressed as men, there is no category for serious drag. But opera takes its cross-dressing quite seriously, even in comic operas. Women dressed as men function in operatic narrative not as reductive caricatures of stereotyped male behavior but as actual male characters. But in mainstream popular culture, transvestism presents too subversive an image to allow such disturbing transgression to play itself out in a serious context. When men put on women's clothes in familiar comic drag, the hysterical atmosphere of the performance tends to (or at least appears to) derail the transgression. Farce becomes a way to deal with the category crisis that Garber outlines.

Even more, mainstream drag often uses comedy not only to deflect panic but to counteract it by reinforcing traditional gender categories. In a patriarchal society, men who represent the sources of societal power dress as women in order to induce laughter, implying that women deserve ridicule and that men have the right to appropriate female identity.[10] This kind of drag happens occasionally in opera, notably in the final act of *La Bohème,* when the four male bohemians do a comic drag dance just before Mimi returns for her death scene. Men dressed as women in mainstream media are funny, because they caricature marginalized women while maintaining their powerful position at the masculine center. The gynophobic comic male-to-female cross-dresser presents himself as an ugly woman, both as a kind of ridicule of femininity and as a means of controlling the image of women. It is not surprising, then, that the more "dangerous" variety of male-to-female cross-dresser, the one who emerges from the margins of society and often self-identifies as gay, normally chooses to appear as an attractive woman in order to wield his/her attractiveness to other men as a means of inducing gender category crisis rather than reinscribing normative gender divisions.

The female-to-male cross-dresser, however, always poses a threat. Women dressed as men violate male hegemony by attempting to reject their secondary social role and to assume male power or, more powerfully, to reject the whole concept of binary gender division. Unlike the caricatured ugly man in a dress, the woman in man's clothing opens diverse and problematic categories of desire. The man watching a woman *en travestie* may find himself attracted to her as a woman or, much more dangerously, attracted to her as a man, simultaneously worrying that his obedient wife sitting next to him may have exactly the same feelings and not knowing which of her potential desires is worse. Mainstream male-to-female drag quells panic by purporting to obliterate desire; female-to-male drag induces panic by proliferating desire. Men in drag are funny; women in drag are powerful, and so dangerous.[11]

But that danger turns to productive use within the eroticized confines of the opera house. Opera normalizes drag primarily because it employs transvestism as a means toward its larger erotic ends. Opera has no need to distance its audience from the transgressions of drag, nor to relieve the embarrassing erotic tension generated by the cross-dressed body. Instead, this tension merely enhances opera's pansexual free play. The female body in drag seems normal on the operatic stage, because, within the rules that govern that space, it *is* normal. If there is anything unusual about cross-dressing in opera, it is that the drag singer is often the most attractive figure on the stage; the transvestite violates the norm not by being excessively different from her surroundings but by being even more excessive than the normative excess of opera. The transgressive desire generated by the female-to-male transvestite gets magnified by the desire generated through her music, and I have almost no choice but to fall in love with her. I typically do not make an erotic investment in women's bodies, but Cherubino and Octavian turn me on.

But if opera employs the dangers of female-to-male cross-dressing to enhance its erotic atmosphere, since the beginning of the nineteenth century it has shied away from the rampant and overtly erotic terror represented by the bodies of the castrati. Instead, opera generally has buffered the panic of women in drag by placing them in the safer representational role of the adolescent or preadolescent boy. The castrato singers enacted the roles of fully sexualized adults via their sexually incapacitated bodies; the female singer in drag uses her sexually intact body (*pace* Freud and his theories of penis envy) to enact the roles of presexual or protosexual male youths. After the decline of the castrati, by far the majority of drag roles in opera are boys: adolescent youths, pages, shepherds, and the like. By the middle of the nineteenth century this practice becomes codified and conventionalized; virtually any time an opera plot requires a boy, the composer gives it to an adult female soprano in drag.[12] The expectation of this convention, in turn, quells the sense of anomaly inherent in drag performance.

Garber argues that the female body in male clothing becomes eroticized through assuming the sexually ambiguous role of the boy. The boy figure, partaking of both the masculine and the feminine, offers a powerful example of eroticizing gender category crisis. Garber outlines the erotic power of the boy actor playing female roles, especially during the Renaissance on the Elizabethan stage, where the boy's sexual ambiguity becomes the site for both same-sex and opposite-sex desires. She notes in particular that at this time the term "boy" did not refer exclusively to prepubescent males but could indicate any comparatively young male figure under the power or authority of someone else, especially when employed for sexual services.[13]

Later, especially in the repressive Victorian atmosphere of the nineteenth century, the Elizabethan theatrical formula was reversed. Rather than boys playing women on the stage to heighten erotic tension, women frequently portrayed boys in the theater as a ploy to eroticize the otherwise sacrosanct female body. The act of putting a woman in men's clothing eroticized her, intentionally for the male spectator, more covertly for the female spectator. Standard women's roles in nineteenth-century spoken melodrama provided little room for erotic fantasy. The good girls were too pure to excite the imagination, and the bad girls, though momentarily alluring, brought danger with them and always wound up dead. In either case, the heavy drapery of women's clothing did little to enhance the desirousness of the female body on stage. But a woman dressed as a boy became highly eroticized, both by her transgressive act of cross-dressing and, most importantly, by the pants or tights that she wore, making her nether regions intensely visible. The eighteenth-century spoken stage, even more so the nineteenth-century spoken stage, saw an explosion of female-to-male cross-dressing, with women taking on male roles in everything from pantomime to Shakespeare, to the erotic thrill of the audience.[14]

But if the image of a woman dressed as a boy is erotic, it also preserves a cover of public respectability for the dangerous figure. As Freud would point out at the end of the Victorian era, even though children are intensely sexual, no adult wants to believe it. By assuming the role of the boy, the woman in drag cloaks her eroticism beneath a heavy layer of socially condoned repression, just as opera masks its intense eroticism under a heavy layer of upper-class paraphernalia. The woman-as-boy figure represents the ideal balance for nineteenth-century opera, a figure of open eroticism who also maintains an inviolable mask of respectability.

Out of this cloak of respectability emerges a parade of powerfully eroticized boy figures on the operatic stage. I would like, then, to look more closely at three of opera's most prominent erotic boys, one from each of the three centuries of standard repertory opera—Cherubino in Mozart's *Le Nozze di Figaro,* Oscar in Verdi's *Un Ballo in Maschera,* and Octavian in Strauss's *Der Rosenkavalier*—and the differing contexts in which their boyishness becomes eroticized. These three characters, though at times pushed to the margins of the narrative, become the focal points of the audience's sexual desire, and they represent some of the most dangerous bodies in opera.

The Masturbating Androgyne

When Mozart wrote *Le Nozze di Figaro* in 1786, few regulations governed operatic transvestism. Gender representation in the first century and a half of opera history was a rather chaotic affair. The baroque opera situated most of its roles in the treble range, and so it required singers who could negotiate these roles: women, boys before puberty set in, falsettists, or castrati. Well into the eighteenth century, any of these varieties of treble voice might find their way into any type of operatic role, male or female, as long as they could handle the notes (though boy singers, with little training, were the last resort). Given the vicissitudes of travel, health, and temperament, opera impresarios would often have to make do with whatever voice was available and capable, putting the appropriate costume on the body that contained the voice, no matter what its biological sex might be. Only in Rome, with its ban on female performers, was there any consistency in the use of drag in opera.[15] In the baroque era, drag induced a truly thrilling category crisis, because the audience literally could never be sure what kind of body might be under the costume.

But by the 1770s, the heroic *opera seria* had begun to decline in popularity. Cristoph Willibald von Gluck had initiated his reforms during the previous decade, advocating a less flamboyant, more gender-normalized style for serious opera. At the same time, the popularity of *opera buffa* was growing, with its greater reliance on narrative over vocal fireworks and its subsequent disdain of the castrati. Both of these trends worked to reduce the potential for the random mix-and-match cross-dressing of the baroque period. The huge success of *Le Nozze di Figaro* did a great deal to cement these trends by demonstrating that opera that placed narrative and characterization over florid vocal display could also engage the audience's interest—and its erotic attention. To replace the allure of the castrato hero, Mozart offered to his audience two butch baritones, Figaro and the Count, two attractive female sopranos, Susanna and the Countess, and, most importantly, a female soprano taking on the role of an eroticized adolescent boy. Cherubino was certainly not the first instance of female-to-male cross-dressing in opera. But Mozart and Da Ponte brought Cherubino to the stage at a crucial moment in operatic history. The brilliant success of Cherubino established the figure of the drag boy on the opera stage, and the seductive power of this figure served to normalize the practice of operatic drag for all subsequent opera.

Cherubino is defined by his sexuality. He is the quintessential "naughty boy," the youth with too many hormones to keep his sexuality in check and too little maturity to keep his passions private. He exemplifies what Foucault, in *The History of Sexuality,* labels the "masturbating child," the youth whose inability to repress his sexual urges amounts to a pathology.[16] Watching Cherubino reminds me of my youthful bathroom adventures of sexual discovery. He spends the entire opera in a state of sexual frenzy, madly chasing anything of the opposite sex (or, rather, of the same sex—the cross-dressing lets me plug in my own proclivity). I laugh at his inexperience, but his predicament cuts close to home. Obviously, neither Cherubino nor any other operatic character (at least before the twentieth century) literally masturbates on stage. But if the opera deprives me of the literal act, I certainly get to witness his sexual fantasies in detail. Cherubino's aria "Non so più" is a masturbation fantasy, an encyclopedic litany, set to rapid triplets, of what he finds sexually arousing (which is virtually everything he sees). The music is halting, fitful, erratic. It is, quite literally, breathless. When he sings repeatedly "ogni donna mi fa palpitar" (every woman makes me palpitate), the words merely confirm what the music has already said. By the end of the aria the music collapses into sexual exhaustion. The hormone attack has passed.

Even more than his open declaration of frenzied sexuality (a freedom that the more decorous *opera seria* never allowed its castrato heroes), Cherubino is sexually charged by his gender ambiguity. Brigid Brophy, in her study *Mozart the Dramatist,* evokes the open space around Cherubino's gender with a chapter entitled "Seduction in Mozart's Operas, with a Note on Who Is Cherubino, What Is He?" Unfortunately, Brophy dodges the question, at least that regarding Cherubino's seductiveness. She calls Cherubino a lot of different names—poltergeist, fairy, spirit, demoted god, youth, baby, and especially cherub and Cupid—and argues that Cherubino represents exactly what his name implies, the mischievous boy-god of classical mythology. Even though Cherubino talks about sex, she argues, the Count is really the center of the opera's seduction.[17] But Brophy's literal-minded reading looks exclusively at the narrative and entirely ignores the conditions of the performance, most importantly the fact that Cherubino is a woman in drag. The Count may try to seduce Susanna, but Cherubino is the one who seduces the audience, because we don't quite know what s/he is. Cherubino represents a child, but the character is played by an adult woman, with a powerful sexual presence. And that power, as Garber argues, becomes multiplied because the body simultaneously evokes the male and the female. The confusion that my college friend felt in identifying Cherubino is, in fact, the character's primary erotic power, a power that Beaumarchais, in his original drama, also recognized in specifying that Cherubino should be performed by a woman in male clothes.

Mozart and Da Ponte highlight Cherubino's gender ambiguity even further in the Act II episode of counter-cross-dressing. As with Shakespeare, who intensifies the sexual play in his comedies by having female characters who are played by boys counter-cross-dress as boys, Da Ponte has Cherubino, a boy played by a woman, counter-cross-dress as a woman. Susanna and the Countess, the objects of Cherubino's erotic interest, dress him/her as a woman in order to escape from the Count (who is his/her rival for those objects), but also as an excuse for getting their hands on him/her. The perpetual-motion door-slamming farce of this scene only lightly masks an intense sexual play, in which erotic attraction and jealousy bounce among all of the characters onstage at once. By the end of this act (the end of Cherubino's major action), I become giddy with the whirl of layered gender signals, a fitting lead-in to the more serious sexual jousting of the last two acts, in which Cherubino almost disappears.

Cherubino's erotic stage presence demonstrates the seductive force of Garber's ambiguous category crisis. I feel this power whenever I listen to *Nozze;* in the opera, Cherubino's scenes absorb me completely, almost as fully as the *Rosenkavalier* trio. I once attended a performance of *Nozze,* directed by Jean-Pierre Ponelle, at the Vienna Staatsoper. I was in standing room, which in Vienna means waiting in line for hours in the wind and cold (it was December) to have the privilege of fighting for a few square inches of space from which, if you are lucky, you can see a corner of the stage over the heads of the other patrons. The cast was not brilliant, and I had seen a much better rendition of the Ponelle production (sitting down) at the Met the year before. But when Cherubino began to sing "Non so più," my attention was suddenly riveted. Just then, a woman in front of me began a conversation with her date. I tried the standard withering look, but she didn't see me. I then tried to tap her lightly on the shoulder to get her attention. But in my pent-up frustration from having my erotic engagement with Cherubino disengaged, I instead gave her a solid blow to the back. She shut up, but I spent the rest of the performance imagining myself, à la *Die Fledermaus,* sitting in a Viennese prison on assault charges. The rest of the performance failed to engage me, but Cherubino's seductive presence, and the possibility of being deprived of that seduction, drove me to violence.

Cross-Dress Patterns

Cherubino sets the pattern for cross-dressing in the romantic opera of the nineteenth century. But in romantic opera, the most powerful sexual energy switches largely from the free-wheeling spirit of the *opera buffa* into the more serious tragic opera of the bel canto composers, and of Verdi and Wagner. Cherubino's youthful sexual energy continues in the nineteenth century to reside in the practice of cross-dressing female singers as boys; but rather than major players in the action, the drag figures most often appear in secondary roles, as one of the bouncy pages or children who hover at the margins of the tragic narrative. Occasionally a drag figure will come to the center (Arsace in Rossini's *Semiramide,* Maffeo Orsini in Donizetti's *Lucrezia Borgia,* Romeo in Bellini's *I Capuleti e I Montecchi,* Hänsel in Humperdinck's *Hänsel und Gretel*). More often, though, rather than representing the central erotic presence on stage, the transvestite soprano teases us, a transgressive figure on the margins of the more normalized erotic tale. We get, for example, the mezzo roles of Siebel in Gounod's *Faust* and Nicklausse in Offenbach's *Les Contes d'Hoffmann,* both youthful, androgynous figures whose peripheral presences contrast with the more aggressive central stories of frustrated sexual desire; we also get the even stranger androgyny of Orlofsky, in *Die Fledermaus,* whose ambiguity creates a license for the heterosexual free play of the main plot.

The most vibrant peripheral drag figure in nineteenth-century opera, though, is certainly Oscar, the boyish page in Verdi's *Un Ballo in Maschera.*

Oscar, in his own way, plays as pivotal a role as Cherubino. Like Cherubino, he is androgynous. But he also evokes an intense sexuality, though much less overtly so than Cherubino. Cherubino declares openly his erotic desire for all women; Oscar demonstrates a more covert but equally powerful attachment to one man, his master, Riccardo. Verdi plays an even trickier reversal game here than Mozart. Instead of having a woman in man's clothes singing about "heterosexual" love for women, Verdi puts on stage in the figure of Oscar a woman in male drag who evinces a suppressed "homosexual" attachment to a man.

Oscar has three arias, each indicating an increasingly close attachment to Riccardo, though this attachment always manifests itself in a deflected context. The first aria, "Volta la terrea," is ostensibly a defense of the gypsy Ulrica, but its plaintive tone aims directly at Riccardo, and its bouncing energy sounds much more like a playful seduction than a defense. In the second aria, "Alle danze questa sera," in which Oscar invites the conspirators to the ball, Oscar actually stands in for Riccardo, a metonymic presence among those who wish to murder the governor. In the final aria, "Saper voreste," Oscar acts as the protective lover, hiding Riccardo's presence from his assassins. Throughout the opera he hovers around Riccardo, far more devoted and doting than Riccardo's reluctant lover, Amelia. And, though Riccardo and Amelia have only one love scene together (but admittedly a most powerful one), Riccardo and Oscar are rarely out of sight from one another.

Some will protest the suggestion of a homoerotic attachment between Oscar and Riccardo. Oscar certainly does not give any literal, outward show of sexual feeling for Riccardo, and Riccardo focuses his sexual attention elsewhere. But Oscar occupies a well-defined erotic role on the nineteenth-century stage: the hopeless lover, prevented from marrying the hero by barriers of class or other impediment. This role normally goes to a female character, such as Eboli in *Don Carlos* or Amneris in *Aïda,* but the dynamics are almost identical here. Further, Oscar does not fit the typical servant role. He is flip and flirtatious, in violation of social propriety and the practice of other opera pages, and he is deeply stricken by Riccardo's death. Oscar is the "other woman," like the servant Liù in *Turandot,* cherishing an impossible love for an eroticized father figure, an amusing and pitiable creature who garners our sympathy but never gets the chance to act on "her" desires.

I do not mean to suggest that Verdi, in creating Oscar, wanted to infiltrate his opera with a subtle gay aesthetic. Verdi is as straight as they come. If there is a homoerotic content in the relationship between Oscar and Riccardo, it emerges from the category crisis induced by Oscar's transvestism. More importantly, in the nineteenth century, despite the male drag, audiences probably did not even think of Oscar as a man at all, but rather as a female body eroticized by a fetching period male costume. Old recordings indicate that earlier singers sought to emphasize Oscar's femaleness. In Luisa Tetrazini's recording of "Saper voreste" in 1911, the diva makes no attempt to "masculinize" her voice. She fills the aria with coloratura trills and embellishments, derailing any notion that there is a male body under the cute clothes. Tetrazini truly turns Oscar into the second female lead, the not-very-bad girl to Amelia's not-very-good girl.[18] The implied erotic attachment between Oscar and Riccardo would not shock a Victorian audience, because the audience could see Oscar as a woman, and the male audience members could feel heterosexual attachment to her, especially as she wore the eroticizing clothes of the boy page.[19]

The importance of maintaining Oscar's female presence was highlighted by David Alden's production of Verdi's opera, which I saw in 1990 at the English National Opera. Rather than the typical vision of Oscar, in boyish eighteenth-century clothes that emphasize the singer's curves, Alden's characterization of Oscar obliterated all signs of the female in the character. The production, set vaguely in the nineteenth century, put Oscar in a long, dark overcoat and glasses, with pale, almost ghostly makeup and, most notably, facial hair of a Mephistophelean red. The costume gave no visual indication of cross-dressing, so that when this figure began to sing in a soprano range, the effect was extremely jolting, even to those of us in the audience familiar with the opera. Rather than doting on Riccardo, Alden had Oscar hover around the action as a sinister presence, more an accomplice to the murderers than Riccardo's protector. The effect was highly unsettling; without the normal implied romantic role for Oscar, and without his feminine side, he lost his erotic allure and became instead a terrifying, uncanny figure.

Drag Races

The proliferation of cross-dressed roles, even those in secondary positions, diminishes sharply as opera moves into the twentieth century. Transvestism becomes less vital to opera for several reasons. First, Verdi and Wagner dominate operatic composition after the mid-nineteenth century. You could be either a Verdian or a Wagnerian, but whichever master you chose to follow, neither provided substantial incentive to write major drag roles. Verdi and Wagner both rely heavily on the tenor-soprano-baritone triad for their plots, and other than Oscar, neither employs the drag boy figure with any regularity. More importantly, the increased audience desire for realism after mid-century diminishes the viability of these roles. Gounod, in 1859, could create the cross-dressed role of Siebel in *Faust* without calling attention to the gender anomaly, because Siebel's sexuality is gentle, pastel-shaded, and idealized. But Bizet, in 1875, had no use for cross-dressing in the sexually charged world of *Carmen*. The raw and obvious sexuality of verismo precludes the sexual ambiguity of the transvestite figure. Siebel in drag is charming; José in drag would be ludicrous.

When Richard Strauss and Hugo von Hofmannsthal wrote *Der Rosenkavalier* in 1911, they broke away from the verismo pattern and made a conscious effort to hark back to the free-wheeling style of operatic cross-dressing in the late eighteenth century. Strauss and Hofmannsthal make no secret of the Mozartean parentage of their leading character. Octavian springs from an odd pair of progenitors; he gets his chief character outlines and behavior patterns from Cherubino, the lovesick man/woman. His other parent and namesake is Ottavio, the less-than-butch nonhero of *Don Giovanni,* who provides Octavian with his windy bravado and questionable masculinity. Strauss and Hofmannsthal transform the rather effeminate and ineffectual tenor of the serious Mozartean plot into the gender-ambiguous cross-dressed mezzo of their comedy, adding in Cherubino's lust and playfulness. The opera offers other clear Mozartean parallels, in the setting in the courts of Viennese nobility and in the *opera buffa* intrigues of the complex plot. In the middle of this world stands Octavian, part eighteenth-century icon of heroic youth, part twentieth-century Freudian erotic child, swaying to a nineteenth-century Viennese waltz. Strauss and Hofmannsthal use Octavian not only to throw gender into category crisis but to create a dizzyingly ambiguous mélange of three centuries of opera history. *Der Rosenkavalier* is the first postmodern opera.

In its prototypical postmodernism, *Rosenkavalier,* unlike its eighteenth- and nineteenth-century predecessors, puts a frame around its transvestism. By making Octavian a drag hero, Strauss and Hofmannsthal want to bring to mind Octavian's historical ancestors and to highlight both the similarities and the differences. The similarities are fairly obvious, but the differences are more significant and amplify the sexual tensions already raised by the transvestism. First, Octavian is not exactly a boy. If he behaves like the childish Cherubino, he occupies the social role of the marriageable nobleman Ottavio. Octavian has not yet reached emotional maturity, but he has attained sexual maturity; Cherubino fantasizes about sex, but Octavian actually has sex. After the orchestral prelude in which Strauss depicts, quite literally, the sexual liaison between Octavian and the Marschallin, the curtain opens on them rolling out of bed. This opening scene precludes the possibility of completely equating Octavian and Cherubino. Even more, it places in immediate and intense focus the serious gender category crisis here by foregrounding the phallus that is not there, represented by the detachable sword. As in *opera seria, Rosenkavalier* foregrounds the leading singer's phallic lack.

This foregrounding continues throughout the opera, in the continued play with Octavian's sword,[20] and especially with the two Mozartean counter–cross-dressing scenes in Acts I and II. Just as Mozart and Da Ponte

put Cherubino in a dress to escape the wrathful Almaviva, Strauss and Hofmannsthal call further attention to the gender ambiguity by putting Octavian in skirts dressed as the maid Mariandl, pursued by the randy Baron
Ochs. But again, the twentieth-century work calls attention to its differences from the eighteenth-century model. Mozart's Cherubino makes an escape by dressing as a woman, but whereas *Nozze* uses this switching device
as a brief farcical moment, *Rosenkavalier* makes it the core of the opera's
subplot. Octavian spends fully half of the opera in women's clothes, most
of that time in direct sexual pursuit by Ochs. The gender play here flirts
with the edge of a Derridean abyss: a butch woman dressed as a man making love to a beautiful woman, then dressed as a caricatured woman fend-
ing off the sexual advances of an unattractive man, then falling in love with
another beautiful woman, ending with a sexually charged musical orgasm
for all three women, one back in male drag.

But even in the midst of this category crisis, audiences have willingly embraced *Rosenkavalier* and found a way to normalize its dizzying gender
play. The sexual free play energizes the opera, but we do not see Octavian
as a subversive drag role, primarily because of the historical distance provided by the period setting. The mask previously afforded by the figure of
the woman-as-boy now is provided by history.[21] *Rosenkavalier*'s persistent
popularity arises from the skillful game played by Strauss and Hofmannsthal, where they push sexual ambiguity to the edge of terror while
masking fear by maintaining a reliable safety line of historical distance to
protect the audience. Sexually, *Rosenkavalier* is opera's version of bungee-
jumping.

In their later works, Strauss and Hofmannsthal continue to experiment
with cross-dressing, most notably with the Composer in *Ariadne auf Naxos*
(and halfheartedly with Zdenka in *Arabella*). But after *Rosenkavalier,* they
no longer play these dangerous games and revert to cross-dressing as a conventionalized theatrical device. In *Rosenkavalier* Strauss takes the raw sexuality of *Salome* and *Elektra* and sublimates it within the elegant cloak of
eighteenth-century comedy of manners; *Ariadne* is merely the comedy of
manners without the sexual tension. The Composer is male here only because composers are supposed to be male, and the role goes to a mezzo to
blend with the dramatic soprano of Ariadne and the lyric soprano of Zerbinetta to perpetuate the vocal balance that Strauss employed so effectively in
Rosenkavalier. But *Ariadne* has no hint of the sexual tension that charges
the cross-gender casting of the earlier work. Even when the Composer toys
romantically with Zerbinetta, the effort seems mechanical, not erotic. I like
Ariadne very much, but, compared to *Rosenkavalier,* it is about as sexually
adventurous as *Hänsel und Gretel.*

After Strauss, few twentieth-century operas engage the erotics of eigh-
teenth- and nineteenth-century cross-dressing technique. Instead, rather

than an adult woman portraying a boy, recent opera more often will employ real boys for erotic purposes.[22] For example, Benjamin Britten, the most successful operatic composer after Strauss, frequently writes youthful male roles in the treble voice, not for adult women but for actual preadolescent male singers: Harry in *Albert Herring;* four fairies in *A Midsummer Night's Dream;* four boys in *Let's Make an Opera!;* four more in *Billy Budd;* several in the Church Parables; and especially Miles in *The Turn of the Screw.* Britten also gives us the silent youths John in *Peter Grimes* and the highly eroticized young dancer Tadzio in *Death in Venice.* And in *Midsummer,* besides the boy fairies, Puck is performed by a speaking boy actor while the adult Oberon sings in a ·countertenor range that·rivals Titania's. Britten also uses young girl singers, but not nearly so frequently as boys.[23]

The free-wheeling gender crisis induced by transvestism has inspired one more variation on operatic cross-dressing in the twentieth century: opera travesty, where male performers take on standard women's roles in a parody of opera. Charles Ludlam's Ridiculous Theatrical Company has performed several operatic drag parodies, but with a difference. Rather than men in dresses singing in falsetto to make opera look foolish, this kind of drag gets at the roots of opera's paradoxical gender stereotypes. By using mostly men to perform *Der Ring Gott Farblonget, Galas* (a thinly veiled parody of the life of Maria Callas), and *Camille* (nonmusical, but heavily indebted to *La Traviata*), Ludlam's plays challenge the assumptions about how gender roles pervade our assumptions about opera.[24] Similarly, the cross-dressed performers of the all-male company La Grand Scena subvert virtually every overblown convention in opera in their drag performances, but only because they know those conventions inside out.[25] By reversing the typical drag formula of opera, with men playing women's roles, travesty opera highlights the intensely erotic, and homoerotic, nature of opera, especially the allure of the grand diva.[26] When men enact the role of diva they redouble opera's sexual ambiguity, thrusting the invisible conventions of operatic drag into the spotlight.

Opera's uncanny ability to embrace and normalize drag performance gives me hope for the future of opera, especially in the postmodern context of late-twentieth-century performance. If opera seems like a dead, archaic form to so many people, it appears so only in the context of modernist, realistic standards of theatrical representation. If we hold realism as the ideal of performance, then opera, which has nothing to do with realism, has no place. But to a generation raised on MTV, where computer-generated virtual reality seems more real than reality itself, opera may once again have something to say. The gender-image overload generated by the castrati and the operatic transvestite function in much the same way as the visual-image overload of the rapid-fire music video. Like MTV, operatic drag normalizes subversion within a broader realm of sensual, eroticized display. It is only a short leap from Strauss and Hofmannsthal to the historical survey of drag roles performed by RuPaul and Elton John in their joint video rendition of "Don't Go Breakin' My Heart." If the subversive drag of RuPaul can find its way into mainstream popular discourse through MTV, then the transvestite category crisis of *Der Rosenkavalier* can still engage an audience, even today's media-raised generation.

11

OPERA THROUGH THE MEDIA

One group of records contained the closing scenes of a certain brilliant opera, overflowing with melodic genius. . . . Hans Castorp had learned something of the plot, knew the main lines of the tragic fate . . . he understood perhaps not every word they said, but enough, with his knowledge of the situation, and his sympathy in general for such situations, to feel a familiar fellow-feeling that increased every time he listened to this set of records, until it amounted to infatuation.

—Thomas Mann
The Magic Mountain[1]

Can opera fit into the home? Does opera disrupt home values? What happens when Adelina Patti's voice emerges from the furniture?

—Wayne Koestenbaum
The Queen's Throat[2]

Massive Media

In the last ten years or so, entertainment technology has grown so rapidly that the average consumer can barely keep pace with new developments. We've been thrown into amusement overload. The volume and diversity of these innovations have become so overwhelming that nostalgia for outdated technology has become a major growth industry. Now that I have finally managed to switch from vinyl LPs to CDs, I discover that I am supposed to adopt another new technology, Digital Audio Tape, which I must obtain lest I face the stigma of technological backwardness (so far I've held out, at least until the price drops). A composer friend of mine now works exclusively via computer, so that he becomes not only his own recording engineer but also the exclusive performer of his compositions. The college where I teach has recently added a master's degree program in electronic music. We can now talk back to the impassive television and craft our entertainment to suit our personal tastes. As I write this paragraph, the latest and by far the most frightening innovation is virtual reality, an all-encompassing multisensual environment that will envelop me so thoroughly that I will no longer be able to tell the difference between my life and performance. Virtual reality scares me not because I fear it will turn my life into a personal opera (I could live with that) but because I fear it will turn my life into a big, three-dimensional, shoot-'em-up video game.

Like opera, these innovations threaten me because they are both attractive and sensually enveloping. They have the appeal of new toys to small children, but with the added danger of keeping us permanently in their thrall; each new video game or expansion of our home-entertainment system means more time and money we must devote to its service. Like opera, entertainment technology is a powerful master, and also like opera, its appeal depends on the allure of embarrassing excess. We run to each new innovation, no matter how silly, with a strange combination of innocent curiosity and eroticized anticipation of pleasure. But these changes are hardly innocent; they profoundly affect the way we shape our lives and our perception of the world. The advent of electronic mail on my campus has eliminated the need for me to talk to anyone in person or over the telephone (and my students now turn in their papers via the computer, I correct them electronically, and send them back with comments over the wires); just so, the explosion of entertainment technology threatens to keep us in a state of artificially generated bliss that will eliminate all further need for human contact.

The most significant impact of the technology tidal wave on opera, as well as on other forms of live performance, comes in this aspect of mediated entertainment, its elimination of direct communication between human bodies. The whirlwind of high-technology games puts us in perpetual danger of forgetting the appeal of traditional nonmediated performance, in which performers and audience members occupy the same space at the same time. The more sensually involving technology becomes, the greater this threat looms. It is as if we were to allow our sex lives to be overwhelmed entirely by pornography and let the mediated version of our pleasure substitute for the reality of human contact. Certainly, there are people who live with this substitution, but something vital gets lost in the process. By obviating the traditional performer-audience dynamic that stands at the core of live performance, technology threatens to eliminate the fundamental purpose for opera's existence, the direct sensual appeal of sexually charged live performance.

More disturbingly, we seem not even to have noticed this loss, because of technology's ability to substitute for live interaction the illusion of an even more intimate contact. The most concrete appeal of live performance—the erotic interest of the spectator in the physically present body of the star—is subsumed by the prying camera, which, if it cannot get me near a live body, can at least generate the illusion that I am much closer to that body than live performance allows. Two-dimensional pictures replace three-dimensional bodies as the objects of my desire. If my emotional stake in opera depends so heavily on the sexual exchange between live bodies in the same space, what will happen as these bodies become ever more remote from my own body through the distancing of the media? What happens to the sexual dynamic of opera when it becomes a wholly mediated experience, when the bodies become merely an electronically generated image?

The question is especially acute for opera, because opera adapts much less easily to mediated performance than realistic prose theater. To go from the photographic realism of a standard Broadway drama to the actual photography of the film camera requires a comparatively small leap. A realistic play is essentially the same work on stage or on screen; both media ask the audience to make the same kinds of choices about sympathy and identification, and the realistic conventions of the fourth wall that distance the audience in live theater employ many of the same techniques as those by which film separates spectator and performer. But even the most firmly veristic opera connects with its audience in a way entirely different from film. The sympathy and identification games of realistic narrative have little to do with the way an audience responds to opera, and the fourth-wall distance of realism has no place in the erotic interaction of the audience with the singer's body. When opera moves into a mediated form, it changes in profound ways, especially in the physical response of the audience to the body of the singer.

Distant Voices

Nominally, live performance remains the paradigm for opera; radio and television broadcasts and many recordings tout themselves oxymoronically as "live" performances and even hold up that immediacy as a major selling point. But it is getting increasingly hard to justify live opera's continued claim to primacy. Today, audiences get their exposure to opera mostly in mediated form. Far more people, at least in the United States, listen to opera at home via recordings, television, and radio than attend opera in live performance. More fans may listen to a single Saturday afternoon broadcast from the Met than attend performances in that vast theater in a whole season. And even though the repertories of major houses like the Metropolitan continue to stagnate in the romantic era, the economics of mediated opera has allowed a revival of interest in long-forgotten works from earlier periods and has put contemporary opera in a concrete form from which it can eventually find an audience. In significant ways, opera via the media today is more important, more vital than opera done live.

But this shift toward mediated opera has a price. Prior to this century, the most important element of popular entertainment was size. The quality of a performance was measured by its scope, in the mode of P. T. Barnum. Opera fit this bill of epic scale to a tee. Everything about opera is big, and its hugeness was commensurate with popular taste. In the twentieth century, popular taste has shifted drastically: Everything must now be small, condensed, miniaturized. We still want epic productions but ones that we can put in our pocket through mediation. Instead of grandeur, we want accessibility. Opera, so monumental in scope, must downscale to the dimensions of the television screen. As technology has developed, this process has become the central trope of popular entertainment: taking huge things and making them ever smaller. We go from full-screen films to in-home video, from LPs to compact discs, mainframe computers to personal computers to laptops. Opera, to keep pace with this trend, has had to find ways to compress its vast scale into increasingly smaller forms in order to make itself marketable to the public via the media.

In reducing opera's size, mediation also reduces its capacity to command my attention. In the nineteenth century, if I wanted to learn an opera I would have to go to the opera house many times, listening intently to the work and following its story. I would also have to learn to read the score, perhaps playing it on the piano and attempting to sing it myself. A hundred years ago, I could not listen to opera casually. With the advent of electronic recording, however, I need make no particular commitment of time or effort to gain access to opera. All I have to do is buy it. I can simply throw a recording of *La Bohème* onto the stereo and listen to it while I make dinner. (I currently have Britten's *The Prodigal Son* playing, and I *really* should be listening to it more attentively.) Opera, divorced from the commitment of the listener, becomes a kind of background noise, devoid of the complex emotional and erotic engagement that characterizes opera in the theater. This familiarity, in turn, encourages me to perceive opera this way in the theater as well, so that I look at the proscenium arch as merely a gargantuan wide-screen television. Bit by bit, mediation makes me forget how to pay attention.[3]

But even as the easy access to technologically sophisticated (if not intellectually sophisticated) entertainment within the home poses an increasing threat to the grandeur and immediacy of live opera performance, this explosion of technology also makes opera vastly more accessible. If I cannot always to go to the opera house, prevented by distance or money (and what percentage of the population could ever afford to go?), I can turn on my radio on a Saturday afternoon and get the Metropolitan Opera in my living room, and for a much lower price. In a sense, the mediation of opera has brought it back to its popular impulses, made it more accessible and less daunting. The popular phenomenon of the Three Tenors concerts could only have happened through mediated performance. Wagner envisioned his music-drama as the theater of the common people, but the *Ring* has only found a popular audience on the scale Wagner imagined in recent years, removed from the intimidating trappings of the opera house (and its related expenses), placed instead in the familiar guise of the family TV set, with close-ups and easily readable subtitles. But if television finally gives Wagner the audience he wanted, he would hardly recognize the product as his own.

Mediation, then, creates another operatic paradox, by simultaneously bringing opera closer to its audience and further away from it. On the one hand, media puts opera at a distance; the event is not live, the performers are removed by both time and space, there is no group audience experience, sound and visual quality are artificially altered, and all sense of danger, the thrill that something might go wrong before my eyes and ears, is lost.[4] On the other hand, mediated opera can make me feel considerably more intimate with the work; I can see much more detail of facial expression than when I sit in the balcony of a cavernous opera house; I can set my home stereo to suit my individual taste for sound quality; I can follow the words more directly. More importantly, the mediated experience is—or seems— personal, a one-on-one interaction between me and the performer. My sexual fantasy has more freedom to wander around an image on a screen or a voice on a stereo than with a live body on stage when I am in the middle of a huge audience; and the privacy of my home allows me more behavioral leeway in responding to these fantasies. In the sexual free play of opera, mediated performance does not necessarily blunt sexual desire, but it certainly alters its form in fundamental ways.

Opera Without Pictures

Technology has had a profound impact on opera from the first days of the media explosion. The voice of Enrico Caruso was committed to records as early as 1902; these recordings soon became the most popular of the era, and they were in many ways responsible for the initial growth of the recording industry. If the popular mystique of Caruso as the greatest tenor of all time still lingers, it is largely due to the overwhelming impact of these recordings, in spite of their marginal sound quality (and sometimes less than stellar performances). Caruso on record was more than an opera star; he became an icon of desire. During Caruso's engagement with the Metropolitan in the early years of this century, he drew audiences of a size that no other singer could match.[5] The audience flocked to the theater because they anticipated hearing the voice they already knew on records; the audience had focused its erotic attention on a sound coming from a machine, and it expected the live voice in the opera house to imitate the reproduction.

The operatic voice projected over a loudspeaker wields a mysterious, almost unworldly power to attract the listener. Thomas Mann, toward the end of his metaphysical novel *The Magic Mountain,* introduces a Victrola into the strange world of the novel's Swiss tuberculosis sanatorium; it rapidly becomes more than mere entertainment, especially for the novel's hero, Hans Castorp. Castorp, who through the novel grows from a shallow youth into a profound observer of human nature, develops a growing fascination with the record player, especially with a recording of the final scenes of *Aïda.* Mann explains his hero's response as a kind of sympathy for the human condition, saying that he knows just enough of the opera's plot to discover a "familiar fellow-feeling" with the characters. But this sympathy is really an infatuation with the recording itself and its uncanny power to engage his emotions. Notably, Mann has Castorp stay up alone through the night playing opera recordings over and over again, in the same room that witnessed his earlier failed love affair with a mysterious woman. The Victrola becomes his sexual partner, his most successful love relationship in the novel.[6]

Desire in the opera house is a two-way erotic exchange between the singer and the audience, depending heavily on the audience's visual contact with the singer's body. But when the body of the singer disappears through mediation, via radio or recordings, the voice transforms from an integral part of a human body into an isolated object. The voice-object, rather than the embodied voice, becomes the erotic focus for the listener. In short, the mediated voice becomes a fetish, an object charged with erotic attractiveness. Without the presence of the singer's body to complicate things, the voice becomes abstracted, divorced from the complex psychological responses with which human bodies relate to each other, and so subject to the processes of fetishization that a live, whole human body is not. Rather than an exchange between my body and the singer's body, heightened by the presence of several thousand other bodies responding in similar ways, mediated opera becomes a private, personal sexual experience. A fetish requires no two-way erotic interchange; I do not expect a fetishized object to interact with me; I only want it to present itself for my contemplation. When I go to the opera house, the performance is a physical sex act between my body and the singer's voice-body. When I listen to an opera recording, the erotic experience becomes a private masturbation fantasy.[7]

When I listen to a recording, I feel no impulse to applaud at the end of the performance, as I do in the opera house. I have not engaged with the singer's body, and so I have built up no need to relieve the pressure of my physical desire through applause. Listening to the live radio broadcasts from the Met, even the diminished volume of applause—the sound engineers reduce the level to make room for the announcer's voice-over describing the curtain call—sounds strangely hollow and distant, entirely without the thrill that the same response generates when I am in the house applauding in person. Rather than a need for applause, at the end of a recording or radio broadcast performance I experience a sense of relief and completion—not a desire to perpetuate the erotic exchange through applause, but a feeling of closure. When I listen to the *Rosenkavalier* trio on record, I do not even feel a strong need to hear the opera out to the end; once I am past the peak erotic experience of the trio, I want to get on to other things in my life. (This desire is why recordings of opera "highlights"—collections of abstracted peak erotic moments—are so popular.)

Poizat's notion of operatic *jouissance* as pure voice, then, happens not in the opera house but only when the visual elements of opera disappear through mediation. What I feel toward the radio or a recording is an intense response to the details of the voice itself as an object, particularly in climactic musical moments. As with any fetishized object, small details of the voice-object take on disproportionately large significance. I pick out minute points of vocal interpretation, the differences between the way singers interpret a particular phrase or word, and the differences between different performances by the same singer. This kind of obsessive wrangling over interpretative minutiae pervades Koestenbaum's study of opera queens and forms the central issue of Act I of McNally's *The Lisbon Traviata,* in which Mendy and Stephen debate the relative merits of Callas's numerous performances of *La Traviata.* Such obsessive analysis becomes possible only through recording, partly because the recording allows more intimate study of the voice through repetition, but even more because the recording turns the voice into an object, distanced from the physical presence of the singing body.

Radio broadcasts and commercial recordings often attempt to compensate for the lack of the singer's physical presence in several ways, either with verbal descriptions of the opera or with photographs and drawings. The Texaco Metropolitan Opera broadcasts always include a physical description of the scenery and costumes, a practice that harks to the pretelevision days of radio, when listeners were encouraged to sit by their radios and use their imagination to create the missing visual element. To assist this process, *Opera News* publishes several key photographs of the opera being broadcast each week. Boxed sets of opera recordings sometimes include images of scenery and costumes, but more often they contain pictures of the singers themselves, mostly out of costume and in elegant concert clothing. If I cannot have the singer's body, I can at least have a picture to fuel my fantasies. But these pictures do not really compensate for the lack of the singer's body; they are, ultimately, irrelevant to the erotic process once the opera leaves the theatrical space. The visual images satisfy my curiosity, but they are not necessary to my fetishizing of the voice as object.

Wayne Koestenbaum takes his fetishizing of the singing voice one step further; he sexualizes not only the voice but the objects that produce the voice—his recordings and stereo equipment. He equates his desire to collect long-playing vinyl recordings with his sexual desire for other men:

> Yes, I fetishize records; and yes, I fetishize men's bodies, make a fetish
> out of groove and label and hole, spindle and turntable and speaker,
> credenza and box, and the hiss that precedes the moment of music, the
> unintended "click" that tells me the needle has found the first groove,
> and the song is about to start. . . . I loved the idea of opera before I
> loved opera: and what I loved, in this idea of opera, was the boxed set.
> . . . I wanted to own the boxes before I knew that opera was what the
> boxes contained. . . . I felt that boxed sets were waiting for me to dis-
> cover them, waiting for me to adore them.[8]

Koestenbaum eroticizes every physical object connected to opera recordings: not only the records themselves, but also the stereo and its spindle, the
album covers, old issues of *Opera News;* any object that partakes of the
mediated opera experience becomes sexually exciting. If he cannot get hold
of an actual opera or its performers, then he will shift his desire to the objects that represent or contain opera.

Opera recordings have one major advantage over opera live in the theater:
I can hold them in my hands and own them. Along these lines, opera proliferates eroticizable objects for its fans: books on opera (especially books with
lots of pictures), posters, programs (the larger the better—my La Scala program, an actual hardbound book, is the best one I own), autographed pho-
tos of opera stars, souvenir T-shirts, mugs, calendars, postcards, anything by
which I can acquire a concrete piece of the opera experience. Major opera
houses all have gift shops, which thrive on hoards of fans looking for objects
to fetishize. I get particularly excited about things from European opera
houses, which I can imbue with an extra degree of erotic exoticism (besides
using them to prove that I was there). All of these objects function as an extension of the eroticized voice-object, physical things, all more tangible than
the voice itself, upon which to project my desire.

But opera recordings surpass all of these toys, because the recording is
an object that will actually create the erotic experience. I invest a remarkable degree of emotional energy in opera recordings (not to mention a remarkable amount of money). When trying to impress house guests, the
first thing I do is show off my wall of over 1,000 CDs, mostly opera sets.
Opera recording companies buy into this fetishizing process unashamedly.
The illustrations on the covers of these boxes are heavily eroticized, with
alluring pictures of the stars featured prominently.[9] These illustrations are
one reason (besides years of erotic investment) why opera fans who grew
up on vinyl are the last of the die-hards, fighting fiercely to hold onto their
old recordings: LPs may be clunky and collect dust, but they have much
bigger pictures than CDs. If opera without pictures distances me from the
singer's body, it gives me any number of other objects to satisfy my sexual
desires.

Pictures Without Opera

In the performance of Verdi's *Il Trovatore* that ends the Marx Brothers spoof *A Night at the Opera,* I don't get to hear much of the opera, only some phrases of the overture, snatches of a few of the more famous arias, and a little of the gypsy dancing. But if I don't hear much, I do get to see a great deal—too much, in fact. I see not only the scenes that I'm supposed to see, but everything that I'm not supposed to see as well: the comic antics in the orchestra pit, in the loges, in the wings, in the fly space. The camera violates the conventions of traditional opera by entering forbidden territory, just as the transgressive tomfoolery of Chico, Harpo, and Groucho violate opera's self-important pretensions. The Marx Brothers camera intrudes opera's sacred spaces, and I laugh because I know the camera is showing me things I'm not supposed to see.

The camera that films a serious opera event, though less obviously obtrusive, also violates opera's visual norms. In the theater, opera does not allow me to get as close to the action as the camera does. If opera on radio and record removes the visual, opera on film and television makes the visual the central element of the performance. I get to see the singers at close range, sometimes idealized in a Hollywood vision of perfection, at other times without the glamorous filter, sweating, panting, and much less pretty than when they remain at a distance. The scale of the performer shifts as well, the singing body occupying virtually all of the visual space, rather than framed by a huge proscenium and scenery. Through the agency of the camera, the visual comes close to overwhelming the musical altogether. Film relegates music to the background; repeated filmgoing trains us to ignore the sound track. The balance between auditory and visual stimuli provided by physical distance in the theater gets lost when the camera virtually crawls down the throats of the singers, and the orchestra, instead of standing between me and the singers as a constant physical presence, disappears into the sound track (except for the occasional moments when, in a video recording of a live performance, the camera chooses to show the orchestra). The immediacy of the visual image takes over the performance.

In a sense, then, opera on television and film is not opera at all; it is instead a kind of realistic theater with music. The video medium does not merely transfer the opera to a different form intact; the camera radically shifts the way we read operatic narrative. In the opera house, I need not pay much attention to the story line; the physical presences of the singing bodies allow me to engage erotically with the performers and bypass the narrative altogether, if I so desire. But the narrative becomes harder to ignore on film and television. The conventions of film highlight storytelling, so that every aspect of the visual representation reinforces the words. (For example, in Zeffirelli's film version of *Otello,* in the Act I love duet, rather than Otello describing his heroic exploits, they are enacted visually.) Even more directly, the subtitles make me pay more attention to the words. In the opera house I can let the text drop out of my perception; on screen I almost have no choice but to follow the story word for word. All of the sympathy and identification games that realistic film and theater expect me to play, and which opera in the theater problematizes, return full force when opera transfers to the screen.

On film, opera's sensual excesses become so realistic that they no longer seem excessive. Tosca can actually leap from the top of the Castel Sant'Angelo; Violetta can really inhabit nineteenth-century salons. The visual anomalies, especially those of the singer's body, that I have to work to ignore on the stage can often be erased, or at least minimized, on film. Zeffirelli makes remarkably lavish opera both live and on film, but, unlike his productions in the opera house, on film the lavishness becomes subsumed within the historical frame and the realism of photography. He selects singers who are particularly suited to the romantic character stereotypes; thus, he casts Teresa Stratas as Violetta in his film of *La Traviata,* a singer small and gaunt in her own right, made to seem even more so by makeup and lighting, in order to make Violetta's death from consumption much more plausible than is usually the case on the stage.[10] Operas on film work the same way as do the Hollywood epics of Cecil B. DeMille: they overwhelm the audience with their scope, but at the same time they convince us that the spectacle is to be accepted as reality.

In order to compensate for this realism, and the subsequent loss of direct erotic contact with the singer's body, opera films often consciously magnify the narrative's sexual elements. Zeffirelli plays this game in his rendition of Verdi's *Otello.* He minimizes the more static and pathetic scenes (for example, he excises Desdemona's Willow Song from the last act), and he interpolates scenes into the film's more overtly thrilling or erotic moments. Besides the battle scenes during the love duet, Zeffirelli adds a controversial scene to the point in Act II when Iago describes Cassio's supposed dream of Desdemona. In this scene—which, of course, Iago invents to rouse Otello's jealousy—Zeffirelli dissolves to an image of Cassio in bed, lying on his back, dreaming of Desdemona. Not only does Zeffirelli show Cassio as being sexually aroused, but he is pretty clearly masturbating, though the camera places his crotch conveniently outside the frame. Zeffirelli leaves nothing to the imagination here. If the film prevents sexual connection with the singer's body, it makes up for it with direct erotic enactment.

Other opera films use similar techniques. Rosi amplifies the overt sexuality in his film version of *Carmen.* He casts as Carmen the very seductive Julia Migenes-Johnson, who heightens her eroticism by lifting her skirts and rubbing her thighs at key moments. Unlike most stagings of the opera, the film provides concrete suggestions of sexual activity between Carmen and José. Joseph Losey's film of *Don Giovanni* is also intensely eroticized, though with techniques somewhat less blatant than those Zeffirelli and Rosi employ. Losey provides Giovanni with a body double, a shadowy figure who appears on the edges of the action, a kind of evil genius for the Don's lustful plans. This shadow figure adds to Giovanni's sexual mystique and connects him more directly with sin and the devil than the opera usually does. Also of particular note here is the staging of Leporello's list aria; instead of the typical book or several-foot-long scroll used on stage, Losey uses the freedom of the camera to make the list of unbelievable length; as Leporello reads it out, the scroll unwinds endlessly, out the door, down the steps, into the garden, a simultaneously comic and frightening image of the endlessness of Giovanni's lust, and, metaphorically, of the length of his penis.[11]

Televised "live" opera performances (these are rarely really live, as the PBS "Live from Lincoln Center" title implies, but are rather edited compilations of several performances recorded well in advance) work rather differently than these filmed operas, negotiating a strange compromise between mediated and unmediated performance. They do not function realistically in the same way that opera on film does. The broadcast maintains the illusion of a live performance by recording a performance in its actual venue and keeping changes in staging to a minimum (normally just changing light levels for the cameras). But, of course, the television experience is entirely unlike going to the theater. The camera directs the attention of the audience in ways that might not happen at all with the live audience. The camera also magnifies elements of the staging that are not nearly so visible in the vast auditorium of the Met. What looks good on a live stage does not always look as good when seen through a television camera. A camera close-up shows what the live audience is too far from the stage to see: that the costumes may be fraying at the seams; that the singers sweat profusely; that they wear extremely heavy makeup; that they can't act very well. An overweight singer on television much more obviously violates a character's stereotypical image than the same singer in person at a distance.

All of these factors, of course, tend to diminish the romantic ideal of the performance. If opera "live" on television has widened the popular audience for opera, it has also left the impression with that audience that opera is nothing very special. The televised performance, by reducing opera's scale, assures the audience that they have nothing to fear from opera.[12] But in reducing its potential terror, television also deprives opera of its erotic edge. If film turns opera into a Hollywood epic, television turns opera into a nighttime soap opera, a lurid melodrama where the actors happen to be singing along with the sound track. By eliminating the distance of the opera house, the television camera makes opera look just a little silly, and therefore harmless. By defusing its erotic terrors, the camera may make opera more accessible and popular, but it also derails opera's central power as a performance genre.

Which brings me back to *A Night at the Opera.* The first scene from *Il Trovatore* that we see in the film is the opening of Act II, with the gypsies around the campfire listening to Azucena singing "Stride la vampa." The staging is classic, the low-voiced gypsy mother portrayed as a mannish old hag. But the camera comes in closer than I care to get to this horror; I can see her too-heavy makeup and the absurd stereotyping of her character. Just at the point when the camera's intimacy gets a little too much to take, the scene cuts to Groucho watching from his box. I become Groucho; his eyes are mine. He takes one look at the scene, finds it as repulsive as I do, and, with a squiggle-fingered gesture using both hands to cast an evil spell on the foolish scene, he says, "Boogie, boogie." I scream with laughter. All he has done is give voice to the stereotype, saying only what I already know. But the laws of opera tell me that I shouldn't point out the stereotypes or get too close to them. Groucho breaks the rules and I collapse in laughter—but only because the camera, by letting me see the opera stage up close while remaining physically outside of it, permits me to step back from my engagement with the singers. The camera lets me off the hook.

Invading the House

Radio, recordings, film, and television all separate opera from the site of live performance. But technology has not remained exclusively outside of the theater. Increasingly over the last few years, technological innovations have found their way into the live performance space itself, leading to intense and often vitriolic controversies. Many opera fans who support broadcast opera and recordings vehemently oppose any introduction of electronic mediation into the theater space itself. The media may appropriate opera performance and modify it in any number of ways, but opera on radio, recording, film, and television is distinct from opera performed live in the opera house; the original remains intact, even if at a considerable distance from most of the audience. I may not get the experience of live opera when I listen to the Met on radio, yet at least I know that someone is. But when mediation enters the sacred space of the theater itself, the fundamental experience of live performance becomes threatened. Can the interaction of human bodies in opera, with its complex balance of desire and fulfillment, survive the addition of supertitles, amplification, and other technologies in the performance space itself? Or do these innovations turn the theater into merely a more complex version of big-screen television?

What many people find so disturbing about technology in the opera house is its invisibility. Often, the technology involves small modifications in the performance, which do not call attention to themselves. When I listen to a recording or see an opera on film, I begin with a full awareness of the technological mediation, and I can modify my expectations accordingly. But if, for example, a singer with a weak voice wears a body microphone, and the voice is bolstered through the subtle use of amplification, I may remain entirely unaware of the mediation. I have, in a sense, been cheated, made to believe that the singer has more power and erotic appeal than he or she actually has. To return to the analogy of pornography, it is as if a porn star has used extra padding or trick lenses to create a sense that there is more to certain key parts than actually exists. In a porn film, I expect such tricks. But in a live strip show, I want to see the real thing, and I feel cheated when smoke, mirrors, and rolled-up socks replace reality. Similarly, in the opera house, if I am going to expend my erotic energy on the performance, I want to know that the object of my desire can really deliver the goods.

Of course, the theater has always used technological tricks to mask the inadequacies of its stars. Carefully applied makeup and artistic lighting effects can enhance the facial beauty of the singer and make old divas seem youthful. Costumes with yards of flowing fabric frequently hide a star's unsightly obesity. The simple fact of physical distance in a large house serves to diminish the physical failings of the singers. But we generally draw the line at the voice. We will accept any remodeling of the body, as long as the sounds coming out of that body have the ring of authenticity. The voice eroticizes the singing body; the voice induces in the audience the opera's moments of orgasmic climax. If the voice's power is not legitimate, then there is virtually no difference between the live voice and the recorded voice. Or, rather, once we discover that we have been fooled, we *believe* that there is no difference, and so no reason to come to the opera house.

It is particularly interesting to see the vehemence with which opera audiences resist electronic modification of the singer's voice, since this practice is now widespread in the Broadway musical theater. Electronic mediation and miked singers came to the Broadway stage in the late 1960s, with the advent of the first rock musicals, but now every commercial musical uses sophisticated sound mixing equipment in the theater. Broadway audiences have not heard a live singing voice for years. Done well, the effects can be relatively unobtrusive. Done poorly, the effects can be disastrous, or at least intensely disconcerting (as when, as is often the case, the singing body appears on one side of the stage and the singer's voice emerges from the other side or from another part of the theater altogether). But the audience of a Broadway musical can forgive these sins more easily than the opera audience. The musical relies far more heavily on the conventions of realistic narrative theater than does opera, and so it does not depend on the same kind of obsessive eroticizing of the voice. The Broadway musical (with the exception of some works by Bernstein and a few others) does not induce many musical orgasms. On Broadway, we want a spectacle, with all available means of amplification in its service. In the opera house, we want the eroticized voice, and we want it real.[13]

Other than sound modification, the most popular, widespread, and controversial innovation in opera has been the addition of projected supertitles (usually on the upper proscenium arch) so that the audience can understand operas sung in a language that it does not speak. There has been extensive debate about the use of these titles; some companies, such as New York City Opera, have embraced them, whereas others, notably the Met, have (at least until recently) firmly resisted the trend. Experts debate at length about the most unobtrusive way to project titles while still making them easily available to the audience: Should they be projected high on the proscenium, or just above the scenery? Should they be on screens on the backs of the seats, with the option for individual viewers to turn them off? How bright should they be?[14] More important than all of these questions, though, is the effect that projected titles have on the experience of the opera itself. What happens to the response of the operagoer when meaning-bearing language becomes separated from the body that is supposed to be the source of that language?

On the surface, supertitles in the house have the same impact as subtitles in film. When I can understand every word of the dialogue, the narrative grows in importance. As in film and television, the addition of supertitles makes the experience of opera much more like realistic theater, and there is a greater tendency to engage in identification and sympathy games than in a normal opera performance. But the case of supertitles is more complicated, because, unlike film subtitles, supertitles in opera occur in a separate field of vision. In film, I can read the subtitles and still keep my eye on the action. In the opera house, if I want to look at the titles, I must take my gaze off of the singer, especially if I am sitting toward the front of the house. When I attend a performance with supertitles, I feel as if I am at a tennis game, with my focus constantly shifting back and forth from stage to titles. This bifurcated field of vision, besides being rather annoying, disrupts the eroticizing of the singer's body through my gaze. Supertitles force me into a choice between looking at the singer or following the words.

In the heated debate over supertitles, there is a widespread and problematic assumption that we, in fact, want to understand all of the words of the performance. But, as I have argued, the most powerful impact opera has on its audience is sensual and erotic, not verbal and intellectual. It does not hurt to know all the words the characters are singing, but it is not a necessary part of the opera experience. The problem comes when, as is often the case with supertitles, the presence of projected words actively disrupts the contact between stage and audience. Not only do the titles prevent me from looking at the singer; they also disrupt my ability to listen to the music. If I look up every ten seconds during an aria to catch the words—and I tend to do this when supertitles are present, even when I know the aria word for word in the original language—then I lose track of the climactic build of the music. Listening to an orgasmic aria with projected supertitles is like having sex with the television on: It not only distracts you from the business at hand but it can disrupt and prevent the possibility of the orgasmic climax altogether.[15]

Other technological innovations in the opera house are less controversial and also less clear in their ultimate impact on the opera experience. Technological innovations in scenery have been with opera from the beginning; indeed, most advances in techniques for changing scenery since the seventeenth century have originated in opera. The scenic wonders of Philip Glass and David Henry Hwang's *The Voyage,* or the elevator spectacles of Zeffirelli, or any number of recent opera stagings by Robert Wilson represent only the latest applications of modern scenic technology that threaten, temporarily, to overwhelm the music with their impact.[16] Ultimately, as with any scenic innovations, audiences quickly assimilate the wonders, and the balance of effects returns. Some operas, such as Dominick Argento's *The Dream of Valentino,* have incorporated film and video into their stagings, though this practice dates back at least to Berg, who employs a film scene in *Lulu.*[17] And in *The Cave,* composer Steve Reich and video artist Beryl Korot have created a work incorporating a coordinated performance of instrumental musicians, singers, and video that, for lack of any other available genre classification, most critics called an opera.[18] Technology has pushed the definitional bounds of opera in ways that challenge our entire perception of the medium.

I am deeply afraid to predict where the media will take opera in the next decades. Things are moving too fast to begin to know what will happen. I can imagine some possibilities: holographic performance; personal audio systems in the opera house; or even interactive opera in virtual reality, where I can become Rodolfo or Mimi myself.[19] There is already opera karaoke, where I can pretend to be able to sing a role with a recorded orchestral background. But I still cling desperately to the notion that, no matter how widely mediated opera becomes, nothing will replace traditional live performance altogether, at least not for a while. No amount of mediated opera gives me the thrill I get from a single live performance. Human nature being what it is, the simple notion of being in the same place as a star-level opera singer will drive people relentlessly to the opera house, to capture a moment of stardom themselves. I also like to think that as live opera becomes a smaller and smaller percentage of all opera performance, its very rarity will keep it alive. A few live opera performances can infuse all of mediated opera with excitement. My greatest fear is that technology will price live opera out of the market, that opera through the media will become so accessible, and opera on the stage so prohibitively expensive, that the weight of economics will drive out even the most powerful desire for erotic fulfillment with the body of the singer. If there is one thing that can kill the joy of sex, it's unpleasant worries about money. I desperately hope that live opera does not become an erotic pleasure I cannot afford to enjoy.

12

THE END OF OPERA

*Given its centrality in the manipulation of affect, social formation, and
the constitution of identity, music is far too important a phenomenon
not to talk about, even if the most important questions cannot be defin-
itively settled by means of objective, positivistic methodologies. For
music is always a political activity. . . .*

—Susan McClary
Feminine Endings[1]

The Grand Finale

The best part of an opera is the ending. True to its melodramatic impulses
(and "melodrama" really only means "drama with music"), opera builds
inexorably toward its final moment, when the overwhelming crisis of the
story finally gets resolved, either in triumph or in death. This kind of last-
minute resolution often does not characterize spoken theater, which frequently takes time for philosophical speculation or a few final jokes after
the narrative concludes. The two most thrilling moments of Sophocles's
Oedipus the King, the scenes when the narrative comes to its climax, are
the revelation of Oedipus's incestuous and murderous past and his subsequent self-blinding, but there is quite a bit of the play to get through after
these climaxes. Shakespeare spends a few dozen lines of dialogue musing
on the deaths of Hamlet and Lear, on the marriages of Beatrice and
Benedick and Rosalind and Orlando, while tying up the last remaining
threads of the narrative. But operas, especially romantic operas with tragic
endings, more typically wait until the very last moment to reach their peak.
Tosca sails off her parapet; José rids himself of Carmen; Butterfly stabs herself; Isolde consummates her love; Gilda dies in Rigoletto's arms, and he be-
moans his cursed fate: Whatever the details, the most thrilling point of the
narrative tends to happen within the last bars of the music.

But beyond the obvious climax of the narrative, the final notes are the most thrilling of the evening specifically because they are the final notes. At this moment the opera reveals its true relationship with the audience. The fictional narrative disappears, leaving only the underlying sexual narrative, the erotic negotiations that have been happening all evening between the bodies on either side of the proscenium. When we hear the notes that lead up to the final cadence the tension in the audience rises noticeably, not only because the heroine is about to die but because we in the audience know we must soon play our part and perform our approval back to the stage. The final bars leading up to the coda tell us that the end is approaching. We have a few moments to build our expectation for the last note, to anticipate our cue, and to prepare our response. Such anticipatory moments happen at the end of every set aria and each act, but they happen most powerfully at the end of the performance, when we know the fictional frame will not return, when we will be left alone to consummate our relationship with the performers. The ending of the opera reveals the end of opera, its ultimate purpose in our aesthetic and social lives.

In the realistic spoken theater, the endings of plays create definite lines of demarcation. The last moments of a play do not invite the audience to continue its participation in the event, nor does a play help us anticipate its last moments. A dramatic text offers few signals that say with precision when the final moment will come. Unlike opera, the last line of a play comes as something of a surprise. The ending of a realistic play disengages us from the spectacle, tells us firmly that the story is over and that we should no longer worry about the characters on the stage, nor about the actors. Notably, many performances of realistic drama end not with the curtain falling but with the lights going out, either in an instantaneous blackout or a slow fade. The fictional world of the play literally disappears when the narrative ends, vanishes palpably from before our eyes. The lights go to black, the play recedes from view, and when the lights come back on, we have returned to the "real" world. We are asked to stop suspending our disbelief, to acknowledge the actors for their work, and then to go home and return to our normal lives.

In opera, on the other hand, the final note does not produce the same feeling that the performance has concluded. The curtain comes down, but the lights that illuminate the singers and scenery usually stay on, implying that the world behind the curtain still exists. Unlike the blackout of the realistic drama, in opera the performance does not literally disappear. Instead, the curtain sweeps down, covering the spectacle momentarily from our vision, rising again to reveal a tableau, or parting slightly to allow the singers to emerge for their curtain calls. The opera's grandly decorated curtain plays with the audience a variation of Freud's *fort/da* game, a teasing peekaboo that hides the eroticized spectacle from our eyes, a spectacle we gleefully expect to return, as indicated by our applause and cheers. When the show does, inevitably, return, we redouble the volume of our response, just as the child does when the parent's face emerges from the covering cloth. The singers leave and return again and again, replaying the *fort/da* tease to the increasing thrill of the audience.[2]

The last notes do not place a frame around the opera; instead they induce a crisis of uncertainty and possibility for the audience. They dare us to blur the lines between opera and "reality." The audience often has considerable difficulty negotiating these last moments of the performance. Most often the applause begins too soon, the moment the curtain begins to fall but before the music is actually over. The anticipatory tension of the final moment is too great, someone starts to clap, and the rest of us follow, overwhelming the last notes with our applause. Or there is an uncomfortable silence after the music ends before someone begins the applause, a situation that often happens when the opera does not end with a loud bang or when the piece is unfamiliar. In both of these cases, the line that separates the performance from reality is unclear; the fictional world of the opera and the "real" world of the audience intrude upon one another. These moments represent a crisis of shifting categories: our uncertainty about how to deal with the transition from fiction to reality. As the opera drops its narrative, as Carmen ceases to be Carmen and rises from the dead in the persona of a famous singer, we in the audience must redefine our relationship to the stage. But unlike the spoken theater, opera does not set up a clear line for this transition; it defies us to let the fiction bleed outside the narrative frame. Our anticipatory energy for the final moment spills beyond the end of the narrative, into the curtain call and still beyond. Such crises do not happen in mediated opera, where the endings are as solidly framed as in the spoken theater and where Carmen will stay resolutely within the television screen, dead. Only when live bodies are present does the operatic ending force a crisis of negotiation between opera and the real world.

But, as Marjorie Garber argues, category crisis is itself erotic. The sexual excesses that opera presents throughout its performance, and which play on opera's wide range of erotic ambiguities—cross-dressing, the seductive duet, the musical orgasm—get thrown into a whole new level of crisis by the ending. The last moments of the opera and the curtain call that follows serve only to intensify the ambiguities of the performer-audience relationship. The standard Broadway musical always has a grand finale; the show has to go out with a bang, providing a sensual climax of singing, dancing, and scenic spectacle. The Broadway finale is erotic, but it also gives the sense of a definitive ending to the performance. But an opera, no matter how climactic the finale, never really ends. The last moments of the opera spill injudiciously outside the frame of the narrative, outside the frame of the opera house itself. Opera provides such a powerful sexual lure, because the ending of the opera never lets us disengage from the performance entirely, and we are never quite certain how to deal with the leftover sexual ambiguities and excesses. The power of operatic discourse—the end of its sexual politic—arises from its challenge to the sharp demarcations we posit between art and life. For the opera fan, as Koestenbaum argues, opera *is* life.

The Postmodern Paradox

Because it refuses to come to a definitive ending, because it defies clearly defined frames of erotic reference, opera is, arguably, the quintessential postmodern art form. Opera's sexuality permits multiple readings more readily than realistic theater, and it resolves less often to a single, unambiguous vision of "reality" for the audience to accept. Opera, the most stolid and traditional of the performing arts, the genre that clings to its past most desperately, becomes, in the light of contemporary postmodern analysis, also the genre most in tune with current artistic sensibilities: a postmodern paradox. Opera has become postmodern because of its efforts to stay resolutely premodern in the face of encroaching modernism. On the sexual plane, opera offers an endless string of possible interpretations, each validated by the sensibility brought to it by the audience of the moment. The further contemporary society travels in time from opera's historical roots, the more eighteenth-century rationalism and nineteenth-century romanticism become remote and inexplicable to us, the more this disjuncture appears, and the more postmodern opera becomes.

Opera in the late twentieth century has an advantage over spoken theater in playing the postmodern game. Realistic theater is stuck resolutely in modernism; the linear narrative of realism expects unified readings from its audience, marked by clear points of identification and sympathy. Realism tells us how to read its images and expects us to follow its univocal vision of reality without protest. Realism never intrudes upon the ambiguities of reality. But opera, clinging so tenaciously to the traditions of a past in which a modern audience has little investment, makes fewer coercive demands than realism and opens the possibility of multiple representations. Opera can be both straight and queer, normative and subversive, serious and camp, all in the same moment. Even more, it can transcend these simple binary divisions, through its undifferentiated paneroticism. Opera has always banked on its potential for multiple visions, but the inexorable retreat of realistic theater behind the formidable frames of the proscenium and the camera, and the subsequent disengagement of live bodies from the audience, make the open-ended sexual tensions of opera all the more visible and significant.

Opera not only refuses to represent a single vision of reality for the audience; it also evades a single representation of itself within critical literature.

Opera will not sit still for our definition. Since its earliest days, opera has eluded the efforts of critics who want to give it a solid, unambiguous genre label. Whether approaching opera from an Aristotelian or a Newtonian desire to categorize, modernist critics have never found an adequate answer to the vexing question of what, exactly, opera *is*. Is it *really* music? Is it *really* drama? Is it a hybrid genre that partakes of both forms? Is it a category unto itself? Which camp in the academic community "owns" opera? This debate began with the earliest discussions of the Florentine Camerata when they invented the form, and in the subsequent four hundred years no one has yet come up with a satisfactory solution to the problem, though the issue continues to rage unabated in the critical literature.[3]

But blame for the failure to define opera's genre status does not lie with the critics. Opera cannot be placed within a single genre definition, because opera transgressively defies definitional boundaries. Opera is, in Garber's terminology, the "third thing," the embodiment of category crisis that refuses to fit into binary genre definitions.[4] Opera is a crossover form, not in that it embodies a clearly defined genre situated between two already existing genres, but because it refuses the concept of genre classification altogether. Opera performs, to borrow Garber's analysis, a kind of aesthetic transvestism, embodying one genre while wearing the aesthetic trappings of another, never admitting which is its "real" self. Opera entices us and maddens us by its refusal to stand still for our contemplation. Like the photon, the unit of light in quantum physics that is sometimes a wave and sometimes a particle, as soon as you think you know what opera is, it becomes something else. This postmodern elusiveness stands at the core of opera's endless fascination and fuels its powerfully ambiguous eroticism. And opera, in its position as the "third thing," the elusive undefinable other, wields great powers of cultural production, powers that make it a foundation for the very possibility of cultural production.[5]

It is hardly surprising, then, that so many contemporary performance artists have begun to work in operatic or quasioperatic forms in their attempts to break free of traditional genre boundaries. Nor is it surprising that the most vibrant postmodern staging experiments have appeared in opera rather than in spoken theater. This postmodern defiance of categories also explains the recent explosion of critical interest in opera, especially among contemporary literary theorists. The union of music and text in performance creates a space of ambiguity, a field where meaning can shift and slip, where the emotional and the logical can clash and unite with alarming ease. Music in the theater disarms me, makes me more willing to accept ideas and feelings that my more logical mind resists. Music makes theater dangerous. The people who invented realism believed wholeheartedly in the concepts of logic and Newtonian physics, formulas that applied to the world a century ago. Those simple linear formulas no longer describe the world in the late twentieth century. If theater wants to continue to speak to a paradoxical world, then it needs to embrace the postmodern paradoxes of opera.

I have always thought that realism in the theater never had much of a future. Realism on stage is too transparent, too accessible. Realism works on film and television, because these artificial modes of mediation keep everything at a distance. They leave a gap between the real and the artificial that retains some of the mystery of performance. But live theater needs something more than literal representation to make it interesting. For the stage to capture my erotic interest, I need mystery and ambiguity and paradox. I need men dressed as women and women dressed as men; I need verse and metaphor; I need people to sing. (Is it accidental that the historically acknowledged periods of high tragedy—Classical Greece and Elizabethan England—both filled their theater with music, dance, verse, and drag?) If live performance wants a running chance to compete with the current media and entertainment explosion, it had best grow beyond realism, which mediated performance does so much better than live performance. Many opera critics—notably Koestenbaum—assert that opera has reached its end as an art form. But opera has died only within the standards of older criteria. Opera is not dead; it is, I would argue, the most viable form of live performance in the foreseeable future.

In this crazy world at the turn of the millennium, where religious fundamentalists do battle with pornography for my attention on consecutive cable-TV channels, opera plays both ends of the sexual spectrum. Opera poses as the bastion of traditional images of gender and sexuality, the last refuge for the eighteenth- and nineteenth-century views of the moral order. It appears as a safe haven for the elite who feel threatened by the seemingly unstoppable tide that threatens to undermine their social and political power. It wears the mask of moral simplicity, showing a world where I can pretend that the good are rewarded and the evil punished. But under its mask, opera is, as it always has been, the site for remarkable levels of sexual transgression. The sexual order of opera is a very thin illusion, the most fragile of Apollonian shells over a churning Dionysian well of chaotic sensuality, a shell that disintegrates as soon as I begin to test its viability. Even more, opera seems perpetually drawn in two opposing directions, yet it simultaneously refuses to be bound into this binarism. It claims chastity and purity, and it teases me with overt sexuality and decadence, but it is both, and it is neither. Opera spins in a whirlpool of sexual chaos.

But was chaos ever made more attractive? Chaos frightens with its threat of the dark abyss, but it can also reveal remarkable beauties. Chaos means lack of control, but it also means sensual abandonment. The color images of fractal clusters, those excruciatingly detailed, infinite regressions of patterns within patterns in James Gleick's 1987 best-seller *Chaos*, display a stunning, hypnotic beauty.[6] They look like the exquisite baroque details on a period costume. They look, in fact, as if they belong on the opera stage. Only the barely controlled sexual chaos of opera can fully embody the terrifying beauty of the erotic. The orgasm is a moment of chaos, a loss of reason, a plunge into the abyss. Opera makes the orgasm palpable; it turns sexual oblivion into art. Opera lets me taste the moment of chaos, then it rescues me at the end and returns me to a world—a less satisfying world— where things once again seem to make sense. But opera never completes that transition, and in its frenzy of unbounded eroticism, I can take some of that chaos back with me to the "real" world, even after the performance ostensibly has ended.

Opera, Sex, and Reality

By spilling outside the frame of the opera house, operatic sex challenges the very concept of "real" sex. Opera defies me to compare my private sex life with its public eroticism and to ask which is more "real," which is more potent. Operatic sex is not like sex in the bedroom. Sexual relations between human bodies can never embody the monumentality of operatic sex, but at the same time operatic sex can never embrace the intimacy of sex in the bedroom. As I listen in the audience, operatic sex stands apart from me, touching my body only through sound waves and visual stimuli sent from a distance. But its distance is also its power. Opera performs its sexual acts with thousands of bodies at the same time and induces orgasmic fulfillment on a scale impossible for my individual body. My desire for opera's superhuman sexual power forces me to reevaluate my own abilities to give and receive erotic pleasure. If opera causes physical revulsion in so many people, perhaps it is because opera's excessive sexuality is too powerful, too serious a challenge to their own sexual powers, too serious a challenge to their received notions about "real" sex.

But then, superhuman sex always seems more erotic than sex in the bedroom, the fantasy more stimulating than the practice. If opera challenges my notion of sexual reality, its fictional frame lets me believe that it is not reality. Just as the partially clothed body, held just out of reach, teases my erotic imagination more than a fully nude body within my grasp, opera, with its distant, extreme sexuality, feeds my imagination more powerfully than more directly physical sexual activities. Even more, I never get the postclimactic letdown that biological sex invariably involves; I never have to make opera breakfast in the morning or hold a conversation with it. Opera is the ideal lover, because it never makes demands on me (or makes only demands of a fiscal nature, which I willingly offer). Like Mendy in *The Lisbon Traviata,* opera provides me with a sexual refuge from the demands of human relationships.

But I cannot live like Mendy. I do not want opera's crisis of sexual reality to overwhelm my ability to engage in sex in the bedroom. I refuse to limit my definition of reality to one world or the other. I will not sacrifice either version of sex, neither the intimacy of human relationships nor the remote intensity of operatic relationships. I want everything, every kind of reality. Opera's postmodern refusal of binary categories teaches me to expand my definition of "real" sexuality. I'll take my lover to the opera, but I also want him real and warm in bed next to me in the morning. Koestenbaum might argue that I am not a full-fledged member of the opera-queen cadre, that my desire for a physical, functional sex life in the bedroom precludes my complete devotion to opera. But I see no reason why I can't have both operatic sex and biological sex, no reason why I should not let the two versions of sexual reality spill into one another and reinforce each other's pleasure.

Opera wields its powerful sexual reality over me, but I can avoid being overwhelmed by its force with a simple realization: Sexually, opera needs me as much as I need opera. Opera's sexual power becomes meaningless without an erotic object. Painting and sculpture can survive through the centuries with a casual audience. Visual art has the patience to sit still in a museum, waiting for its occasional admirers, content with a passive, contemplative relationship with its audience. Visual art can live with a few devotees and a small but steady tourist trade. A loudly appreciative crowd in a museum feels wrong, because visual art is shy. But brazen opera needs a crowd of screaming fans. It needs my passion to respond to its seduction. Opera is about public display, and public display needs an audience. An exhibitionist gets no thrill when no one watches the self-exposing performance.

Opera transforms sex into a unique theatrical force. Opera is the theater of sexual abandon, the illegitimate child of the arts. And, like an illegitimate child, no matter how hard it tries to establish its respectability, opera cannot escape its tainted sexuality. Opera has tried desperately, almost maniacally at times, to deny its sexual nature in public. Music library shelves overflow with endless tomes explicating the formal and intellectual attractions of opera. But opera's chaste pretense forms a vital part of its game; it winks at its audience, promising a pure experience while flaunting its eroticism openly. The surface trappings of polite society and Victorian morality really do not fool anyone, though many people buy into the discourse of public respectability. No matter how hard we may try to deny it, the sexual nature of opera always manifests itself sooner or later. Opera cannot pretend it is not about sex.

Nor would I want it to; without sex, opera loses its unique place in the world of the stage. Opera legitimizes the illegitimate, makes sexual transgression acceptable. It puts sexual transgression into an elegant frame, makes it beautiful and idealized. Just as the lurid lives of film stars become attractive within the fictionalizing frame of stardom, so the sexual irregularities that make up opera's public image become thrilling because of their separation from quotidian life. Opera creates a world where extraordinary passion becomes the normal means of existence, where everyone feels Herculean passions and monumental emotions. Here everything is big, everything is beautiful, everything exists to its fullest. I cannot live that way all the time; I would burn out, probably without the aesthetic form of an operatic character's lovely death. But I like to have that level of passion available to me, an alternate reality to the safer sexual world of my nonoperatic life.

Opera, Sex, and the Future

I cannot imagine a future without opera, just as I cannot imagine a future without sex. But Wayne Koestenbaum and a steady stream of other critics tell me that opera is already dead, or at least on the edge of demise. The great era has, they say, certainly past. There are no more great singers, there are no more great composers, and it is only a matter of time, they say, before the form will collapse altogether under the weight of its own glorious past. Is opera really doomed? Am I among the last of those who will find sexual pleasure in the overblown world of opera?

No living art form can survive solely as a museum. But opera is not a museum; classical museums do not engage their spectators in postmodern whirlwinds of erotic ambiguity. Opera's flagrantly transgressive sexuality lets it transcend its museum status and, by using the archaic past as a means of postmodern production, provides its audience with a continuing reason for returning to the opera house. Many kinds of artistic expression do not survive the passage of time, but sex endures. When I teach the comedies of Aristophanes in my theater history course, my students cannot appreciate the political humor or the subtle puns, but they always get the toilet humor and they always get the sex jokes. Opera can survive the ravages of static repertory, inept singers, misogynist stereotypes, electronic mediation, and anything else time cares to throw in its way, because it connects with its audience through the eternal language of sex.

Opera is—or at least it has been and can once again be—a laboratory for human sexual relations, a place where we can look under a microscope and see the rules, the prejudices, the thrills of our sexual interactions made visible. And because it has a foot so firmly in the past, opera has a unique ability to demonstrate the complex ways we construct our sexual roles in the postmodern present. Take, for example, the Berlin Komische Oper's staging of that mainstream warhorse, *La Bohème*. Harry Kupfer's production, which premiered in 1982, showed how even the most retrograde opera can serve as a model for rethinking sex. This stunning production challenged Catherine Clément's argument that in opera characters such as Mimi exist only as victims, sacrificed for the sake of the perpetuation of masculine power structures. Here Mimi was no willing sacrificial lamb: She actively sought Rodolfo's love; she controlled the relationship at every stage; and she fought against her inevitable death, even if in the end she still lost her life. In the familiar frame of nineteenth-century romanticism, Kupfer restaged Mimi's fate and offered a model for redefining sexual categories.

In the final scene of Kupfer's production Mimi, though deathly ill, refused to be quiet and passive; she was defiant from the minute she entered the stage. She did not accept the help of Musetta and the men, as she struggled to drag herself up the stairs to the garret (the stage setting, with a visible exterior, allowed her to stay outside of the room, only entering at the line "Ah! come si sta bene qui!"). In a powerful denial of the traditional staging of the scene, Mimi forcefully refused to be put onto a mattress when one was brought for her; she wanted to remain standing, and only her illness forced her to collapse into a chair, propped up by pillows. When the others finally left, she did not wake up tenderly to embrace her lover; she grabbed him violently by the lapels, used her last strength to give him a passionate kiss, and dragged him to the floor with her. As she died, Mimi controlled the relationship entirely; she became the dominant partner, empowered by her illness. Mimi's consumption made her into a different person, not the sparkling little girl but a mature, potent sexual force, disengaged from the conventions of society. Instead of being a punishment for sexual laxity, mortality gave her sexual freedom. Rodolfo was rather upset by all of this; he did not know how to handle this shift in power, and he was left standing coldly, unable to respond. He was still upset with Mimi when she died (sitting up, catatonic), and was too self-absorbed by her unruly behavior to notice the moment of her death. Rather than being cathartic, this *Bohème* was upsetting and demanded that the audience rethink the sexual relationships being portrayed. Opera, with its open space of sexual representation, need not be a static museum of older sexual norms. It can force us to rethink our sexual lives, even in the framework of the most seemingly traditional of operas.

Kupfer's productions, along with those of the other "young turk" directors of opera staging—Patrice Chéreau, Robert Wilson, Peter Sellars, David Alden, Jonathan Miller—raise the hackles of many of opera's traditionalists. Robert Donington, in his polemic against nontraditional opera staging, *Opera and Its Symbols*, virtually accuses these directors of mental illness.[7] But these directors have not violated some fundamental purity of operatic form. Instead, they have explored alternate ways of expressing opera's excessive and ambiguous sexuality, finding new language to reinforce the power of opera's sexual expression. If Donington and other traditionalists shy away from overt challenges to opera's mask of sexual purity, it is because they still want to pretend that Victorian norms operate in the late twentieth century. If opera is to remain alive, it must not limit its expression to the sexual mores of the past, but instead must open its freewheeling sexuality even further to push the limits of our definitions of sexual reality.

Samuel Johnson remarked, in his epitaph for Oliver Goldsmith, "When a man is tired of London, he is tired of life." One might equally say that when people are tired of opera, they are tired of sex. Far more people enjoy sex than enjoy opera, of course, and I'm sure there is no direct correlation between levels of participation in the two amusements. But erotic energy is the mainstay of opera's appeal; sex makes opera thrilling in ways that the spoken theater can only approximate. Now, individual people have been known to become jaded about sex, even give it up altogether (at least for a time). But the population as a whole is unlikely to abandon its interest in sex. Nor is opera likely to lose its sexual appeal. The queer paradoxes of opera let me make of this grand and overwrought world anything I like. In it I can find a world as complex and contradictory as the one I find outside the opera house, a place where I can abandon my feelings as I cannot in my nonoperatic life. And when I leave the opera house, I can return, energized and more fully attuned to that paradoxical place that we call the "real world," carrying along with me a little bit of opera's queer transgressive license as I negotiate my way through life as a sexual being.

NOTES

Chapter 1

1. Wayne Koestenbaum, *The Queen's Throat: Opera, Homosexuality, and the Mystery of Desire* (New York: Poseidon Press, 1993), 42–43.

2. Susan McClary, *Feminine Endings: Music, Gender, and Sexuality* (Minneapolis: University of Minnesota Press, 1991). In her book McClary eloquently explodes the misogyny and antiphysicality that plague traditional musicology, especially in chapter 1, "Introduction: A Material Girl in Bluebeard's Castle." For a specific discussion of the sexual language of traditional musicology, see pages 7–19. Musicology, for McClary, is so deeply entrenched in the male worldview that it cannot see its own patriarchy. Music is supposed to be "pure," without reference to the real world, above such mundane matters as sex and gender. McClary rips the cover off this argument, revealing it as a rather weak excuse to keep these issues out of musicology—and to keep women and other marginalized populations out of music. Opera, she argues, has always given mainstream musicology headaches. Opera can never quite live up to musicology's ethereal illusion of purity—you can't do *Carmen* without Carmen—and so becomes suspect among musicologists. But because of opera's "impurity," it and other "tainted" forms such as rock, blues, and music-based performance art, become prime sites for an exploration of sexual issues in music.

3. Joseph Kerman, *Opera as Drama* (New York: Vintage, 1956). More recently, Herbert Lindenberger has explored the theatricality of opera in *Opera: The Extravagant Art* (Ithaca, N.Y.: Cornell University Press, 1984). Lindenberger makes many valuable observations (some of which I will cite in later chapters), but his study focuses more on the literary and historical manifestations of opera's theatricality, less on the dynamics of theatrical performance.

4. Catherine Clément, *Opera, or the Undoing of Women,* trans. Betsy Wing, with a foreword by Susan McClary (Minneapolis: University of Minnesota Press, 1988). Clément approaches opera as an outside viewer, a woman looking at a male-dominated art, and she does not like what she sees. Why, she asks, must she see herself abused in operatic narrative, murdered, withered away by illness, and otherwise victimized? She tells the stories of the heroines of the standard repertory, the litany of doom and destruction, in which opera audiences find beauty and truth. She outlines the many ways opera abuses women and how audiences relish this abuse. Clément's analysis forces unsettling questions: Why am I in ecstasy watching women die horribly as they sing beautifully? How can I possibly become engaged erotically (as I do) with this misogynist torture chamber we call opera? And can I assume that women in the audience will respond with the same physical abandon that I feel in my male-identified body?

5. Michel Poizat, *The Angel's Cry: Beyond the Pleasure Principle in Opera,* trans. Arthur Denner (Ithaca, N.Y.: Cornell University Press, 1992). For Poizat, operatic *jouissance* lives in the unbridled, Dionysian ring of the singer's voice; opera in its sexual climax becomes an angelic, orgasmic cry. For me, Poizat unlocks one moment of opera's physicality and offers an inroad toward understanding the relation between opera and my body. But this book annoys me at the same time that it inspires me. Poizat's style can be maddeningly erratic; he regularly drops hints of issues that he fails to develop. He reduces opera's sexuality to a single high note and fails to account for the hours of music in between. And he constructs operatic desire entirely within a heterosexual context, a major problem with Lacanian analysis as a whole. (For a criticism of the sexist assumptions of Lacanian psychoanalysis, see Judith Butler, *Gender Trouble* [New York: Routledge, 1990].)

6. Anne Rice, *Cry to Heaven* (New York: Ballantine Books, 1982). In telling the story of the castrati, Rice takes on the most sexually explosive topic in opera—and the most hidden. The overwhelming eroticism of the castrati makes musicologists squeamish, and only a few sanitized accounts of their history are in wide circulation. *Cry to Heaven* may not be a perfectly reliable historical document, but Rice has done her homework, and she knows the castrati to the core: the simultaneous attractiveness and repulsiveness of their sexual ambiguity; the glory and torture of being put on public display for the audience's erotic gaze; and, most of all, the deeply sexual nature of opera itself. Rice says things that no other writer will say, things too shocking or too embarrassing for the staid discourse of academia.

7. Koestenbaum, in his second chapter, "The Shut-in Fan: Opera at Home," also talks about his erotic fetishizing of boxed opera sets. Unlike Koestenbaum, however, I did not fetishize every detail of my boxed sets—only their size and contents.

Chapter 2

1. Michael Moon and Eve Kosofsky Sedgwick, "Divinity: A Dossier/A Performance Piece/A Little-Understood Emotion," in *Tendencies,* by Eve Kosofsky Sedgwick (Durham, N.C.: Duke University Press, 1993), 216.

2. The sixteenth edition of Bartlett's *Familiar Quotations* (Boston: Little, Brown, 1992), traces the saying in its operatic format to 1978. The book lists an anonymous popular saying from the U.S. South, "Church ain't over till the fat lady sings." A footnote attributes to San Antonio sportscaster Daniel John Cook "the most familiar and recent" variant on this saying, "The opera ain't over till the fat lady sings," a remark he apparently made first on the air in April 1978 and, subsequently, in print (*Familiar Quotations,* 782). I would assume, however, that the saying had been in usage, at least locally, for some time before then. Certainly, the stereotype of opera singers as being overweight long predates this construction (see note 4). J. D. Salinger, at the conclusion of *Franny and Zooey* (Boston: Little, Brown, 1961), evokes the image of a "Fat Lady," a powerful symbol in the book's moral and religious discourse, but Salinger makes no connection between the figure and opera.

3. For examples of cartoon representations of the Fat Lady, see Mick Stevens's cartoon "Grand Ole Opera" (*New Yorker,* 30 December 1991, 35), which depicts

the Fat Lady, a Minnie Pearl tag on her helmet, screeching "Howww-Deeee!"; or a political cartoon by Dana Summers (*New York Times*, 27 September 1992, sec. 4, 4), which shows President George Bush, just before the election, saying, "I don't care about the polls, it's not over yet," as the Fat Lady, behind a curtain and with the word "Economy" written on her shield, sprays her throat in preparation to sing. The album covers are *The Anna Russell Album*, Sony CD MDK 47252; *Heavy Classix*, Angel CDM 0777 7 64769 2 6; *Heavy Classix II*, Angel CDM 7243 5 65172 2 6. The Bugs Bunny cartoon is "What's Opera, Doc?" dir. Chuck Jones, Warner Brothers, 1957. It is especially telling that the producers of the *Heavy Classix* albums chose the image of the Fat Lady, since these recordings are clearly aimed at a wide popular market rather than at more experienced listeners to classical music. The Fat Lady is to classical music what the sexy model is to advertising in the automobile industry, the displaced physical symbol of the product's erotic allure. The album cover of the second volume even picks up the lingo of popular advertising: "She's back! She's bad! She's pumping up the volume louder than ever! The roar of Heavy Classix goes off the charts in Heavy Classix II—63 all-new minutes of the boldest, heaviest, loudest music ever unleashed!" There is little operatic music on the albums, though the first starts off, notably, with "Ride of the Valkyries." Instead, they offer heavily butchered excerpts of familiar concert and encore pieces and are in every way musically unexceptional.

4. There is no consistent construction of an iconic Fat Gentleman to accompany the Fat Lady on the operatic stage. But this absence of a male image may be due in part to the overwhelming power of the female-embodied icon. In 1949, Chuck Jones provides a parallel male image in his cartoon, "Long-Haired Hare." Bugs Bunny's nemesis and the object of ridicule here is a large male singer; at one point Bugs, after humiliating the singer, says in mock consolation, "There's the fat opera singer." This image, though, is a one-shot deal, perhaps even a male transformation of the Fat Lady, who could not appear in the virtually all-male world of Warner Brothers cartoons. In any case, the gender stereotypes surrounding the Fat Lady, as with all such stereotypes, tend to rest on figures gendered female. For further exploration of this issue, see my article, "The Rabbit in Drag: Camp and Gender Construction in the American Animated Cartoon," *Journal of Popular Culture* 29(3) (Winter 1995). If he were not seen as a serious pseudo sex symbol, Luciano Pavarotti might singlehandedly generate an icon of the Fat Gentleman of opera.

5. The other major popular icon for obese women is, of course, the Fat Lady of the circus and carnival sideshow. For a particularly pertinent discussion of the conflicted sexuality of this figure, see Sharon Mazer, "'She's So Fat . . . ': Facing the Fat Lady at Coney Island's Sideshows by the Seashore," *Theatre Annual* 47 (1994):11–28. See also Catherine Gallagher, "The Body Versus the Social Body in the Works of Thomas Malthus and Henry Mayhew," in *The Making of the Modern Body: Sexuality and Society in the Nineteenth Century*, ed. Catherine Gallagher and Thomas Laquer (Berkeley: University of California Press, 1987), 83–106. For a discussion of gender issues surrounding obesity, see Marcia Millman, *Such a Pretty Face: Being Fat in America* (New York: Norton, 1980). On rampant consumerism in recent American culture, see Barbara Ehrenreich, *The Worst Years of Our Lives: Irreverent Notes From a Decade of Greed* (New York: Pantheon, 1990).

6. Moon and Sedgwick, "Divinity," 231–232.

7. Ibid., 218.

8. The glorious excess of opera is a continuous underlying theme of Herbert Lindenberger's *Opera: The Extravagant Art* (Ithaca, N.Y.: Cornell University Press, 1984). In this context, Lindenberger quotes Theodor Adorno's essay "Bourgeois Opera," published in its entirety in *Opera Through Other Eyes,* ed. David J. Levin (Stanford, Calif.: Stanford University Press, 1994). Adorno argues that embarrassing excess is essential to opera's appeal. He remarks: "The closer opera gets to a parody of itself, the closer it is to its own most particular element. . . . This may explain why some of the most authentic operas, like *Der Freischütz,* but also *The Magic Flute* and *Il Trovatore,* have their true place in the children's matinee and embarrass the adult, who imagines himself too sensible for them, simply because he no longer understands their pictorial language" (Levin, 26). Opera's implicit excess also explains why so-called "semistaged" opera performances, which have become increasingly popular in the face of current budget cutbacks, performed in concert halls with sort-of scenery, sort-of costumes, and sort-of acting, usually seem so uniquely unsatisfying.

9. Note also the case of *Tosca.* Joseph Kerman reviles the opera as an embarrassing display of excess sentimentality and melodrama; adapting a phrase from George Bernard Shaw, he labels it a "shabby little shocker," capable of pleasing only the lower-class elements in the gallery (*Opera as Drama* [New York: Vintage, 1956], 17–20, 254). Kerman is, in a sense, right; *Tosca* certainly is embarrassingly emotional, but only a little more so than other operas. And its popularity has lasted unabated (among all of the audience's social strata) for nearly a century. (In the recent second edition of the book, Kerman softens his condemnation of *Tosca* to a degree, but he still sees it as a second-rate opera.)

10. Angus Heriot details this pattern of public denial in his study (still the only book-length assessment of the castrati), *The Castrati in Opera* (London: Secker and Warburg, 1956). See in particular pages 24–26 on the papal injunctions against the castrati, pages 42–44 on the secrecy surrounding the operation.

11. At least until recently, when the number of critical considerations of the castrati has multiplied considerably. See Chapter 9 for a more extended discussion of the castrati.

12. The insider/outsider division appears regularly in critical discussions of the camp sensibility; camp is seen as a private language, especially among marginalized groups, most especially among gay men. See, for example, the essays in the first section of David Bergman, ed., *Camp Grounds: Style and Homosexuality* (Amherst: University of Massachusetts Press, 1993). Scott Long, in his chapter "The Loneliness of Camp," remarks: "Camp . . . is a system of signs by which those who understand certain ironies will recognize each other and endure. It is a private language for some who intuit that public language has gone wrong" (78–91, at 90). Further theoretical discussions of camp can be found in Moe Meyer, ed., *The Politics and Poetics of Camp* (London: Routledge, 1994).

13. Judith Butler, *Gender Trouble* (New York: Routledge, 1990), especially chapter 3, "Subversive Bodily Acts."

14. Wayne Koestenbaum, *The Queen's Throat: Opera, Homosexuality, and the Mystery of Desire* (New York: Poseidon Press, 1993), 102.

15. Traces of this view can be found in print as recently as 1968. Julian Gardiner, in *A Guide to Good Singing and Speech* (London: Cassell, 1968), suggests that female singers, when faced with depression connected with bouts of laryngitis, take the following advice: "At such times the prudent female singer would do well to bolster her morale by treating herself to a new hat, good food, and an afternoon at the cinema" (265). A few pages later, in a remarkably sexist section entitled "Singing ladies," he implies strongly that women may use extra weight to compensate for their lack of physical strength: "Women find the exercises in Chapter 2 considerably harder than men. They do not have the same interest or pride in physical achievements, nor are their bodies so well adapted for such things. . . . Singing is an energetic business, and all singers should eat heartily. Inevitably they will get fat unless they eat sensibly, cutting out the odd snack of biscuits, sweet cakes, chocolate and gin, which ruin so many figures. Some fat people may have good voices, but it is not true that singing makes people fat! Admittedly the expansion of the chest is increased and the part immediately below the breastbone becomes slightly more conspicuous" (268).

He goes on to make suggestions to female singers about how to dress, with special emphasis on the presentability of their legs and an admonition not to wear glasses at auditions. Male singers, of course, need not worry about such things.

16. For a concurring opinion, see Richard Miller, *The Structure of Singing: System and Art in Vocal Technique* (New York: Schirmer Books, 1986). He remarks: "What is the ideal weight for the singer? Is it true, as has often been stated in interviews given by prominent overweight artists, that additional avoirdupois is needed in order to project the voice in the opera house, or to 'improve resonance' (as if padding contributed to resonance). Certainly not! The ideal weight for singing is the ideal weight for any physical activity. . . . The oft-repeated story of the famous diva who lost weight and acquired a wobble as a result is incorrect; the tendency to oscillate in the top voice was always there, simply becoming more marked with the passage of years. Waistline had nothing to do with it" (236). Richard DeYoung, in *The Singer's Art: An Analysis of Vocal Principles* (Chicago: DePaul University, 1958), concurs: "Eating rich foods taxes the digestive system and invites the singer's worst enemy, obesity" (109).

17. For example, in several *Opera News* reports on the film, the writers consistently point out that her voice is small, and only the technology of recording allowed her to play this role. She even says of herself that she is more at home in musical comedy (she appeared in the original cast of *Fiddler on the Roof*) and that she is not a "real" opera singer. See John W. Freeman, "Records," *Opera News*, September 1984, 68, and Leslie Rubinstein, "Gypsy!" *Opera News*, October 1984, 11–13 et seq.

18. Peter G. Davis, "Music," *New York Magazine*, 7 June 1993, 58. Maria Ewing has also gained notoriety for full nudity in her performance as Salome.

19. Lindenberger observes that "the power and the ranges of pitch with which the soprano voice can fill a large house with sound allow it to simulate willfulness in an extraordinarily persuasive way. . . . However much the social scale has subordinated women in life, the musical scale has allowed operatic heroines to remain securely on top" (269). If women are indeed "on top" in opera, Clément might argue, it is only so that they may more effectively be brought down.

Chapter 3

1. Gustave Flaubert, *Madame Bovary*, trans. Francis Steegmuller (New York: Vintage Classics, 1992), 255.

2. In regard to this episode, Herbert Lindenberger, in *Opera: The Extravagant Art* (Ithaca, N.Y.: Cornell University Press, 1984), remarks: "The *Lucia* performance represents both a culmination of what went on before and a preparation for Emma's final hectic phase, the consummation and collapse of her relation with Léon" (159).

3. Quoted in Gary C. Thomas, "Was George Friedrich Handel Gay?" in *Queering the Pitch: The New Gay and Lesbian Musicology*, ed. Philip Brett, Elizabeth Wood, and Gary C. Thomas (New York: Routledge, 1994), 185.

4. Michel Poizat, *The Angel's Cry: Beyond the Pleasure Principle in Opera*, trans. Arthur Denner (Ithaca, N.Y.: Cornell University Press, 1992), 12–13. My own expenses are actually quite minor in comparison to some of these Parisian fanatics.

5. Critical discussions of the sensual appeal of music are as old as Plato and constitute a vast literature. The notion that music has more subconscious abilities to manipulate desire is more recent. Susan McClary, for example, outlines the ways in which the music of Carmen literally creates a desire in the audience for the title character's death. *Feminine Endings: Music, Gender, and Sexuality* (Minneapolis: University of Minnesota Press, 1991), 54–67.

6. Joseph R. Roach provides an insightful analysis into the oratorical influences on acting styles in the periods prior to modern realism in *The Player's Passion: Studies in the Science of Acting* (Ann Arbor: University of Michigan Press, 1993).

7. Gustave Flaubert, *Madame Bovary*, trans. Francis Steegmuller (New York: Vintage Classics, 1992), 264–265.

8. Wayne Koestenbaum, *The Queen's Throat: Opera, Homosexuality, and the Mystery of Desire* (New York: Poseidon Press, 1993), 199.

9. Brecht develops his theory of the *Verfremdungseffekt* in various critical essays, especially "Alienation Effects in Chinese Acting" and "A Short Organum for the Theatre," both included in *Brecht on Theatre*, ed. John Willett (New York: Hill and Wang, 1964).

10. Catherine Clément, *Opera, or the Undoing of Women*, trans. Betsy Wing, with a foreword by Susan McClary (Minneapolis: University of Minnesota Press, 1988), 9–10.

11. *Moonstruck*, dir. Norman Jewison, with Cher, Nicholas Cage, Vincent Gardenia, Olympia Dukakis, and Danny Aiello. MGM/UA, 1988.

12. Janelle Reinelt wonders, after reading Clément, if she should abandon her pleasure in going to the opera altogether, since what she sees there, in the light of Clément's critical knowledge, distresses her so intensely. See her "Women Who Love Too Much: The Ambiguity of Deadly Desire" (unpublished paper, 1989). As a male fellow-traveler with the feminist critical project, I find myself asking the same question, though without being able to engage in the same process of nonidentification with opera's female victims. My situation is rather like that of the Puritans, feeling I ought to give up my physical pleasure because of its fundamental sinfulness.

13. Clément, *Opera, or the Undoing of Women*, 5–8.

14. The Player says, "The catastrophe is manifestly wrong, for an opera must end happily." The Beggar responds, "Your objection, sir, is very just, and is easily re-

moved; for you must allow that in this kind of drama, 'tis no matter how absurdly things are brought about." John Gay, *The Beggar's Opera,* in Katharine Rogers, ed., *18th and 19th Century British Drama* (New York: Meridan, 1979), 247.

15. Ralph P. Locke, "What Are These Women Doing in Opera?" *Opera News,* July 1992, 36.

16. Lindenberger confirms their iconic status; he states: "The two celebrated tubercular deaths [Violetta and Mimi] reflect what we now recognize as a peculiarly nineteenth-century way of symbolizing human frailty." *Opera: The Extravagant Art,* 267.

17. Many recent critics have elucidated the theory of the male subject position in narrative performance, most powerfully Laura Mulvey in her now classic "Visual Pleasure and Narrative Cinema," first published in *Screen* 16(3) (1975):6–18. Teresa de Lauretis has been especially instrumental in developing Mulvey's concepts. See, for example, de Lauretis's study *Alice Doesn't: Feminism, Semiotics, Cinema* (Bloomington: Indiana University Press, 1984).

Chapter 4

1. Michel Poizat, *The Angel's Cry: Beyond the Pleasure Principle in Opera*, trans. Arthur Denner (Ithaca, N.Y.: Cornell University Press, 1992), 19.

2. *Carreras, Domingo, Pavarotti in Concert,* Zubin Mehta, cond. London CD 430 433–2; videotape London 071 223–3LH, 1990. *Carreras, Domingo, Pavarotti: The Three Tenors in Concert 1994,* Zubin Mehta, cond., Atlantic CD 82614; videotape WarnerVision Entertainment 50822–3. Tenors II was broadcast over PBS on 16 July 1994 (prod. Tibor Rudas, dir. Bill Cosell). The marketing phenomenon surrounding this concert, and the remarkable volume of popular sales, are documented in Susan Elliott, "In Concert, or The Making of a Hit," *Opera News,* 30 March 1991, 34–35. See also Jennifer Clark, "Over 1.5-Billion People Served Opera During Live, Global Show," *Variety,* 18 July 1990, 65; and Allan Kozinn, "The Three Tenors, Guess Who, To Sing," *New York Times,* 14 July 1994, C11.

3. Eric Salzman, in reviewing the video of Tenors I, evokes the competitive spirit of the event, as well as its sexual content: "Although the concert was held in an unprecedented atmosphere of friendliness and collegial cooperation—especially in the final medley and encores . . . there is inevitably a bit of macho rivalry between champion vocal athletes like these. There is something about the male tenor voice . . . that evokes images of swooning females, territorial aggression, the gorilla thumping his chest, the alpha male howling down all other males. . . . It is certainly a traditional and refined version of male sexuality and aggression." "Champion Tenors," *Stereo Review,* December 1990, 127.

4. For a more in-depth discussion of the Three Tenors phenomenon and its competitive dynamics, see my article, "The World Cup of Opera, or A Sale of Three Tenors," *Theatre Annual* 48 (1995):1–13.

5. Ethan Mordden outlines this dynamic throughout his study of the diva phenomenon in *Demented: The World of the Opera Diva* (New York: Simon and Schuster, 1984). Wayne Koestenbaum similarly argues for his seemingly arbitrary choice of Anna Moffo as his favorite soprano.

6. Much recent writing on performance has theorized the eroticized body on stage. See, for example, Joseph R. Roach, "Power's Body: The Inscription of Morality as Style," in *Interpreting the Theatrical Past,* ed. Thomas Postlewait and Bruce A. McConachie (Iowa City: University of Iowa Press, 1989). This theory of audience response also resonates in Laura Mulvey's film theory and much of Koestenbaum's approach to audience response to opera.

7. Poizat, *The Angel's Cry,* 34.

8. In Chapter 11, I will discuss the differences between the erotic appeal of the live singing body and that of the disembodied voice of radio and recordings.

9. Michel Foucault, *Discipline and Punish: The Birth of the Prison,* trans. Alan Sheridan (New York: Vintage, 1979). I draw the analysis that follows largely from the Roach article cited in note 6, which makes the connection between Foucault's theories of the body on display and stage performance.

10. Herbert Lindenberger comments, "Although the record player has made the fortunes of many singers since Caruso's time, it has never proved an adequate substitute for the singer's physical presence. If anything, recordings serve to whet the audience's appetite for the star's actual presence, which it still is willing, as it was centuries ago, to reward with high fees." *Opera: The Extravagant Art* (Ithaca, N.Y.: Cornell University Press, 1984), 253.

11. For example, Peter G. Davis, in *New York Magazine* ("Lame Salome," 3 December 1990, 178), complains acidly: "An odd change has come over Metropolitan Opera audiences lately, one that must make the Met's artistic director, James Levine, pleased and proud. Everything is acclaimed, loudly and indiscriminately, no matter what happens on stage. . . . The audience loved [the new production of *Ballo*], enthusiastically applauding the garishly inappropriate sets, the dumb staging, and the bad singing. They even cheered the recent revival of *Salome*, despite the gravely flawed production. . . . [In the past] a particularly hideous misconceived production was sometimes even booed. No more. Apparently Levine's artistic policies and the Met's development department have successfully cultivated a new breed of operagoer, one who may not know much and is reluctant to learn but unhesitatingly endorses everything."

I saw the production of *Ballo,* and it was, indeed, awful. But its flaws did not preclude my need to release my erotic energies at the end of the evening. If Met audiences have ceased to boo (which is not true; they roundly disapproved of the new production of *Lucia* in 1992), there are more complex factors at work than the Met's artistic policies.

12. Poizat, *The Angel's Cry,* 35.

13. Ibid., 35–36.

14. See Elaine Showalter, *The Feminine Malady: Women, Madness, and Culture in England, 1830–1980* (New York: Pantheon, 1985). Foucault discusses the construction of hysteria in *The History of Sexuality,* vol. 1, 104, 121, and 146–147, and vol. 3, 115–117. See also Catherine Clément, *Opera, or the Undoing of Women,* trans. Betsy Wing, with a foreword by Susan McClary (Minneapolis: University of Minnesota Press, 1988), 176.

15. In light of current heated debates in gay and lesbian studies, it is problematic to label these men as "homosexual," since the drawing predates the contemporary medicalized construction of the homosexual. But they are certainly drawn as effem-

inate, with clear implications of sexual attraction to each other and to the equally effeminized male singer.

16. See in particular the writings of the early sexologists Magnus Hirschfeld and Richard von Krafft-Ebbing, as well as Foucault, on the pathologization of homosexuality.

17. This pathologization of the hysterical opera fan also underlies much of the discussion of the opera queen in Wayne Koestenbaum, *The Queen's Throat: Opera, Homosexuality, and the Mystery of Desire* (New York: Poseidon Press, 1993).

18. Tom Stoppard, *The Real Thing* (London: Faber and Faber, 1982), 25.

19. Koestenbaum, *The Queen's Throat*, 134.

20. Laurie A. Finke, in "Painting Women: Images of Femininity in Jacobean Tragedy," *Theatre Journal* 36 (1984):357–370, analyzes the process by which, in artistic representation, male figures preserve their ideal images of femininity by killing women, as exemplified by Jacobean revenge tragedy. The only way to preserve a woman's paradoxical position as sexual object and pure virgin is, Finke argues, to "kill her into art."

Chapter 5

1. Wayne Koestenbaum, *The Queen's Throat: Opera, Homosexuality, and the Mystery of Desire* (New York: Poseidon Press, 1993), 18.

2. Neil Bartlett, *Who Was That Man? A Present For Mr Oscar Wilde* (London: Serpent's Tail, 1988), 40.

3. Terrence McNally, *Three Plays by Terrence McNally* (New York: Plume, 1990). McNally himself, unlike Koestenbaum, disdains the term "opera queen," but he paints a dead-on portrait of the stereotype in his play. See Will Crutchfield's interview with McNally, "Dishing About Divas and Other Opera Chat," *New York Times,* 4 June 1989, sec. 2, 5 et seq.

4. McNally wrote several versions of the play over a five-year period. The initial versions end with the Carmen-like stabbing. After the New York opening, in response to critical complaints about the violent conclusion, McNally rewrote the final scene, with amplified references to *Carmen* (using the actual dialogue from the last scene of the opera), but where Mike leaves unharmed. This version appears in the "official" published edition, though some subsequent productions of the play have opted for the original violent ending. For a further elaboration of the critical dispute over the play's ending, see my article, "The Death of Queens: *The Lisbon Traviata* Controversy and Gay Male Representation in the Mainstream Theatre," forthcoming in *Theatre History Studies* 16 (1996). David Román discusses the play, especially in relation to the AIDS crisis, in his essay, "'It's My Party and I'll Die If I Want To!': Gay Men, AIDS, and the Circulation of Camp in U.S. Theatre," in *Camp Grounds: Style and Homosexuality*, ed. David Bergman (Amherst: University of Massachusetts Press, 1993), 206–233.

5. Koestenbaum, *The Queen's Throat*, 241.

6. Koestenbaum, *The Queen's Throat*, 76.

7. Ethan Mordden, *Demented: The World of the Opera Diva* (New York: Simon and Schuster, 1984).

8. T. R. Witomski, *Kvetch* (Berkeley, Calif.: Celestial Arts, 1989), 40.

9. Alex Ross, "Grand Seductions" *New Yorker,* 12 April 1993, 115. Bruce Bawer, in *A Place at the Table* (New York: Poseidon, 1993), says he does not like opera himself and cites an interviewee who rejects the label of opera queen, arguing that he loves opera for its art and not (in a statement that parallels Ross) because it has any connection with being gay (167). I appreciate the sentiment, though the quotation, like much of Bawer's work, smacks of the musty smell of the closet.

10. Writing in response to Koestenbaum, Paul Robinson, in "The Opera Queen: A Voice From the Closet," *Cambridge Opera Journal* 6(3) (1994):283–291, muses on the phenomenon of the opera queen and whether there are any real connections between gay men and opera. He offers a series of tentative answers, many of which parallel ideas that I was developing as I drafted this volume. (It is encouraging to find authors who confirm your ideas before you publish them.) I differ with Robinson, though, on a number of central issues. Like Koestenbaum, he suggests that the connection between opera and gay men is mysterious; as I argue later in this chapter, I think the connection, through opera's queer sexuality, is quite tangible and explicable. He posits that going to the opera acts as a metaphor for sex for gay men; as I will argue in Chapter 6, I think opera is actual, not metaphorical, sex, a phenomenon experienced by every audience member, not just gay men. At the end of the essay, he reverts to the idea of the closet. Even though (as he relates) he had once written a piece highly critical of closeted opera queens, he suggests here that the love of opera may really be a function of the closet and, waxing nostalgic, that the closet might not be an entirely bad thing. He concludes, in a sentiment that I reject entirely, "Coming out of the closet may also mean coming out of the opera house" (290–291). I find Robinson's essay suggestive but often circular and self-contradictory; it stalls out at the end and backs away from making use of the fertile ideas it brings up.

11. Eve Kosofsky Sedgwick, *Epistemology of the Closet* (Berkeley: University of California Press, 1990), 82–86.

12. Opera has gained a strong following in many Asian capitals, witnessed in the rising number of Asian-born opera singers and the popularity of the form in Hong Kong, Seoul, and other cities. This phenomenon, though, seems to reflect the much larger embracing of Western culture in Asia during this century. This situation can lead to frequently uncomfortable situations, when Asian opera singers and companies perform orientalist works such as *Madama Butterfly,* with their condescending views of Asian society (a situation depicted in David Henry Hwang's play *M. Butterfly*).

13. Some recent studies have noted the intense problems raised by the impulse to generalize about the feelings, opinions, and desires of any group that identifies as a community, especially a marginalized one. The powerful political incentive for the community to speak as one voice runs headlong into the inevitable individual differences within the community. In other words, who and what do "we" mean when "we" say "we"? These conflicts have plagued numerous social activist groups, from the National Organization for Women to ACT UP, an AIDS awareness organization. For extended discussions of the problematics of identity politics, see Sedgwick, *Epistemology of the Closet;* Judith Butler, *Bodies That Matter: On the Discursive Limits of Sex* (New York: Routledge, 1993); and Peggy Phelan, *Unmarked* (London: Routledge, 1993). In the latter two works there are especially interesting dis-

cussions of the problematic gay identity politics raised by Jennie Livingston's independently released 1991 film *Paris is Burning*.

14. Eve Kosofsky Sedgwick, *Tendencies* (Durham, N.C.: Duke University Press, 1993), 7–8.

15. Elizabeth Wood, "Sapphonics," in *Queering the Pitch: The New Gay and Lesbian Musicology*, ed. Philip Brett, Elizabeth Wood, and Gary C. Thomas (New York: Routledge, 1994), 27–28. Robinson also cites similar feelings expressed in Terry Castle's book *The Apparitional Lesbian: Female Homosexuality and Modern Culture* (New York: Columbia University Press, 1993).

16. Bartlett, *Who Was That Man?* at 72. For an even earlier depiction of queer opera lovers, see the illustration "A Dandy Fainting or—An Exquisite in Fits," in Chapter 4.

17. See Joseph Horowitz, "Coming to America," *Opera News*, 27 March 1993, 14–20 et seq., for a discussion of Wagner's intense sexuality as perceived in the nineteenth century, as well as Wagner's attachment to his protégé, Anton Seidl.

18. Witomski writes: "Some operas attract more gays than others. Operas in German, operas longer than four hours, operas featuring fading divas are big favorites. Put these criteria all together and they spell *Parsifal*, which is where all nice opera queens spend Good Friday." *Kvetch*, 43.

19. Ross, "Grand Seductions," 119. Joseph Kestner discusses *Parsifal*'s repudiation of women in "The Dark Side of Chivalry," *Opera News*, 30 March 1991, 18–21 et seq.

20. For an evocative discussion of the problematic relationship that a gay Jewish man feels toward Wagner, see Lawrence D. Mass, *Confessions of a Jewish Wagnerite* (New York: Cassell, 1994), with a foreword by Wagner's great-grandson, Gottfried.

21. In fact, he has little to say about Wagner at all. He recognizes the suppressed homoeroticism in Wagner, but only with disdain. For Koestenbaum, gay men can only experience desire in opera when it is displaced onto the figure of the female diva, preferably singing in Italian. See *The Queen's Throat*, 188–189.

22. Koestenbaum, *The Queen's Throat*, 219–220. It is, admittedly, a very queer moment.

23. Eve Kosofsky Sedgwick, *Between Men: English Literature and Male Homosocial Desire* (New York: Columbia University Press, 1985).

24. Heartfelt thanks to neophyte opera queen Craig Palmer for these observations on *Turandot*, as well as for suggesting ideas about homosocial bonding in *Otello*.

25. Koestenbaum, *The Queen's Throat*, 208. My thanks to Vicki Patraka for bringing the *Lakmé* duet to my attention.

26. The erotics of operatic cross-dressing will be explored further in Chapter 10.

27. Brett has written extensively on Britten, most notably in his contribution to the Cambridge Opera Guide series, *Benjamin Britten: Peter Grimes* (Cambridge: Cambridge University Press, 1983), especially the sections "Britten and Grimes" and "Postscript"; Brett includes further discussions of Britten in his contributions to *Queering the Pitch*. For other discussions, see three articles by Clifford Hindley, "Contemplation and Reality: A Study of Britten's 'Death in Venice,'" *Music and Letters* 7 (1990):511–523; "Homosexual Self-Affirmation and Self-Oppression in

Two Britten Operas," *Musical Quarterly* 76 (1992):143–168; and "Platonic Elements in Britten's 'Death in Venice,'" *Music and Letters* 73 (1992):407–429; also see John Evans, *"Death in Venice:* The Apollonian/Dionysian Conflict," *Opera Quarterly* 4 (1986):102–115, and especially Humphrey Carpenter's recent *Benjamin Britten: A Biography* (New York: Scribner, 1992), which includes for the first time extended discussions of the composer's private life. The continued skittishness toward admitting homosexual desire in Britten can be seen in Graham Elliott, "The Operas of Benjamin Britten: A Spiritual View," *Opera Quarterly* 4 (1986):28–44.

28. The critical resistance to the homoerotic content of Britten's operas, especially *Death in Venice,* is outlined in an article that I wrote with Craig B. Palmer, "Disappearing Acts: Opera, Cinema, and Homoerotic Desire," in *A Night In at the Opera: Media Representations of Opera,* ed. Jeremy Tambling (London: John Libbey/Arts Council of England, 1994), 169–192.

29. The first substantial application of gay and lesbian studies to questions of musicology is Brett, Wood, and Thomas's *Queering the Pitch;* several essays in this collection have already figured in these discussions.

30. It is notable that Brett, who also has two earlier essays in the collection, waits until the very end of the book to bring up the topic of Britten's sexuality.

31. Again, see Abel and Palmer, "Disappearing Acts: Opera, Cinema, and Homoerotic Desire," which also deals with issues of critical erasure in Berg's *Lulu.*

32. For a sympathetic portrayal of Bernstein's conflicted sexual life, see Humphrey Burton, *Leonard Bernstein* (New York: Doubleday, 1994).

33. Peter Galvin, "A Royal Opera," *Advocate,* 30 May 1995, 59.

34. Lawrence Mass, in *Confessions of a Jewish Wagnerite* and earlier works, castigates gay people in the opera world for not being more open about their sexuality and for not bringing gay issues into their work (109–113).

Chapter 6

1. Wayne Koestenbaum, *The Queen's Throat: Opera, Homosexuality, and the Mystery of Desire* (New York: Poseidon Press, 1993), 43.

2. Quoted from a personal conversation between Thomson and Susan McClary, *Feminine Endings: Music, Gender, and Sexuality* (Minneapolis: University of Minnesota Press, 1991), note, 193. McClary buries this quotation in an endnote; I could not in good conscience let it stay there.

3. Anne Rice, *Cry to Heaven* (New York: Ballantine Books, 1982), 311–312.

4. In Philip Brett, Elizabeth Wood, and Gary C. Thomas, eds., *Queering the Pitch: The New Gay and Lesbian Musicology* (New York: Routledge), 78–79. Paul Robinson, in "The Opera Queen: A Voice From the Closet," *Cambridge Opera Journal* 6(3) (1994):283–291, comes close to making the same assertion. He notes that singing involves the erogenous zones of the mouth and throat, that singing is a strenuous physical activity, that operatic music expresses erotic emotions, and that music produces a physical response in the audience. From these factors, he concludes: "There is, in other words, an isomorphism between operatic singing and sexual performance. . . . Vocal electricity, I'm persuaded, is a sublimation or upward displacement (as the Freudians like to say) of the bodily vibrations and tinglings of

the sexual act" (288). But Robinson, despite this evidence, clings to the notion that opera is only sex metaphorically; he remains reluctant to follow his ideas to their logical conclusion, that opera really is a physical sex act.

5. Koestenbaum, *The Queen's Throat,* 16; see also 183–184.

6. Both Michel Foucault, in the first volume of *The History of Sexuality,* trans. Robert Hurley, three vol. (New York: Vintage, 1980, 1986, 1988), and Eve Kosofsky Sedgwick, in many of her writings, especially *Epistemology of the Closet* (Berkeley: University of California Press, 1990), and *Tendencies* (Durham, N.C.: Duke University Press, 1993), explore the coercive social forces that limit our notion of "real" or "proper" sexual practice to insertive vaginal intercourse between and a man and a woman, arguing forcefully that such limitations are artificial social constraints that serve the purpose of control and subordination. These forces are similar to the ones outlined by Adrienne Rich in her famous and powerfully titled essay, "Compulsory Heterosexuality and Lesbian Existence," reprinted in *The Lesbian and Gay Studies Reader,* ed. Henry Abelove, Michèle Aina Barale, and David M. Halperin (New York: Routledge, 1993), 227–254.

7. Koestenbaum, *The Queen's Throat,* 40.

8. Roland Barthes, *The Pleasure of the Text,* trans. Richard Miller (New York: Hill and Wang, 1975).

9. This implication of sexual activity is brought to the front with particular vividness in Francesco Rosi's film version of *Carmen.* At the end of the second act—after singing "La liberté!"—all of the gypsies pair off with their lovers, including Carmen and José, and retire to individual bedrooms, slamming the doors behind them in time to the music.

10. Jonathan Demme's film *Philadelphia* features a scene where the narrative structure of musical orgasm becomes powerfully evident. Tom Hanks's character, dying of AIDS, tries to convey his love of opera to his lawyer. He puts on a recording of Callas singing "La mamma morta" from *Andrea Chenier.* As he translates the words and explains the circumstances, the emotional intensity of his story-telling builds along with the music while the camera sensually envelops Hanks in his growing ecstasy, rising to a moment of orgasmic climax. It is, unfortunately, the only truly electric scene in the entire film.

11. These theories have been developed largely by the French feminist literary theorists, particularly Julia Kristeva.

12. Michel Poizat, *The Angel's Cry: Beyond the Pleasure Principle in Opera,* trans. Arthur Denner (Ithaca, N.Y.: Cornell University Press, 1992), 156.

13. Poizat, *The Angel's Cry,* 179.

14. Barthes, *Pleasure of the Text,* 13.

15. McClary, *Feminine Endings,* 124–125.

16. McClary, *Feminine Endings,* 124–131. McClary presents this concept as a basis for discussing contemporary feminist composers who look for alternatives to these "necessary" rules of musical structure.

17. The art of film scoring depends almost entirely on this kind of physical response in the listener.

18. There is a more detailed discussion of this exchange in Chapter 7.

19. Foucault, *The History of Sexuality,* vol. 2, 117–131; also vol. 3, part 4. Leo Bersani traces the threads in contemporary psychoanalytic theory linking sex (espe-

cially anal sex) and death in his powerful essay "Is the Rectum a Grave?" in *AIDS: Cultural Analysis, Cultural Activism,* ed. Douglas Crimp (Cambridge: MIT Press, 1988), 197–222.

20. Several recent articles in *Opera News* have picked up on this notion of sex linked with death, both written, notably, by theater professionals: playwright Albert Innaurato's "The Gong Show," *Opera News,* 1 February 1992, 8–11, and critic John Simon's "Daughter of Death," *Opera News,* 11 April 1992, 14–16 et seq. Theater critic Jan Kott also makes some poignant personal comments on sex and death in *The Memory of the Body* (Evanston, Ill.: Northwestern University Press, 1992).

21. McClary, *Feminine Endings,* 22.

22. Koestenbaum, *The Queen's Throat,* 44.

Chapter 7

1. Michel Poizat, *The Angel's Cry: Beyond the Pleasure Principle in Opera,* trans. Arthur Denner (Ithaca, N.Y.: Cornell University Press, 1992), 4.

2. Catherine Clément, *Opera, or the Undoing of Women,* trans. Betsy Wing, with a foreword Susan McClary (Minneapolis: University of Minnesota Press, 1988), 99.

3. The Spur Posse incident is described in David Gelman, "Mixed Messages: Spur Posse Sex Scandal at Lakewood High School, California," *Newsweek,* 12 April 1993, 28–29, and Joan Didion, "Trouble in Lakewood," *New Yorker,* 26 July 1993, 46–50 et seq.

4. Sexual violence in opera only seems violent when the music is not pretty, most obviously in the two operas by Alban Berg, *Wozzeck* and *Lulu.* Neither of these operas has appreciably more sexual violence than, for example, *Cavalleria Rusticana* and *I Pagliacci,* but their atonal music makes the violent acts seem much more horrible, the actions of deranged minds rather than scorned lovers' justified gestures of revenge.

5. The classic discussion of how rape imagery is embedded in the media appears in Molly Haskell, *From Reverence to Rape: The Treatment of Women in the Movies* (Chicago: University of Chicago Press, 1987).

6. Despite critical attempts to rescue his masculinity, Ottavio, to be blunt, is a wimp. If masculinity is defined by aggressive and effectual activity, Ottavio is almost entirely devoid of masculinity. He talks a good game, but he does almost nothing. He cannot even make love properly. Both of Ottavio's arias declaring his love for Donna Anna are beautiful and lyrical, but they are not particularly aggressive; they are slow, meditative, repetitious in ways that never characterize the music of Giovanni, and neither of them has any particular effect on the plot. The first, "Dalla sua pace," he sings alone, after Donna Anna leaves the stage, and the aria is mostly about himself anyway; the second, "Il mio tesoro," is a message sent to Donna Anna that he will avenge her father's murder, a vengeance that Ottavio never gets around to, leaving the dead man to avenge himself. Ottavio may be virtuous, but he never achieves the power to put that virtue into action. By contrast, Donna Anna's arias are assertive and proactive; justifiably, in "Non mi dir," she rejects Ottavio's feeble advances, leaving him to follow foolishly behind her. If there is a locus of virility, as defined by concrete action and resolve, outside of Giovanni, it is Donna Anna, whose vocal range and florid style

more closely approximates that of the castrato heroes of the *opera seria,* still popular in Mozart's time. Donna Anna is the butch half of this couple.

7. Clément argues that Giovanni is really bisexual and that his inability to maintain a relationship with a woman arises from his failure to adjust to his sexuality. *Opera, or the Undoing of Women,* 36.

8. Eric Bentley (among many other critics) discusses Giovanni's sexual battles in "Conquests: Man vs. Eros in *Don Giovanni,*" *Opera News,* 14 April 1990, 16–19 et seq.

9. Soren Kierkegaard, *Either/Or,* ed. Steven L. Ross, trans. George L. Stengren (New York: Harper and Row, 1986), and George Bernard Shaw, *Man and Superman* (New York: Penguin, 1946).

10. Joseph Kerman, *Opera as Drama* (New York: Vintage, 1956), 119.

11. Northrop Frye, for example, asserts in *Anatomy of Criticism* (Princeton, N.J.: Princeton University Press, 1957), that, even though Da Ponte labels the piece a *dramma giocosa,* the "verbal action" of Don Giovanni is tragic, yet the "audience is exalted by the music above the reach of tragedy" (289). The seriousness with which this opera has been treated since the late nineteenth century, in any case, certainly problematizes its status as a comedy.

12. Foucault's central argument in the first volume of *The History of Sexuality,* trans. Robert Hurley (New York: Vintage, 1980), is that sexual discourse is not actually repressed in the Victorian era but rather that this period represents a proliferation of sexual discourse in numerous fields. But if sexual discourses spread at this time, it is still the case that nineteenth-century censorship kept direct reference to sexual intercourse on stage to a minimum.

13. Susan McClary, *Feminine Endings: Music, Gender, and Sexuality* (Minneapolis: University of Minnesota Press, 1991), 54–67. See also McClary's comments in her contribution to the Cambridge Opera Guide series, *Georges Bizet: Carmen* (Cambridge: Cambridge University Press, 1992). Nelly Furman also provides an insightful analysis of Carmen's allure in "The Languages of Love in *Carmen,*" in *Reading Opera,* ed. Arthur Groos and Roger Parker (Princeton, N.J.: Princeton University Press, 1988), 168–183.

14. Susan McClary (in a personal conversation) tells of a profoundly disturbing production of *Carmen* in which the Carmen character refused to die at the end of the performance. She was stabbed as usual in the last scene by José but continued to crawl around the stage, dripping blood, all the way through the final chords, and beyond, in the silence left by the stunned and unbelieving audience.

15. Gustav Kobbé, *The Definitive Kobbé's Opera Book,* ed. Earl of Harewood (New York: Putnam, 1987), 655–656.

16. Clément, *Opera, or the Undoing of Women,* 95.

17. Bertolt Brecht discusses his theories on opera in his essay "The Modern Theatre is the Epic Theatre," included in *Brecht on Theatre,* ed. John Willett (New York: Hill and Wang, 1964), 33–42.

Chapter 8

1. Anna Russell, "The Ring of the Nibelungs: An Analysis," *The Anna Russell Album,* Sony MDK 47252 (1991).

2. George Bernard Shaw describes this incident extensively in *The Quintessence of Ibsenism* (New York: Hill and Wang, 1957), 86–93.

3. Herbert Lindenberger, *Opera: The Extravagant Art* (Ithaca, N.Y.: Cornell University Press, 1984), 36.

4. Arguably, since operas are often adapted from plays, the play, coming earlier, takes the brunt of the censorship, removing pressure from the subsequent operatic adaptation. This certainly seems to be a factor in Mozart's ability to stage *Nozze* as an opera in the wake of the furor over the spoken play.

5. One of the few examples of sexual censorship of opera arose at the premiere of *Der Rosenkavalier*. As related in Gustave Kobbé, *The Definitive Kobbé's Opera Book,* ed. Earl of Harwood (New York: Putnam, 1987), 816–817, the opening scene, with its onstage depiction of postcoital repose, was modified in the original Berlin production, the censors having deemed the literal depiction of two lovers in bed too racy.

6. Recently there has been a fascination in the American media with the idea of televised executions; Ted Tally's play *Coming Attractions* raises this idea, as does a 1994 made-for-TV film on the topic. A few editorial writers debating the issue of capital punishment have proposed the idea, some ironically to highlight the perverse nature of the punishment, others quite seriously. Unlike earlier public executions, which were undeniably real, a televised execution would stand in an odd world between reality and illusion, in much the same way that the high-tech graphics of the televised accounts of the Gulf War against Iraq in 1991 made the bloody conflict seem like little more than a sophisticated video game.

7. This analysis of adultery as property right is a central theme in contemporary feminist legal criticism. See, for example, Annette Lawson, *Adultery: An Analysis of Love and Betrayal* (New York: Basic Books, 1988), especially the section titled "Adultery is Theft," 41 ff.

8. A partial list of popular operas with plots involving adultery in some form would include: Mozart's *Le Nozze di Figaro, Don Giovanni,* and *Così fan tutte;* Cherubini's *Médée;* Bellini's *Norma;* Donizetti's *Lucia di Lammermoor;* Verdi's *Rigoletto, Un Ballo in Maschera, Don Carlos, Otello,* and *Falstaff;* Wagner's *Tristan und Isolde, Die Walküre,* and *Götterdämmerung;* Ponchielli's *La Gioconda;* Leoncavallo's *I Pagliacci;* Mascagni's *Cavalleria Rusticana;* Massenet's *Manon;* Puccini's *Manon Lescaut* and *Il Tabarro;* Cilèa's *Adriana Lecouvreur;* Zandonai's *Francesca da Rimini;* Debussy's *Pelléas et Mélisande;* Berg's *Wozzeck* and *Lulu;* Shostakovich's *Lady Macbeth of Mtsensk;* and Janacek's *Katya Kabanova.*

9. See in particular volume 1, trans. Robert Hurley (New York: Vintage, 1980), 36–49 and 105.

10. In Rosi's film version, Carmen gets very physical with José, and the second act ends with everyone running into bedrooms, but most live stagings do not get this explicit.

11. Michel Poizat, *The Angel's Cry: Beyond the Pleasure Principle in Opera,* trans. Arthur Denner (Ithaca, N.Y.: Cornell University Press, 1992), 191–200.

12. Ibid., 192

13. For further discussion, see Sander L. Gilman, "Strauss and the Pervert," in *Reading Opera,* ed. Arthur Groos and Roger Parker (Princeton, N.J.: Princeton University Press, 1988), 306–327.

Chapter 9

1. Anne Rice, *Cry to Heaven* (New York: Ballantine Books, 1982), 182–183.

2. Angus Heriot, *The Castrati in Opera* (London: Secker and Warburg, 1956), 96–97. Michel Poizat also quotes this passage in *The Angel's Cry: Beyond the Pleasure Principle in Opera*, trans. Arthur Denner (Ithaca: Cornell University Press, 1992), 116–117.

3. Joke Dame, in "Unveiled Voices: Sexual Difference and the Castrato," in *Queering the Pitch: The New Gay and Lesbian Musicology*, ed. Philip Brett, Elizabeth Wood, and Gary C. Thomas (New York: Routledge, 1994), observes, "A closer look at the various descriptions [of the castrati] seems to suggest that the castrato's virility, the phallus, has been displaced into his voice" (144). In Gerard Corbiau's fictionalized film biography of Farinelli, *Farinelli, Il Castrato* (dir. Gerard Corbiau, Sony Pictures Classics, 1994), the famous castrato lures a female sexual partner into bed and conducts the foreplay; when the critical moment of sexual performance arrives, the castrato turns his place over to his uncastrated brother, who then completes the act. In this vision, Farinelli wields the sexual attractiveness; his less attractive brother has the testicles. I know of no historical evidence that documents this practice (or much of what goes on in the rest of the film), but it makes for an amusing scenario.

4. Heriot, in his historical survey of the castrati (a charming book, in its cheerful way, though his 1950s sensibility keeps most hints of transgressive sexuality out of the discussion), documents how the most famous of the singers travelled among the royal courts of Europe, using their fame to gain access to circles of power normally denied to mere stage performers. The fierce rivalries between the castrati that Heriot describes were no mere matter of ego; huge amounts of wealth and power were at stake. Philip of Spain kept Farinelli as his court singer for fifteen years and reportedly sought his advice in matters of state as well as in matters of music (*The Castrati in Opera*, 95–110).

5. Painter Sir Joshua Reynolds, in his third discourse to the students of the Royal Academy on December 14, 1770, remarks that in art, "Nature herself is not to be too closely copied. . . . The genuine painter . . . instead of endeavouring to amuse mankind with the minute neatness of his imitations, . . . must endeavour to improve them by the grandeur of his ideas." Reynolds, *The Discourses of Sir Joshua Reynolds*, ed. Edmund Gosse (London: Kegan, Paul, and Trench, 1884), 32. In eighteenth-century art theory, to create the image of the natural, the artist selects and adapts elements from nature in order to create a unified and beautiful whole. What the mind perceives as natural in art, then, is really a carefully constructed representation. The castrato is to singing what the formal garden is to untamed nature. A tree left unattended will always deviate from the platonic ideal shape of that tree as intended by its "true" nature. The function of the gardener, the artist of nature, is to cut and prune that tree into its most natural shape, the ideal. Similarly, the secret surgeons of Italy pruned and trimmed young singers into a more perfect form, an ideal of masculine vocal beauty. My thanks to Barbara Johnson for providing the Reynolds reference.

6. Rice finds the same sexual dynamic in the figure of the vampire in her more popular novels. Poizat also associates the castrato with the voice of the angel, especially in its transsexual quality (*The Angel's Cry*, 115–120).

7. Enid Rhodes Peschel and Richard E. Peschel, "Medicine and Music: The Castrati in Opera," *Opera Quarterly* 4(4) (1986–1987):21–38. Heriot includes reproductions of a number of these satirical drawings.

8. See, for example, Samuel Johnson's famous definition of opera in his *Dictionary* as an irrational entertainment, and Addison's disdainful analysis of Italian opera in *The Spectator* number 18.

9. But at the same time sexual deviance remains remarkably seductive. The United States of the 1950s was about as sexually normative as an era can get, yet this was the time of the boy groups and their flights of falsetto. Androgynous figures like Prince and Michael Jackson occupied the same space during the 1980s, generating enormous sexual energy by playing against sexual norms. Thanks to Eve Sedgwick for pointing out this connection. See also Marjorie Garber, *Vested Interests: Cross-Dressing and Cultural Anxiety* (New York: HarperCollins, 1993), who discusses Michael Jackson's androgyny in her chapter on Peter Pan.

10. Peschel and Peschel, "Medicine and Music: The Castrati in Opera," 32–33.

11. Heriot, *The Castrati in Opera,* 42.

12. The recordings are available on CD, Pearl Opal CD 9823.

13. It is important to remember, though, that at the time any role in the soprano range might be taken on by a castrato or a female singer, depending on a singer's availability and popularity.

14. The vicious competitions between singers in eighteenth-century opera and their prerogative to alter the scores to suit their demands are documented in the letters and records kept by impresario Luca Casimiro degli Albizzi, presented in William C. Holmes, *Opera Observed: Views of a Florentine Impresario in the Early Eighteenth Century* (Chicago: University of Chicago Press, 1993), especially chapters 6 and 7.

15. When I heard a performance of *Mitridate* in London at Covent Garden, I was struck by the electricity generated by this sudden shift to ensemble singing.

16. Joseph R. Roach, "Power's Body: The Inscription of Morality as Style," in *Interpreting the Theatrical Past,* ed. Thomas Postlewait and Bruce A. McConachie (Iowa City: University of Iowa Press, 1989), 99–118.

17. Ibid., 107.

18. Ibid., 106.

19. Dame, "Unveiled Voices," 148.

20. Ibid., 147.

21. Heriot recounts many of these incidents in his individual biographies of the singers, especially his discussion of the antics of Velluti. *The Castrati in Opera,* 189–199.

22. Marjorie Garber, in *Vested Interests,* also sees the transvestite figure as a space of representational overflow. Garber's ideas are discussed at length in Chapter 10 of this book.

23. Roach, "Power's Body," 108–109.

24. For a description of London's homosexual underground, see Randolph Trumbach, "Gender and the Homosexual Role in Modern Western Culture: The 18th and 19th Centuries Compared," in *Which Homosexuality: Essays from the International Scientific Conference on Lesbian and Gay Studies,* ed. Dennis Altman et al. (London: GMP Publishers, 1989), and Laurence Senelick, "Mollies or Men of

Mode? Sodomy and the Eighteenth-Century London Stage," *Journal of the History of Sexuality* 1(1) (1990):33–67. See also Gary C. Thomas, "'Was George Frideric Handel Gay?': On Closet Questions and Cultural Politics," in *Queering the Pitch*, ed. Brett, Wood, and Thomas, 155–203.

25. Roach, "Power's Body," 105.

26. Elizabeth Forbes, "Velluti, Giovanni Battista," *New Grove Dictionary of Opera*, vol. 4, ed. Stanley Sadie (London: Macmillan, 1992).

Chapter 10

1. Marjorie Garber, *Vested Interests: Cross-Dressing and Cultural Anxiety* (New York: Harper Perennial, 1993), 16.

2. Anne Rice, *Cry to Heaven* (New York: Ballantine Books, 1982), 348.

3. Garber, *Vested Interests*, 28.

4. Ibid., 32.

5. Ibid., 75.

6. Garber argues that drag is, in fact, the norm for all theatrical presentation and that only the strictures of realism have driven it to the margins of theatrical display (ibid., 40).

7. Ibid., 192. Garber's chapter 10, "Phantoms of the Opera: Actor, Diplomat, Transvestite, Spy," addresses cross-dressing in David Henry Hwang's play *M. Butterfly*, the Beijing Opera, the castrato figure in Balzac's "Sarrasine," and the cases of the Abbé de Choisy and the Chevalier d'Eon, but she says virtually nothing about cross-dressing in mainstream opera performance.

8. This invisibility via convention has parallels to the way audiences in ancient Greece, Elizabethan England, and many classical Asian theater forms, especially Kabuki, chose not to see, or not to highlight, the institutionalized cross-dressing that was (and in Japan remains) central to those forms. And, of course, in each of these theaters the cross-dressing also has a substantial, if often hidden, erotic content. See, for example, Sue Ellen Case's discussion of drag in *Feminism and Theatre* (New York: Methuen, 1988), and Stephen Orgel, "Nobody's Perfect: Or Why Did the English Stage Take Boys for Women?" *South Atlantic Quarterly* 88(1) (1989):7–29. The eroticism implicit in the drag roles of the Chinese Beijing Opera is brilliantly depicted in the film *Farewell My Concubine* (dir. Chen Kaige, Miramax Films, 1993).

9. Popular performance in the nineteenth century, as documented below, frequently employed female-to-male drag, but this practice has long since faded out of popular discourse, with the one exception of the Principle Boy in British Christmas pantomime. Garber discusses the lack of popular social categories for lesbian drag. *Vested Interests*, 152.

10. Garber, in chapter 2, "Cross-Dress for Success," discusses private men's clubs, restricted to the wealthy and the politically powerful, who give private drag shows for themselves as a means of playing out their hegemony. She also discusses the politics surrounding drag and gay identity in chapter 6 of her book. For some other recent discussions outlining the basic arguments about the politics of drag, see Case, *Feminism and Theatre;* Jill Dolan, *The Feminist Spectator as Critic* (Ann

Arbor: UMI Research Press, 1988); and Carole-Anne Taylor, "Boys Will Be Girls: The Politics of Gay Drag," in *Inside/Out: Lesbian Theories, Gay Theories,* ed. Diana Fuss (New York: Routledge, 1991). In the current gay rights discussion, members of the drag community have begun to express their dissatisfaction with being marginalized as comic figures and are beginning to demand recognition for their contributions to the gay rights movement, especially their central participation in the Stonewall riots. They are, justifiably, particularly incensed by gay critics like Bruce Bawer who would keep drag queens invisible for fear of inducing panic in the straight population.

11. Some recent women's performance, notably that of Split Britches, a troupe that uses female-to-male drag as a means to explore and empower women's roles on the stage, has challenged the politics of drag and has begun to employ camp and lesbian drag to disrupt normative gender images. When women take on male gender stereotypes in a Split Britches show, the effect is to explode those stereotypes and open the audience's vision to new ways of conceiving gender. See Vivian M. Patraka, "Split Britches in *Split Britches:* Performing History, Vaudeville, and the Everyday," in *Acting Out: Feminist Performances,* ed. Lynda Hart and Peggy Phelan (Ann Arbor: University of Michigan Press, 1993).

12. The list of these conventional cross-dressed roles (and my list is partial) is impressive. First we get the boys or sons of central characters: Jemmy, William Tell's son in Rossini's opera, along with roles in his *La Gazza Ladra, La Donna del Lago,* and *Elisabetta, Regina D'Inghilaterra;* Puck in Weber's *Oberon;* Frédéric in Thomas's *Mignon;* Ascanius in Berlioz's *Les Troyens;* Humperdinck's Hänsel, Fyodor in Mussorgsky's *Boris Godunov;* the orphan Vanya in Glinka's *A Life for the Tsar;* Adriano in Wagner's *Rienzi,* two of the Squires in *Parsifal,* and Yniold in Debussy's *Pelléas et Mélisande.* Marie in Donizetti's *La Fille du Régiment* is supposed to be a woman, but she plays at being a boy. Next come the shepherds and similar figures: two goatherds in Meyerbeer's *Dinorah;* Lehl in Rimsky-Korsakov's *The Snow Maiden;* a shepherd in Gounod's *Mireille,* another in Wagner's *Tannhäuser.* And, finally, there are the endless run of pages and boy assistants: Isolier in Rossini's *Le Comte D'Ory;* Smeaton in Donizetti's *Anna Bolena;* Urbain in Meyerbeer's *Les Huguenots;* Ascanio in Berlioz's *Benvenuto Cellini;* Stephano in Gounod's *Romeo et Juliette;* the Kitchen Boy in Dvorak's *Rusalka;* a nameless page also in *The Snow Maiden* and four in *Tannhäuser;* Dmitri in Giordano's *Fedora;* Tebaldo in Verdi's *Don Carlos;* and, most notably, Verdi's other page, the highly prominent Oscar in *Un Ballo in Maschera.*

13. Garber, *Vested Interests,* 84–92.

14. Kristina Straub outlines the erotics of female-to-male stage cross-dressing in "The Guilty Pleasures of Female Theatrical Cross-Dressing and the Autobiography of Charlotte Charke," in *Body Guards,* ed. Julia Epstein and Kristina Straub (London: Routledge, 1991), 142–166. See also Tracy C. Davis, "The Actress in Victorian Pornography," *Theatre Journal* 41 (1989):294–315, and discussions in the same author's *Actresses as Working Women: Their Social Identity in Victorian Culture* (London: Routledge, 1991). See also Laurence Senelick, "Boys and Girls Together: Subcultural Origins of Glamour Drag and Male Impersonation on the Nineteenth-Century Stage," in *Crossing the Stage: Controversies on Cross-Dressing,* ed. Leslie Ferris (London: Routledge, 1993).

15. Heriot provides the cast list for Scarlatti's *Pompeo* in Naples in 1684, where four castrati play three male roles and one female role; four female singers also perform three male roles and one female role. Three uncastrated male singers appear in male roles (*The Castrati in Opera,* 33). He also discusses the general practice of cross-dressing (ibid., 23–30). William C. Holmes, in *Opera Observed: Views of a Florentine Impresario in the Early Eighteenth Century* (Chicago: University of Chicago Press, 1993), also documents numerous operas where various soprano roles, male and female, are taken on either by castrati or women, dressed or cross-dressed as the role demanded, with little logic other than economic expediency.

16. Foucault, *The History of Sexuality,* vol. 1, trans. Robert Hurley (New York: Vintage, 1980), 104–105.

17. Brigid Brophy, *Mozart the Dramatist* (New York: Da Capo, 1988), 105–108.

18. Included in the recording *Divas, 1906–1935,* Prima Voce NI 7802.

19. In period engravings of female singers in drag, it is clear that the singers are, in fact, female. There is no attempt at realistic illusion; the contours of the ideal feminine body are often more highlighted in drag than in "proper" women's clothes. The male clothes emphasize the female parts. Images of hourglass figures, wasp waists, and large bosoms recur in these engravings, clearly evoking the ideal of feminine sexual allure. The only type of cross-dressed character not constructed in this manner is the figure of the Eastern prince (such as Rossini's Arsace), dressed in flowing robes that obscure the feminine contours. But even here some drawings make an attempt to recoup the lost female figure, at least symbolically. A drawing of Giuditta Pasta (available in the Harvard Theatre Collection) in the costume of Armando in Meyerbeer's *Il Crociato in Egitto,* depicts her with only the slightest hint of a feminine figure, but over her heavy drapery appear two oval breastplates, decorated with spikes looking like outsized nipples. The costume seems a desperate attempt to tell the viewer that under the exotic but unflattering robes lies a fully equipped, sexualized European woman after all.

20. See the discussion of Octavian's sword in Chapter 8.

21. The efficacy of historical distance in derailing transvestite sexual panic was highlighted by Peter Sellar's modern updating of *Nozze* to Trump Tower. When I watch this production, with Cherubino dressed as a modern teenager in a hockey uniform, his sexual desire seems much more real and immediate than in a traditional period production.

22. Transvestite boy roles, however, continue to appear in twentieth-century opera, including works by Debussy, Ravel, Pfitzner, Zimmerman, Delius, Janacek, Martinu, and De Falla.

23. Twentieth-century composers cannot buy into the codes of nineteenth-century cross-dressing with the blind faith in operatic convention of an earlier era. Performance today works between the two poles that have governed all narrative art in our time: mainstream realism and violent avant-garde. We either want stage images to reflect our experience with photographic realism, or we want experiments that completely violate our expectations. Alban Berg uses women in drag for two roles in *Lulu,* but in comparison with the other sexual irregularities on the stage, their ambiguity is hardly noticeable. Modern composers who want to play with marginal gender can either follow Britten and write for real boys or go to the other extreme with Michael Tippett (who, in *The Ice Break* [1977], presents the psychedelic mes-

senger Astron, one role sung by two singers, a mezzo and a countertenor), or with the bizarre sexual carnival of Gyorgy Ligeti's *Le Grand Macabre* (1978) with soprano roles for Prince Go-Go and Spermando, to go along with Clitoria, Mescalina, and the coloratura Chief of the Secret Police, who is really a bird.

24. Charles Ludlam, *The Complete Plays* (New York: Harper and Row, 1989).

25. Brian Kellow, "Golden Age Girls," *Opera News,* August 1991, 28–31.

26. See Chapter 5 on homoeroticism in opera.

Chapter 11

1. Thomas Mann, *The Magic Mountain,* trans. H. T. Lowe-Porter (New York: Vintage International 1992), 643.

2. Wayne Koestenbaum, *The Queen's Throat: Opera, Homosexuality, and the Mystery of Desire* (New York: Poseidon Press, 1993), 66.

3. Plato makes the same argument when he cautions against letting writing overtake recitation as a means of communication, that written language makes people lazy and encourages a loss of cultural memory.

4. This lack of danger was driven home a few years ago, during a live Saturday broadcast of Verdi's *Macbeth* from the Met. During the last intermission, a member of the audience (a longtime employee of the opera company) committed suicide by jumping from the top balcony. The rest of the performance was, of course, canceled, but the radio listeners were spared this information. They were only informed that there were some technical problems, and, after an extended intermission, a recording of the final act was substituted. Only well after the performance was the actual story released in the press.

5. See John Dizikes, *Opera in America: A Cultural History* (New Haven: Yale University Press, 1993), 397.

6. Herbet Lindenberger discusses this episode from *The Magic Mountain.* See *Opera: The Extravagant Art* (Ithaca, N.Y.: Cornell University Press, 1984), 189–191. Later, the record player takes on even greater powers. Working together, Hans and the Victrola are able to conjure from the dead the spirit of his beloved cousin during a strange seance scene.

7. In Anthony Burgess's *A Clockwork Orange* and in Stanley Kubrick's film version, Alex masturbates to the accompaniment of the choral finale of Beethoven's Ninth symphony.

8. Koestenbaum, *The Queen's Throat,* 59–60.

9. Ibid., 52 ff. Teldec/Warner has released two recordings called *Sensual Classics* and *Sensual Classics, Too,* promising music to enhance your romantic life. Each recording features on its cover a photograph of an exceptionally attractive and minimally clothed couple (heterosexual in the first case, a gay male couple in the second) in an erotic embrace. The recordings have sold very well.

10. Koestenbaum argues that this film is Franco Zeffirelli's tribute to the late Maria Callas, especially to her tragic love affairs and to her then-recent death (*The Queen's Throat,* 144).

11. If Losey, Zeffirelli, and Rosi eroticize opera, Ingmar Bergman thoroughly desexualizes his version of *Magic Flute*. Bergman's film is a child's fairy tale, framed by the visual images shown during the overture, with lengthy shots of audience faces, lingering particularly on the very innocent face of a young girl. He focuses on the story's frame, not on its character relations, as emphasized by the enchanted setting of the eighteenth-century Drottningholm stage where the film was shot, with its cartoon-like period scenery. All of Mozart's erotic energy is suppressed here; even the Queen of the Night seems desexualized, no more seductive than the repressed eroticism of the wicked queens of Grimm's fairy tales.

12. A number of recent recordings, both video and audio, have capitalized on this desire to make opera less frightening, with titles such as *Pavarotti's Opera Made Easy* and *Who's Afraid of Opera?*

13. Patrick J. Smith, editor of *Opera News*, in his article "Wired for Bel Canto" (*Opera News*, August 1992, 20–22) writes, "Most opera buffs don't want to hear about [the use of microphones] and profess that it doesn't occur (because they can't hear it), but that if it did occur it would be The Final Death of Opera as We Know and Love It." Smith goes on in the article to discuss the practice and its effects, emphasizing its dangers, especially for young singers. Marge Betley goes on to a further discussion of sound technology in the opera house in the next article in the issue, "Sounding Out" (24–26). Betley discusses a wide variety of uses for sound technology and advocates a balanced use of live and amplified sound, especially in nontraditional performance situations.

14. The various controversies are outlined extensively in an issue of *Opera News* (May 1990) devoted to the topic.

15. Supertitles can make the entire opera experience quite surreal. When I attended a production of *Boris Godunov* in Paris, the combination of Russian singing and French supertitles (my French skills being only moderate, my Russian nonexistent) threw me into an odd linguistic crisis. Even worse is the case when the supertitles get out of synch, a situation similar to the scene in *Singin' in the Rain*, in which the male and female voices get exchanged. Those who know the opera well tend to break out in inappropriate laughter, as happened at a production of *Otello* at Indiana University that I attended, where the titles got hopelessly out of synch; the more neophyte part of the audience was perplexed both by the words and by the random laughter during the tragedy. I can only imagine what the poor singers must have been thinking.

16. For a description of *The Voyage*, see the October 1992 issue of *Opera News*.

17. For a discussion of the Argento work, see Ellen Lampert-Gréaux, "Projections," *Opera News*, 8 January 1994, 22–25.

18. K. Robert Schwartz, "Witnesses," *Opera News*, October 1993, 28–31 et seq.

19. Tod Machover of the Massachusetts Institute of Technology Media Lab has experimented with writing a new work for just such an interactive walk-through setting; see the article by Nancy Malitz on opera and current advances in technology, "HyperReality," *Opera News*, August 1992, 28–30. This entire issue of *Opera News* focuses on the advances of technology in the opera house and the impact they might have.

Chapter 12

1. Susan McClary, *Feminine Endings: Music, Gender, and Sexuality* (Minneapolis: University of Minnesota Press, 1991), 26.

2. Peggy Phelan has some interesting speculations on theatrical presence as it relates to the *fort/da* game in her *Unmarked* (London: Routledge, 1993), especially in the final chapter. Commenting on the political effects of the elusive nature of theatrical representation, she remarks, "Doubt may be the best guarantee of real presence. *Fort. Da.*" (Ibid., 180).

3. See, for example, the discussions of opera as a genre in Susanne Langer, *Feeling and Form* (New York: Charles Scribner's Sons, 1953), and, more recently, Peter Kivy, *Osmin's Rage: Philosophical Reflections on Opera, Drama, and Text* (Princeton, N.J.: Princeton University Press, 1988).

4. Marjorie Garber, *Vested Interests: Cross-Dressing and Cultural Anxiety* (New York: HarperCollins, 1993), 33, along with many other references throughout the text.

5. Garber, *Vested Interests*, 390.

6. James Gleick, *Chaos* (New York: Viking, 1987).

7. Robert Donington, *Opera and Its Symbols: The Unity of Words, Music, and Staging* (New Haven: Yale University Press, 1990), 16.

BIBLIOGRAPHY

Abbate, Carolyn. *Unsung Voices: Opera and Musical Narrative in the Nineteenth Century.* Princeton, N.J.: Princeton University Press, 1991.

Abel, Sam. "The Death of Queens: *The Lisbon Traviata* Controversy and Gay Male Representation in the Mainstream Theatre." Forthcoming, *Theatre History Studies* 16 (1996).

_____. "Good Girls/Bad Girls: Gender Stereotypes in La Bohème." *Opera News,* 2 January 1993, 14–16.

_____. "The Rabbit in Drag: Camp and Gender Construction in the American Animated Cartoon." *Journal of Popular Culture* 29(3) (Winter 1995).

_____. "The World Cup of Opera, or A Sale of Three Tenors." *Theatre Annual* 48 (1995):1–13.

Abel, Sam, and Craig B. Palmer. "Disappearing Acts: Opera, Cinema, and Homoerotic Desire." In *A Night In at the Opera: Media Representations of Opera,* ed. Jeremy Tambling. London: John Libbey/Arts Council of England, 1994, 169–192.

Barthes, Roland. *The Pleasure of the Text.* Trans. Richard Miller. New York: Hill and Wang, 1975.

Bartlett, John. *Familiar Quotations.* Boston: Little, Brown, 1992.

Bartlett, Neil. *Who Was That Man? A Present for Mr Oscar Wilde.* London: Serpent's Tail, 1988.

Bawer, Bruce. *A Place at the Table.* New York: Poseidon, 1993.

Bentley, Eric. "Conquests: Man vs. Eros in *Don Giovanni.*" *Opera News,* 14 April 1990, 16–19 et seq.

Bergman, David, ed. *Camp Grounds: Style and Homosexuality.* Amherst: University of Massachusetts Press, 1993.

Bernstein, Leonard. *The Unanswered Question: Six Talks at Harvard.* Cambridge: Harvard University Press, 1976.

Bersani, Leo. "Is the Rectum a Grave?" In *AIDS: Cultural Analysis, Cultural Activism,* ed. Douglas Crimp. Cambridge: MIT Press, 1988.

Betley, Marge. "Sounding Out." *Opera News,* August 1992, 24–26.

Brecht, Bertolt. *Brecht on Theatre.* Ed. John Willett. New York: Hill and Wang, 1964.

Brett, Philip, ed. *Benjamin Britten: Peter Grimes.* Cambridge: Cambridge University Press, 1983.

Brett, Philip, Elizabeth Wood, and Gary C. Thomas, eds. *Queering the Pitch: The New Gay and Lesbian Musicology.* New York: Routledge, 1994.

Brophy, Brigid. *Mozart the Dramatist.* New York: Da Capo, 1988.

Burton, Humphrey. *Leonard Bernstein.* New York: Doubleday, 1994.

Butler, Judith. *Bodies That Matter: On the Discursive Limits of Sex.* New York: Routledge, 1993.

_____. *Gender Trouble: Feminism and the Subversion of Identity.* New York: Routledge, 1990.

Carner, Mosco. "'La Fanciulla del West': A Re-assessment." *Opera* 28 (1977): 426–433.

Carpenter, Humphrey. *Benjamin Britten: A Biography.* New York: Scribner, 1992.

Carreras, Domingo, Pavarotti in Concert. Zubin Mehta, cond. London CD 430 433–2, 1990; London videotape 071 223–3LH, 1990.

Carreras, Domingo, Pavarotti: The Three Tenors in Concert 1994. Zubin Mehta, cond. Atlantic CD 82614; WarnerVision Entertainment video 50822–3.

Case, Sue Ellen. *Feminism and Theatre.* New York: Methuen, 1988.

Clark, Jennifer. "Over 1.5-Billion People Served Opera During Live, Global Show." *Variety,* 18 July 1990, 65.

Clément, Catherine. *Opera, or the Undoing of Women.* Trans. Betsy Wing, with a foreword by Susan McClary. Minneapolis: University of Minnesota Press, 1988.

Crutchfield, Will. "Dishing About Divas and Other Opera Chat." *New York Times,* 4 June 1989, sec. 2, 5 et seq.

Dame, Joke. "Unveiled Voices: Sexual Difference and the Castrato." In *Queering the Pitch: The New Gay and Lesbian Musicology,* ed. Philip Brett, Elizabeth Wood, and Gary C. Thomas New York: Routledge, 1994, 139–154.

Davis, Peter G. "Lame Salome." *New York Magazine,* 3 December 1990, 178.

_____. "Music." *New York Magazine,* 7 June 1993, 58.

Davis, Tracy C. "The Actress in Victorian Pornography." *Theatre Journal* 41 (1989):294–315.

_____. *Actresses as Working Women: Their Social Identity in Victorian Culture.* London: Routledge, 1991.

DeYoung, Richard. *The Singer's Art: An Analysis of Vocal Principles.* Chicago: DePaul University, 1958.

Didion, Joan. "Trouble in Lakewood." *New Yorker,* 26 July 1993, 46–50 et seq.

DiGaetani, John Louis. *An Invitation to the Opera.* New York: Doubleday, 1986.

Divas, 1906–1935. Prima Voce CD NI 7802.

Dizikes, John. *Opera in America: A Cultural History.* New Haven: Yale University Press, 1993.

Dolan, Jill. *The Feminist Spectator as Critic.* Ann Arbor: UMI Research Press, 1988.

Donington, Robert. *Opera and Its Symbols: The Unity of Words, Music, and Staging.* New Haven: Yale University Press, 1990.

_____. *The Rise of Opera.* New York: Charles Scribner's Sons, 1981.

Drake, John. "Castrati Article Castigated." *High Fidelity,* May 1958, 16.

Ehrenreich, Barbara. *The Worst Years of Our Lives: Irreverent Notes From a Decade of Greed.* New York: Pantheon, 1990.

Elliott, Graham. "The Operas of Benjamin Britten: A Spiritual View." *Opera Quarterly* 4 (1986):28–44.

Elliott, Susan. "In Concert, or the Making of a Hit." *Opera News,* 30 March 1991, 34–35.

Ellison, Cori. "Breaking the Sound Barrier: How Women Finally Made Their Way to the Opera Stage." *Opera News,* July 1992, 14–17 et seq.

Evans, John. "*Death in Venice:* The Apollonian/Dionysian Conflict." *Opera Quarterly* 4 (1986):102–115.

Faner, Robert D. *Walt Whitman and Opera.* Carbondale: Southern Illinois University Press, 1951.

Finke, Laurie A. "Painting Women: Images of Femininity in Jacobean Tragedy." *Theatre Journal* 36 (1984):357–370.

Flaubert, Gustave. *Madame Bovary.* Trans. Francis Steegmuller. New York: Vintage Classics, 1992.

Forbes, Elizabeth. "Velluti, Giovanni Battista." *New Grove Dictionary of Opera,* vol. 4. Ed. Stanley Sadie. London: Macmillan, 1992.

Foucault, Michel. *Discipline and Punish: The Birth of the Prison.* Trans. Alan Sheridan. New York: Vintage Books, 1979.

_____. *The History of Sexuality.* Trans. Robert Hurley. Three volumes. New York: Vintage, 1980, 1986, 1988.

Furman, Nelly. "The Languages of Love in *Carmen.*" In *Reading Opera,* ed. Arthur Groos and Roger Parker. Princeton, N.J.: Princeton University Press, 1988, 168–183.

Freeman, John W. "Records." *Opera News,* September 1984, 68.

Frye, Northrop. *Anatomy of Criticism.* Princeton, N.J.: Princeton University Press, 1957.

Gallagher, Catherine, and Thomas Lacquer, eds. *The Making of the Modern Body: Sexuality and Society in the Nineteenth Century.* Berkeley: University of California Press, 1987.

Galvin, Peter. "A Royal Opera." *Advocate,* 30 May 1995, 59.

Garber, Marjorie. *Vested Interests: Cross-Dressing and Cultural Anxiety.* New York: HarperCollins, 1993.

Gardiner, Julian. *A Guide to Good Singing and Speech.* London: Cassell, 1968.

Gay, John. *The Beggar's Opera.* In *18th and 19th Century British Drama,* ed. Katherine Rogers. New York: Meridan, 1979.

Gelman, David. "Mixed Messages: Spur Posse Sex Scandal at Lakewood High School, California." *Newsweek,* 12 April 1993, 28–29.

Gilman, Sander L. "Strauss and the Pervert." In *Reading Opera,* ed. Arthur Groos and Roger Parker. Princeton, N.J.: Princeton University Press, 1988, 306–327.

Gleick, James. *Chaos.* New York: Viking, 1987.

Groos, Arthur, and Roger Parker, eds. *Reading Opera.* Princeton, N.J.: Princeton University Press, 1988.

Hart, Lynda, ed., *Making a Spectacle: Feminist Essays on Contemporary Women's Theatre.* Ann Arbor: University of Michigan Press, 1989.

Haskell, Molly. *From Reverence to Rape: The Treatment of Women in the Movies.* Chicago: University of Chicago Press, 1987.

Heavy Classix. Angel CDM 0777 7 64769 2 6.

Heavy Classix II. Angel CDM 7243 5 65172 2 6.

Heriot, Angus. *The Castrati in Opera.* London: Secker and Warburg, 1956.

Hindley, Clifford. "Contemplation and Reality: A Study of Britten's 'Death in Venice.'" *Music and Letters* 71 (1990):511–523.

_____. "Homosexual Self-Affirmation and Self-Oppression in Two Britten Operas." *Musical Quarterly* 76(2) (1992):143–168.

_____. "Platonic Elements in Britten's 'Death in Venice.'" *Music and Letters* 73 (1992):407–429.

Holmes, William C. *Opera Observed: Views of a Florentine Impresario in the Early Eighteenth Century.* Chicago: University of Chicago Press, 1993.

Horowitz, Joseph. "Coming to America." *Opera News,* 27 March 1993, 14–20 et seq.

Innaurato, Albert. "The Gong Show." *Opera News,* 1 February 1992, 8–11.

Jacobs, Laura. "No Song of an Ingenue." *Opera News,* 13 March 1993, 16–17.

Kellow, Brian. "Golden Age Girls." *Opera News,* August 1991, 28–31.

Kennicott, Philip. "Song of the Wild." *Opera News,* 11 April 1992, 34–36 et seq.

Kerman, Joseph. *Opera as Drama.* New York: Vintage Books, 1956.

Kestner, Joseph A. "The Dark Side of Chivalry." *Opera News,* 30 March 1991, 18–21 et seq.

_____. "The Feared Woman." *Opera News,* 11 April 1987, 34–37 et seq.

Keyser, Dorothy. "Cross-Sexual Casting in Baroque Opera: Musical and Theatrical Conventions." *Opera Quarterly* 5(4) (1987/1988):46–57.

Kierkegaard, Søren. *Either/Or.* Ed. Steven L. Ross, trans. George L. Stengren. New York: Harper and Row, 1986.

Kivy, Peter. *Osmin's Rage: Philosophical Reflections on Opera, Drama, and Text.* Princeton, N.J.: Princeton University Press, 1988.

Kobbé, Gustav. *The Definitive Kobbé's Opera Book.* Ed. Earl of Harewood. New York: Putnam, 1987.

Koestenbaum, Wayne. *The Queen's Throat: Opera, Homosexuality, and the Mystery of Desire.* New York: Poseidon Press, 1993.

Kott, Jan. *The Memory of the Body.* Evanston, Ill.: Northwestern University Press, 1992.

Kozinn, Allan. "The Three Tenors, Guess Who, to Sing." *New York Times,* 14 July 1994, C11.

Lampert-Gréaux, Ellen. "Projections." *Opera News,* 8 January 1994, 22–25.

Langer, Susanne. *Feeling and Form.* New York: Charles Scribner's Sons, 1953.

Laqueur, Thomas. *Making Sex: Body and Gender From the Greeks to Freud.* Cambridge: Harvard University Press, 1990.

Law, Joe K. "Alessandro Moreschi Reconsidered: A Castrato on Records." *Opera Quarterly* 2(2) (1984):1–12.

Lawson, Annette. *Adultery: An Analysis of Love and Betrayal.* New York: Basic Books, 1988.

Lee, M. Owen. "Heroine Addiction." *Opera News,* 2 March 1985, 25–26 et seq.

Levin, David J., ed. *Opera Through Other Eyes.* Stanford, Calif.: Stanford University Press, 1994.

Lindenberger, Herbert. *Opera: The Extravagant Art.* Ithaca, N.Y.: Cornell University Press, 1984.

Locke, Ralph P. "What are These Women Doing in Opera?" *Opera News,* July 1992, 34–37.

London, Sol. "When Singing Was a Monster's Art: The Golden Age of the Great Castrati." *High Fidelity,* February 1958, 41–44 et seq.

Ludlam, Charles. *The Complete Plays.* New York: Harper and Row, 1989.

Malitz, Nancy. "HyperReality." *Opera News,* August 1992, 28–30.

Mann, Thomas. *The Magic Mountain.* Trans. H. T. Lowe-Porter. New York: Vintage International, 1992.

Mass, Lawrence D. *Confessions of a Jewish Wagnerite.* New York: Cassell, 1994.

Mazer, Sharon. "'She's so Fat . . . ': Facing the Fat Lady at Coney Island's Sideshow by the Seashore." *Theatre Annual* 47 (1994):11–28

McClary, Susan. *Feminine Endings: Music, Gender, and Sexuality.* Minneapolis: University of Minnesota Press, 1991.

McNally, Terrence. *Three Plays by Terrence McNally.* New York: Plume, 1990.

Meyer, Moe, ed. *The Politics and Poetics of Camp.* London: Routledge, 1994.

Miller, Richard. *The Structure of Singing: System and Art in Vocal Technique.* New York: Schirmer Books, 1986.

Millman, Marcia. *Such a Pretty Face: Being Fat in America.* New York: Norton, 1980.

Milner, Anthony. "The Sacred Capons." *Musical Times* 114 (1973):250–252.

Mitchell, Basil. "The Castrati." *Theatre Arts* 36(3) (March 1952):46–47 et seq.

Mitchell, Donald. *Benjamin Britten: Death in Venice.* Cambridge: Cambridge University Press, 1987.

Mitchell, Ronald E. *Opera: Dead or Alive.* Madison: University of Wisconsin Press, 1970.

Moonstruck. Dir. Norman Jewison, with Cher, Nicholas Cage, Vincent Gardenia, Olympia Dukakis, and Danny Aiello. MGM/UA, 1988.

Mordden, Ethan. *Demented: The World of the Opera Diva.* New York: Simon and Schuster, 1984.

_____. *Opera Anecdotes.* New York: Oxford University Press, 1985.

Moreschi, Alessandro. *The Last Castrato.* Pearl Opal CD 9823.

Mulvey, Laura. "Visual Pleasure and Narrative Cinema." *Screen* 16(3) (1975): 6–18.

Nettl, Paul. "Eternal Youth: The Age of the Castrati." *Opera News,* 1 December 1958, 10–12.

Orgel, Stephen. "Nobody's Perfect: Or Why Did the English Stage Take Boys for Women?" *South Atlantic Quarterly* 88(1) (1989):7–29.

Patraka, Vivian M. "Split Britches in *Split Britches:* Performing History, Vaudeville, and the Everyday." In *Acting Out: Feminist Performances,* ed. Lynda Hart and Peggy Phelan. Ann Arbor: University of Michigan Press, 1993.

Peschel, Enid Rhodes, and Richard E. Peschel. "Medicine and Music: The Castrati in Opera. *Opera Quarterly* 4(4) (1986/1987):21–38.

Phelan, Peggy. *Unmarked.* London: Routledge, 1993.

Pleasants, Henry. *The Great Singers: From the Dawn of Opera to Our Own Time.* New York: Simon and Schuster, 1966.

Poizat, Michel. *The Angel's Cry: Beyond the Pleasure Principle in Opera.* Trans. Arthur Denner. Ithaca, N.Y.: Cornell University Press, 1992.

Reinelt, Janelle. "Women Who Love too Much: The Ambiguity of Deadly Desire." Unpublished paper, 1989.

Reynolds, Sir Joshua. *The Discourses of Sir Joshua Reynolds.* Ed. Edmund Gosse. London: Kegan, Paul, and Trench, 1884.

Rice, Anne. *Cry to Heaven.* New York: Ballantine Books, 1982.

Rich, Adrienne. "Compulsory Heterosexuality and Lesbian Existence." In *The Lesbian and Gay Studies Reader,* ed. Henry Abelove, Michèle Aina Barale, and David M. Halperin. New York: Routledge, 1993, 227–254.

Roach, Joseph R. *The Player's Passion: Studies in the Science of Acting.* Ann Arbor: University of Michigan Press, 1993.

_____. "Power's Body: The Inscription of Morality as Style." In *Interpreting the Theatrical Past,* ed. Thomas Postlewait and Bruce A. McConachie. Iowa City: University of Iowa Press, 1989.

Robinson, Michael F. *Opera Before Mozart.* London: Hutchinson University Library, 1966.

Robinson, Paul. "A Deconstructive Postscript: Reading Libretti and Misreading Opera." In *Reading Opera,* ed. Arthur Groos and Roger Parker. Princeton, N.J.: Princeton University Press, 1988, 328–346.

_____. "The Opera Queen: A Voice from the Closet." *Cambridge Opera Journal* 6(3) (1994):283–291.

Rogers, Francis. "The Male Soprano." *Musical Quarterly* 5 (1919):413–425.

Román, David. "'It's My Party and I'll Die If I Want To!': Gay Men, AIDS, and the Circulation of Camp in U.S. Theatre." In *Camp Grounds: Style and Homosexuality,* ed. David Bergman. Amherst: University of Massachusetts Press, 1993, 206–233.

Rosenthal, Harold, and John Warrack. *The Concise Oxford Dictionary of Opera,* second edition. New York: Oxford University Press, 1979.

Ross, Alex. "Grand Seductions." *New Yorker,* 12 April 1993, 115–120.

Rosselli, John. "The Castrati as a Professional Group and a Social Phenomenon, 1550–1850." *Acta Musicologica* 60 (1988):143–179.

Rubinstein, Leslie. "Gypsy!" *Opera News,* October 1984, 11–13 et seq.

Russell, Anna. *The Anna Russell Album.* Sony CD MDK 47252.

Salinger, J. D. *Franny and Zooey.* Boston: Little, Brown, 1961.

Sawkins, Lionel. "For and Against the Order of Nature: Who Sang the Soprano?" *Early Music* 15 (August 1987):315–324.

Schwartz, K. Robert. "Witnesses." *Opera News,* October 1993, 28–31 et seq.

Scott, Michael. "On Wings of Song." *Opera News,* 4 February 1984, 18–22.

Sedgwick, Eve Kosofsky. *Between Men: English Literature and Male Homosocial Desire.* New York: Columbia University Press, 1985.

_____. *Epistemology of the Closet.* Berkeley: University of California Press, 1990.

_____. *Tendencies.* Durham, N.C.: Duke University Press, 1993.

Senelick, Laurence. "Boys and Girls Together: Subcultural Origins of Glamour Drag and Male Impersonation on the Nineteenth-Century Stage." In *Crossing the Stage: Controversies on Cross-Dressing,* ed. Leslie Ferris. London: Routledge, 1993.

_____. "Mollies or Men of Mode? Sodomy and the Eighteenth-Century London Stage." *Journal of the History of Sexuality* 1(1) (1990):33–67.

Shaw, George Bernard. *Man and Superman.* New York: Penguin, 1946.

_____. *Plays Unpleasant.* New York: Penguin, 1946.

_____. *The Quintessence of Ibsenism.* New York: Hill and Wang, 1957.

Shepard, John. *Music as Social Text.* Cambridge: Polity Press, 1991.

Showalter, Elaine. *The Feminine Malady: Women, Madness, and Culture in England, 1830–1980.* New York: Pantheon, 1985.

_____. *Sexual Anarchy.* New York: Penguin, 1990.

Simon, John. "Daughter of Death." *Opera News,* 11 April 1992, 14–16 et seq.

Smith, Patrick J. "Wired for Bel Canto." *Opera News,* August 1992, 20–22.

Stevens, Mick. "Grand Ole Opera." *New Yorker,* 30 December 1991, 35.

Stockdale, F. M., and M. R. Dreyer. *The International Opera Guide.* North Pomfret, Vt.: Trafalgar Square Publishing, 1990.

Stoppard, Tom. *The Real Thing.* London: Faber and Faber, 1982.

Straub, Kristina. "The Guilty Pleasures of Female Theatrical Cross-Dressing and the Autobiography of Charlotte Charke." In *Body Guards,* ed. Julia Epstein and Kristina Straub. London: Routledge, 1991.

Summers, Dana. "I Don't Care about the Polls . . . " *New York Times,* 27 September 1992, sec. 4, 4.

Taylor, Carole-Anne. "Boys Will Be Girls: The Politics of Gay Drag." In *Inside/Out: Lesbian Theories, Gay Theories,* ed. Diana Fuss. New York: Routledge, 1991.

Thomas, Gary C. "'Was George Frideric Handel Gay?': On Closet Questions and Cultural Politics." In *Queering the Pitch: The New Gay and Lesbian Musicology,* ed. Philip Brett, Elizabeth Wood, and Gary C. Thomas. New York: Routledge, 1994, 155–203.

Trumbach, Randolph. "Gender and the Homosexual Role in Modern Western Culture: The 18th and 19th Centuries Compared." In *Which Homosexuality: Essays from the International Scientific Conference on Lesbian and Gay Studies,* ed. Dennis Altman et al. London: GMP Publishers, 1989.

Von Buchau, Stephanie. "Room at the Top." *Opera News,* July 1992, 8–12 et seq.

Westrup, J. A. "Two First Performances: Monteverdi's 'Orfeo' and Mozart's 'La Clemenza di Tito.'" *Music and Letters* 39 (1958):327–335.

"What's Opera, Doc?" Dir. Chuck Jones. Warner Brothers, 1957.

Witomski, T. R. *Kvetch.* Berkeley, Calif.: Celestial Arts, 1989.

Yorke-Long, Alan. "The Castrati." *Opera* 1(3) (1950):26–29; 1(4) (1950):28–32.

ABOUT THE BOOK AND AUTHOR

Verdi, Wagner, polymorphous perversion, Puccini, Brunnhilde, Pinkerton, and Parsifal all rub shoulders in this delightful, poetic, insightful, sexual book sprung by one man's physical response to the power and exaggeration we call opera. Sam Abel applies a light touch as he considers the topic of opera and the eroticized body: Why do audiences respond to opera in a visceral way? How does opera, like no other art form, physically move watchers? How and why does opera arouse feelings akin to sexual desire? Abel seeks the answers to these questions by examining homoerotic desire, the phenomenon of the castrati, operatic cross-dressing, and opera as presented through the media.

In this deeply personal book, Abel writes, "These pages map my current struggles to pin down my passion for opera, my intense admiration for its aesthetic forms and beauties, but much more they express my astonishment at how opera makes me lose myself, how it consumes me." In so doing, Abel uncovers what until now, through dry musicology and gossipy history, has been left behind a wall of silence: the physical and erotic nature of opera. Although Abel can speak with certainty only about his own response to opera, he provides readers with a language and a resonance with which to understand their own experiences. Ultimately, *Opera in the Flesh* celebrates the power of opera to move audiences as no other book has done. It is indeed a treasure of scholarship, passion, and poetry for everyone with even a passing interest in this fascinating art form.

Sam Abel is assistant professor of drama at Dartmouth College.

INDEX

"Adagio for Strings" (Barber), 92
Addison, Joseph, 132
Adultery, 113, 117–119, 206(n8)
  and murder, 118–119
  and social class, 118–119
  and verismo, 118–119
Aïda (Verdi), 7–8, 57, 168
AIDS, 56, 74, 199(n4), 203(n10)
Albee, Edward, 125
Alden, David, 158
Allen, Peter, 26
Amfortas (*Parsifal*), 123
Androgyny, 17, 153–156
Angeles, Victoria de los, 8
Angel's Cry, The: Beyond the Pleasure
  Principle (Poizat), 5, 27, 47, 97,
  192(n5)
Anna Russell Album, The, 13
Applause, 83, 168
  and booing, 198(n11)
  critical view of, 51–52
  curtain call, 50–52
Arabella (Strauss), 160
Arena di Verona, 26
Argento, Dominick, 177
Ariadne auf Naxos (Strauss), 72, 160
Arias, 134–135
Aristotle, 86
Artifice, 20–21
Asia, 200(n12)
As Is (Hoffman), 74
Audience
  as consumer, 18–19
  female, 36–39, 191(n4)
  feminization of male, 53–55
  and grand finale, 180–182
  and identification, 31–35

as performer, 50
and perversion, 114–117
and rape, 101–102, 103–105
and rivalry, 129–131
seduction of, 27–31, 103–105
and singer's body, 47–50, 165
theories of, 20–21
women as, 67

Ballo in Maschera, Un (Verdi), 71, 95,
  153, 156–158
Barber, Samuel, 92
Barthes, Roland, 85, 88–89, 136
Bartlett, Neil, 62, 67
Beaumarchais, Pierre de, 113
Beggar's Opera, The (Gay), 37,
  196(n14)
Behrens, Hildegard, 19, 47
Bel canto, 156
Benedetti, Pietro, 134
Berg, Alban, 73–74, 114, 121, 177,
  211(n23)
Bergman, Ingmar, 213(n11)
Berlin Komische Oper, 187
Bernasconi, Antonia, 134
Bernstein, Leonard, 74
Between Men (Sedgwick), 70
Bickham, George, 139–141
Billy Budd (Britten), 73
Binary categories, 146, 186
Body. *See* Castrati; Female body;
  Singer's body
Bohème, La (Puccini), 7, 8, 35–36, 38,
  71, 108
  popularity of, 112
  and postmodernism, 187–188
  transvestism in, 151